GUIDE TO THE WEIMARANER

GUIDE TO THE
WEIMARANER

Gillian Burgoin

The Boydell Press

© Gillian Burgoin 1985
First published 1985 by The Boydell Press
an imprint of Boydell & Brewer Ltd
PO Box 9, Woodbridge, Suffolk IP12 3DF

British Library Cataloguing in Publication Data

Burgoin, Gillian
   Guide to the Weimaraner.
   1. Weimaraners (Dogs)
   I. Title
   636.7'52   SF429.W33

   ISBN 0–85115–414–X

Library of Congress Cataloguing in Publication Data

Burgoin, Gillian
   Guide to the Weimaraner.
   1. Weimaraners (Dogs)
   I. Title
   SF429.W33B87   1985   636.7'52   85–6705

Printed in Great Britain by St Edmundsbury Press
Bury St Edmunds, Suffolk

CONTENTS

PREFACE

I suppose this book might never have come into existence had it not been for the persistent nagging by one or two 'friends' – goodness knows I have no pretensions about my temporary calling as a writer! However, having started on the job in hand, my primary object was to set the records straight and correct several inaccuracies which have been printed in the past regarding the original stock brought into this country, and some claims to fame which did not stand up to close investigation. Although the breed has been in this country for a relatively short time, early successes in various fields have been dramatised and embellished out of all proportion and I have taken great care to unearth official records wherever the slightest doubt arose. Hence, some items will be missing which may have appeared in earlier so-called breed records.

Of course, the original concept to put into print breed records which could prove to be of use in future years, soon expanded and, like 'Topsy', grew and grew. This leaves me with a list of thanks due to the many, many people at home and abroad who were so patient with my demands and who gave so generously and freely of their memories and treasured photographs. To all I offer my sincere thanks whether their contribution was a chapter, a sentence or just the odd word which may have been the last piece in a particular puzzle.

Very special thanks must go to Eleonore Fearn without whose invaluable help in translating from the German I should still be struggling over the first few lines.

I hope that you will gain much pleasure from looking at the many pictures of our lovely and versatile breed – and that you will instantly recognise them as *Weimaraners*, endorsing Karl Brandt's words written all those years ago: 'Even if the Weimaraner were painted a brown colour, one could instantly recognise him as a Weimaraner.'

Gillian Burgoin

ACKNOWLEDGEMENTS

Special thanks to the following:

Ian Petty and Eric Richardson.
Eleonore Fearn, Josef Jürgen, and Inga Lewis, for translations.
John Gassman, Louise Petrie-Hay and Trevor Horsefield, for their field trial contributions.

And for their overseas data:
Lilian and Ray Taylor, *South Africa*.
Kees Hoekzema, *Holland*.
Wally Finch, John Mayhew and Geoff Redmond, *Australia*.
John Tweedie, *New Zealand*.
Eduardo Victor Costa, *Brazil*.
Dr Werner Petri, *Germany*.
Franz Amon-Hechtenberg, *Austria*.
Lucette Ferragu, Ginette Junillon, and Catherine Lansard, *France*.
Lars Kilborn, *Sweden*.
Wendy McKay, *Canada*.
Manfred Hölzel, *Czechoslovakia*.
Eva Ericksen, *Norway*.
Niels Jørgen Drost, *Denmark*.

Anne Williams – for her cartoons in Appendices V, VI and VII.
Anne Johnson – for her line drawing in Appendix IV (Show Gallery no. 12 and Breed standards).

The Kennel Club, London (Breed standards, statistics, Show/Field/Working Regulations, etc.).
The American Kennel Club, New York (Breed standards, statistics).
Federation Cynologique Internationale (FCI) (Breed standard).
Federacion Cinologica Argentina, Buenos Aires, Argentina.
Societe Royale Saint Hubert, Brussels, Belgium.
Bermuda Kennel Club, Hamilton, Bermuda.
Confederacao do Brasil Kennel Clube, Rio de Janeiro, Brazil.

ACKNOWLEDGEMENTS

Dansk Kennelklub, Solrød, Strand, Denmark.

Suomen Kennelliitto-Finska Kennelklubben, Helsinki, Finland.

Raad Van Beheer op Kynologisch Gebied in Nederland, Amsterdam, Holland.

Magyar Ebtenyésztök Orszagos Egyesülete, Budapest, Hungary.

Ente Nationale Della Cinofilia Italiana, Milan, Italy.

Kennel Club of India, Nilgiris, S. India.

New Zealand Kennel Club, Wellington, New Zealand.

Norsk Kennel Club, Oslo, Norway.

Zwiazek Kynologiczny W Polsce, Varsovie, Poland.

Federation Canofila de Puerto Rico, Santurce, Puerto Rico.

Real Sociedad Central de Fomento de las Razas Caninas en España, Madrid, Spain.

Svenska Kennelklubben, Bromma, Sweden.

Schweizerische Kynologische Gesellschaft, Bern, Switzerland.

Der Weimaraner Vorstehhund, Dr Werner Petri, 1980.

Der Weimaraner Vorstehhund, Von Klaus Hartmann, 1972.

The Weimaraner, Jack Denton Scott, 1952.

The Complete Weimaraner, Wm W. Denlinger, 1954.

Express Newspapers plc, 1953 and 1955 articles by MacDonald Hastings.

Field & Stream (USA), 1947 article by Jack Denton Scott.

Weimaraner Club of Great Britain (magazine extracts, etc.)

Weimaraner Club of America (magazine extracts, etc.)

HOLLAND

Hamburg

Bremen

Lüneburger Heide

Celle

Hanover

Bad Oeynhausen

Lemgo

Düsseldorf

Sondershausen

Eisenach   Erfurt   Apolda

Gotha   Weimar

Saalfeld

BELGIUM

Frankfurt   Fulda

Schweinfurt

Heidelberg

Nuremburg

W. GERMANY

FRANCE

Freiburg

Black Forest

Munich

Bavarian Alps

SWITZERLAND

Innsbruck

ITALY

E. GERMANY

POLAND

Berlin

Magdeburg

Wernigerode

Halle

Leipzig

Dresden

Weissenfels

Prague

CZECHOSLOVAKIA

Lower Austria

Upper Austria

Grunau

Salzburg

Vienna

AUSTRIA

1

Weimar and the Weimar Republic

Today Weimar is an industrial town in the German Democratic Republic (East Germany) in the district of Erfurt on the River Ilm. This is not a very romantic sounding setting for the breed of dog, the Weimaraner, which was named after the area. However, if we go back much further in time, to the sixteenth century, we find that in 1547 Weimar became the capital of Saxe-Weimar, and in the eighteenth and nineteenth centuries it was an important cultural centre of a small principality ruled over by the Grand Duke Karl August (1757–1828). In 1815 it became the capital of the Grand Duchy of Saxe-Weimar-Eisenach and later was the capital of Thuringia. It still has a grand-ducal palace as well as other palaces and a fine eighteenth-century church in which are buried several famous German painters and poets including Lucas Cranach (1472–1553), painter and engraver whose best work, *Christ on the Cross*, is the altarpiece at Weimar. In the latter part of the eighteenth century Weimar became one of the great literary centres of Europe and is famous for its musical associations. Franz Liszt worked in its state theatre from 1849 to 1861. From 1708 to 1717 Johann Sebastian Bach was court organist and chamber musician to Duke Wilhelm Ernst of Saxe-Weimar and it is said that in 1716 he was called upon to accompany his master on a visit to Duke Christian of Saxe-Weissenfels and compose a cantata to be performed after the two noblemen had spent a day hunting. Unfortunately no mention was made of the dogs they may have used! However, its title was 'My whole delight is the merry chase' (Cantata No. 208) and includes the well-known air 'Sheep may safely graze' in which the words were chosen to complement the two listening princely rulers. Goethe and Schiller are two names synonymous with Weimar. Johann Wolfgang von Goethe (1749–1832) the German poet and dramatist and Johann Christoph Friedrich von Schiller (1759–1805) the poet. Other notable intellectuals at that time in Weimar were Johann Gottfried von Herder (1744–1803), German critic and poet who was court preacher, and Christopher Martin Wieland (1733–1813), poet and novelist.

After the First World War (1914–18), Weimar became the seat of the new German republic. Weimar gave its name to the Weimar Republic because the German constitution (established in 1919 after the defeat of Germany) was signed and drawn up there. This constitution, drafted by Hugo Preuss, was accepted on 31 July 1919. It established a federal system with a Reichsrat (house of states) and a Reichstag (directly elected house). This was a noble but ill-fated German effort at parliamentary democracy and the Weimar Republic has gone down in history as the monumental failure of the one democratic state that the Germans ever had up to the time of Hitler. On 31 July 1932 the Nazis polled 37 per cent of the votes cast, the strongest single party in the new Reichstag, and the Communists emerged second. Thus the majority of the German people voted for one or the other form of dictatorship. In 1933 the Republic ended and the Third Reich began with Hitler's assumption of power as Chancellor.

The 'Weimar period' stands out as an era of intellectual ferment; of rich diversity in motivation and idiom, and this ferment affected all branches of the arts. This turmoil, the burning of the Reichstag, and then the Second World War no doubt all played a part in the destruction or loss of so many early Weimaraner breed records and, indeed, the breed itself. For such a noble breed to be unwittingly associated with such ignominy seems unfair, but then people's memories are short and today the breed can stand proudly on its own four feet and hold its aristocratic head high in the world.

2

Theories on the Breed's Origin and its Known History

At school English history was without doubt my worst subject. Perhaps had it been Weimaraner history my school reports might have made slightly better reading. One of my favourite time-wasting pastimes was making lists! It still is. Hence this humble offering of what amounts partly to a book of glorified lists. However, I digress: back to history, which is defined in my dictionary as: (a) the study of the past; (b) a systematic and chronological record of past events relating to a particular period or country, etc.; (c) a recorded or connected series of facts, especially concerning a particular group or subject.

Many previous so-called 'histories' have fallen into none of these three categories and have often resulted in pure fantasy – the products of over-fertile imaginations. In the light of modern knowledge of genetics, some of the theories put forward in the old days may appear extremely fanciful, but in nearly all of them there is just that touch of the unexplained which leaves one wondering if we have really learned all that much over the years. What is certain is that we are really no nearer now to pinpointing the Weimaraner's ancestor than were the old experts in Germany so many years ago.

What is attempted in this chapter is to give a résumé of some of the more acceptable versions of the origin of this fascinating breed, the Weimaraner, as well as the factual documented past history. Résumé it will of necessity be. The old saying 'history repeats itself and historians repeat one another' seems very true. Nevertheless I hope that the reader will find items of interest not previously known to him.

A promise made by the *Reichsjaegermeister* to grant independence to all specialised breeds was finally fulfilled in 1896 when the Weimaraner was accepted, after considerable opposition, as a separate pure breed by the German Delegate Commission. The first German dog show was held in 1863 in Hamburg and the Delegate Commission was founded in 1880 so it was after 1880 that connoisseurs of the grey dogs requested that the Weimaraner be recognised because of its excellent shooting qualities. This was bitterly opposed by many 'canine experts' who were of the opinion that the Weimaraner was merely a colour variation of the German Shorthair. Eventually however, the idea prevailed that *because* of its colour the Weimaraner was a breed in itself and at a show during 1896 in Bernberg the first 'breed standard' was laid down by Major von Bünau.

One year later, on 20 June 1897 the first club was formed. It was named the 'Club for the Pure Breeding of the Silver-grey Weimaraner Vorstehhund' and among its first members were First Lt von Crompton from Weimar, Karl Brandt from Osterode, Dr Lenhobel Lindblohm the painter, Rittmeister Pitzsche of Sandersleben, who was one of the earliest breeders, Baron von Wintzingerode-Knorr of Adelsborn, Wittekop of Hauchenhausen, whose kennel name was Rudemanns, Chamberlain von Altem of Weimar, Paul Schettler, a book publisher from Koetha, E. Stahlecker, an editor from Berlin, Sebastian Tillman of Koblenz, and Forest Ranger Feltens of Dassel, one of the earliest and biggest breeders. The Weimaraner was the fourth specialised breed to be recognised, the others being the *Deutsch Drahthaar*, the *Deutsch Kurzhaar* and the *Deutsch Langhaar*. The rather unwieldy title of the Club was soon changed to the slightly shorter *Society for the Breeding of the Weimaraner-Vorstehhund* and the first President was Herr von Crompton from Weimar. So much has been written about the supposed origin of the Weimaraner but when it is all boiled down, all that can be undeniably proved is that it has *officially* existed as a pure breed since 1896 although obviously it was known long before then. Indeed there were 14 Weimaraners exhibited at a Berlin Show in 1880.

Apart from the plausible *Brache*, *Leithund* and *Schweisshund* ancestor theories, one of the most popular ideas put forward was that the Weimaraner was a degenerated (colour-faded) German Short-haired pointer – a theory I have heard stated quite forcibly as recently as 1981! The *Deutsche Dogge* (Great Dane) was also a well-supported originator, and proposed by that great GSP authority Dr Paul Kleemann. What follows now is a selection of translations from various German writings, and other articles – some mere snippets of information, others more lengthy in content, and from which the reader may decide for himself whence came the Weimaraner of today. These are collected into four groups: the pointing dogs; the *Brache*, *Leithund* and *Schweisshund*; the Great Dane; and the German Short-haired Pointer.

1. The Pointing Dogs

Possibly the first mention of pointing dogs in the German language was in a short note written by Kaiser Maximilian who ruled from 1493 to 1519. He wrote to the Duke of Austria on the subject of falconry and instructed his servants to establish a preserved area for either woodcock (*Waldhuehner*) or partridge (*Feldhuehner*) which were to be caught with a net and a pointing dog. It was at about that time that Austria ruled over Spain and many Spanish pointers were brought to Austria and Germany.

It is well known that up to the year 1700 no German apart from the ruling classes was permitted to keep pointing dogs in Germany.

Diezel (1779–1860) wrote: 'As far as bird hunting goes, the English pointer surpasses the German pointing dogs, but if any pointing breed is capable of taking over the work of the *Schweisshund* (bloodhound) it is the German *Vorstehhund* (pointer) and not the English pointer. I would wager that nobody would be more surprised than the English to learn that dogs were brought from them to make a breed of all-purpose dog.'

In 1902 in *Unser Hund* Dr A. Stroese of Neudamm wrote: 'The silver grey Weimaraner is said to have been descended from a yellow and white smooth-haired English bitch imported into Germany in the 1820s by the Duke of Weimar, and crossed with German dogs.'

In the same year (1902) Oberleutnant Emil Ilgner wrote an unsupported history of the breed in which he said that the Duke of Weimar was introduced to the breed by the Prince Esterhazy and Auersperg on numerous trips he made to Teplitz in Bohemia. He was said to be so impressed with the dogs with which he hunted there that he took several back to Weimar. To this, Major Herber replied: 'Some time ago I received a letter which indicated that the trail of the breed led back to the *Vorstehhund* of Bohemian origin. This was a contradictory statement as among other things, the sharp forehead of the Bohemian was referred to, and the original colour was pointed out to have been yellowish-white which can never be transformed to grey.'

In 1904 in *Die Deutschen Hunde* Richard Strebel wrote: 'Karl Brandt said in the time of the Grand Duke Karl August of Weimar (end of the eighteenth century) a German Shorthaired bitch was crossed with an English pointer. A grey dog resulted and from this grey dog by means

5

of clever breeding, the Weimaraner is said to have sprung. The picture by Van Dyck (1631) proves that these dogs are older and the introduction of the pointer was done as an experiment.'

2. Brache, Leithund, Schweisshund

According to legend, in the seventh and eighth centuries the St Hubert strain of bloodhound was established in the Ardennes (France) and was named after François Hubert, the son of Bertrand, Duc de Guienne. One of Hubert's favourite pastimes was hunting with his home-bred pack of bloodhounds, but after the death of his wife Floribane, he lost interest in living the life of a nobleman and spent all his time out hunting. He was out hunting as usual on one Good Friday when he had a vision which so affected him that he gave up this worldly pleasure and joined a monastery. His vision was the sudden appearance of a stag bearing a shining crucifix between its antlers. There is a beautiful painting, 'The Vision of St Hubert' by the fifteenth-century artist Pisanello which hangs in the National Gallery, London. Hubert was appointed Bishop of Tongern and later Bishop of Liège where in 708 he had a cathedral built and where he died in 825. He was canonised 100 years later. Miraculously his body had remained intact and was taken to a Benedictine cloister in the Ardennes. He is known as the patron saint of all hunters. After his death, his strain of hounds was preserved by the monks and while at first these were all black hounds, they later developed small tan markings, then black and tan; there were also some white hounds thought possibly to be the originals of the famed 'Talbot'. Many years later in England some hounds became a greyish-red colour and these were known as 'dunne houndes' but the true St Hubert strain eventually died out during the nineteenth century.

King Louis IX, the devout Saint Louis, was a renowned huntsman and he is said to have introduced to Europe the grey dogs with which he had hunted gazelle in the Holy Land. These grey hounds were said to have the strength of mastiffs, the speed of greyhounds and the scenting abilities of bird-dogs. Through subsequent cross-breeding several breeds of dogs evolved, each being utilised for a specific form of hunting. The setters were used to flatten themselves against the ground so they did not become enmeshed in the nets being cast; the hounds harried stag for hours and could also hold their own against the fearsome black boar; and the greyhounds were fast and absolutely lethal on quarry such as wolf. According to some old French books, the name greyhound was derived from the Celtic 'grech' or 'greg' which meant dog; according to others it was connected with 'grey' which appeared to be the most common colour of this breed. In the French magazine *Revue du Chien* (5) published in the 1970s, Germain de Brie said that the prized grey colour of the 'Weimaraner' (not known by that name, of course) attracted the kings of France who gave the breed their protection and jealously guarded it until in about 1450 owing to a change in fashion, they turned their attention else-where and thus lost France's monopoly in the breed. De Brie draws attention to the many Van Dyck paintings of later years which depict the breed and also to the two enormous antique bronze statues framing the portals of Las Palmas Cathedral in the Canary Isles which are said to closely resemble the present-day Weimaraner.

A snippet from Diezel – he wrote that *Brachen* are *Waldbodenhunde*, meaning dogs who search the floor of the forest, drive game and bark on trail.

In an old German book, Fama states: 'The ideal hunting dog in old times was the so-called *Leithund*. This dog was set on the scent of a chosen (not wounded) stag or other deer in the herd and was able to lead the hunter to this single animal. For this purpose they developed the *Schweisshund*, brown of colour. Then they had pointers for smaller game, for birds, rabbits and so forth. Then came the idea to cross these breeds to meld the hunting qualities of both. The Weimaraner was the result of this noble experiment; a dog that points, with an exceedingly good nose.'

Chief Justice Richnow of Aurich, a member of the Weimaraner Club (Germany) in 1908 also wrote about the supposed origin of the breed; parts of his article are quoted here:

Looking through the old hunting and shooting classics it is disappointing to find the inadequate and incomplete description of the appearance of the dogs which were used for shooting in those days. The different hair types of the *Vorstehhund* were not distinguished or recognised as breeds in the present sense. From this we can conclude that as changes occurred in shooting in general, a change in the type of dogs used occurred at the same time. The oldest type of shooting dog was the *Brache* (simply called the shooting dog in the classics). The days of the *Leithund* were coming to an end; he was not needed any more. When the *Jägerhof* of Hanover cultivated the work of the *Leithund* into the bloodhound, the days of the *Leithund* were over. . . . a. d.

Winkel describes the colours as white with brown patches, piebald or striped brown, also brown with white markings, black, or white with different coloured markings which, according to the author, are rare. Ash grey and yellow dogs of pure breed are very rare indeed. . . . If one knows how to interpret the classics one has to conclude that from the beginning to the middle of the nineteenth century the *Vorstehhund* can hardly have been bigger than middle-sized. It was only in the time before 1870 that the heavy old German *Vorstehhund* developed, heavy because of the crossing in of the *Leithund*, often loosely-shouldered like the *Leithund* with his heavy ears and overhanging lips, slow and clumsy. Through selective breeding but also through the intake of a lot of English blood, especially with the German Shorthair, a fast field-dog has been created. With the Weimaraner all this has happened a lot more slowly. The Weimaraner was then mainly bred in and around Thuringen, almost exclusively so and used in small shoots where the searching for game with a slow dog was preferred. Even still before the First World War most Weimaraners, even those that had been improved by skilled breeders and whose type had therefore been improved, could not compare with a field trial dog in a stylish search, although his enthusiasm for retrieving, his tenacity and speed were quite adequate. There is hardly a Weimaraner that does not naturally track on every scent and is a born *velorenbringer*. That he has not lost his ability can be attributed to the fact that there has not been excessive pointer blood bred into him which would only have spoiled the Weimaraner. Having said this does not mean that occasionally strange blood has not come into the breed because, after all, each pure breed has started with dogs genuinely believed to be pure bred and which complied with the ultimate breeding aim. The Weimaraner has retained in him in considerable strength the last drop of *Leithund* blood.

Looking ahead a few years to the approach of the First World War and during it, activities were naturally quiet on the Weimaraner scene, but after the war had ended the breed started to surge upwards. This upsurge is inseparably connected with the name Major Robert Herber (1867–1946) who, with his wife Hetty, founded the famous *aus der Wulfsriede* kennels.

It is said that having seen his first Weimaraner whilst a young captain, he never shot over another breed, so impressed was he with it. In 1921 he took over the management of the Club and through his tireless efforts and skilful selective breeding brought about the change in the breed, which was then still slightly slow and clumsy but incomparable for tracking. Today we admire the streamlined shape of the Weimaraner. From 1921 onwards Herber was in the true sense of the word the 'father of the Weimaraner'. As secretary of the magazine

Kennel and Field he wrote numerous articles propounding his theories on the breed's origins, some of which are translated in this chapter; he also published a book on the breed acknowledged in Germany as the 'bible'. His death on 15 September 1946 was indeed a great loss to the breed. He was honoured in 1951 when the first Major Herber Memorial Field Trials took place in Marklohe.

Answering the *Brache/Leithund/Schweisshund* theories, Major Herber wrote the following:

It is not necessary to rack our brains about the colour of the Weimaraner because this colour can be brought about in several ways – out of black, brown and, as Friess says, even due to lack of vitamins, or a mutation. Why, therefore, should we not accept the black colour which occurs within the Bloodhound breed as well as within the breed of the *Brache*, the ancestor of the Bloodhound? Brown, also originating from black, can be deleted. Even if we accepted the brown *Deutsch Kurzhaar* as the father of the Weimaraner, this colour would have had to show up even if only slightly. Which other colour appears now and then as a slight tint on the legs and cheeks? Yellowish-red – which was also mentioned as being the colour of the Bloodhound and the *Brache* on these places. (a.d. Winkel states that these colours are typical characteristics of the *Brache*.) Due to these characteristics of breed, I would like to state my opinion, which I have established over eighteen years, and through all these years I have bred and highly valued the Weimaraner. In *Hunting Press* for 28 October 1923, Richnow states that the Weimaraner can be regarded as being the dog having the largest amount of bloodhound blood which proves that he believes that the Weimaraner originates from the Bloodhound breed. The bloodhound as well as all long-eared hunting dogs in Europe and Asia is a descendant of the *Brache*. When I admit that I agree on a greater part that the *Brache* is the father of the Weimaraner I am not, however, disagreeing with Richnow's point of view. Richnow himself has also thoroughly considered this question and would certainly have made a positive decision if it were possible. The following possibility remains and it is the most probable one. As the Weimaraner cannot be found in the books of our old literates, he did not exist as a breed at that time. But nevertheless, such short-haired grey dogs may have already existed in sporadic numbers at that period. Van Dyck painted a portrait of Prince Rupprecht von der Pfalz with a Weimaraner-coloured short-haired *Huehnerhund* (bird-dog) [see below], also Friess, but please do not consider the few old hunting writers as in their opinion the Weimaraner was a worthless cross-breed even though one or the other had good hunting qualities. A certain dog breeder seemed to like these grey dogs due to their excellent hunting qualities, and he paired them in Thuringen where they then appeared in large numbers. The physical characteristics of the *Brache*, for example the shape of the head, flesh-coloured nose, the very slight onset of the forehead, the slight over-drooping of the lips, the small wrinkle at the mouth, the shape of the tail, the carrying of the full-length tail, are signs which point out that the Weimaraner originates from the *Brache*. Now back to the colour – grey can originate from black or brown. If the colour of the Weimaraner originated from brown then it should somehow have occurred again, instead of the reddish-yellow colour of the *Brache*. Our grey therefore originated from black and is the reason why I assume that the Weimaraner is a descendant of the *Brache*, as Doebel and Hartig point out that black as well as brown are the colours of the bloodhound. When Friess therefore insists on the brown colour, why then must it come from the *Deutsch Kurzhaar*? It could just as well come from the brown of the bloodhound. Let us put together all my researches and enquiries which result in the most likely probability: that the Weimaraner originates from the *Brache*, perhaps as a mutation originating from our oldest hunting dogs.

3. The Great Dane (Deutsch Dogge)

Dr Paul Kleemann, an acknowledged expert on German Short-haired Pointers favoured the Great Dane as the Weimaraner's ancestor. He wrote an article in *Wild und Hund* dated 29 July 1938 to which Major Herber replied. Dr Kleemann's article is not printed here as it is adequately covered by Major Herber's comments, which were as follows:

Dr Kleemann mentions several discussions concerning the Weimaraner in hunting literature, among others published in the magazine *Der Hund* which also assumes that the Weimaraner originates from the Great Dane although the name of the author was not given. The proof thereof was stated as having been the large bodies, the blue-grey colour, the less glossy hair and the narrow cheeks. We must also ask the question here as to how many of our Weimaraners has this anonymous author already seen. Pictures of our oldest Weimaraners reveal absolutely no abnormal size although some dogs may have been very large, but do large dogs not occur also among the other *Vorstehhunde*, for example the *Deutsch Kurzhaar* or the *Deutsch Langhaar*? Is that a breed characteristic? The Weimaraners were never observed to have been of a blue-grey colour; even the mouse-grey is different. Even Friess says that the colour of the Great Dane never occurs in the Weimaraner. The less glossy hair can be noticed on the Weimaraner only if he has not been given the correct food and diet. I have never observed any difference between the gloss of the Weimaraner's hair and, for example, that of the *Deutsch Kurzhaar*. There are individual changes, but not breed characteristics. Now

Prince Rupprecht von der Pfalz with Huehnerhund – Van Dyck.

only the question of the narrow cheekbones remains. Does the Great Dane possess such narrow cheeks?

Dr Kleemann states further: 'The hunting activity of the Dukes of Weimar had nothing to do with the existence of the Weimaraner.' He writes that the proof thereof is the fact that several hunting writers of the Royal Court of Weimar never mentioned the Weimaraner, which they by all means would have done for patriotic reasons. I have been in touch with the *Hofmarschallamt* and the *Hofjagdamt* in Weimar, who had found nothing concerning the Weimaraner despite thorough searching through their files. The name was probably brought into existence because the Weimaraner first occurred in large numbers in Weimar and was bred there. Even Diezel says nothing about the Weimaraner in 1873. The writers of that time did not recognise the peculiarity of the plain-looking colour, states Kleemann, and that is also my opinion. Therefore, the Weimaraner had already existed for a long time, but no one took notice of him as he had not been mentioned in dog-breeding literature.

Kleemann then points out the paw of the Great Dane which the Weimaraner is also supposed to have. I asked a well-known breeder of Great Danes what is meant by the expression *Doggenpfote* (Great Dane foot). He assumed that what was meant was *Spreizpfote* (spreading toes). This has occurred and still does, but not often. I myself have noticed this on the *Bertholdsburger* but this cannot be accepted as a breed characteristic. It has also been observed among other breeds and is therefore no proof for the assumption that the Great Dane is the father of the Weimaraner.

If Kleemann means the *Hasenpfote* (rabbit-foot) I have never seen anything like it on any Weimaraner which I have examined closely. Kleemann says that the head of the Great Dane is the same as that of the Weimaraner, as are the blue eyes. Regarding the head, the breed characteristics of each breed give the best information. Great Dane: distinct onset separating back of nose from forehead. Weimaraner: very slight onset (stop) from forehead. Great Dane: slightly pronounced cheeks. Weimaraner: jowl muscles pronounced. I have given further details of the characteristics of the two breeds in the article published in *Wild und Hund*. Now the blue eyes: the Weimaraner has blue eyes only during his first two months of age; then they turn to shades of amber, never brown or dark colours as those most desired in the Great Dane. The Great Dane may have light-coloured eyes, but this is not the rule. The Griffon and the *Stichelhaar* may also have light coloured eyes and the above cannot, therefore, be accepted as proof.

Kleemann states further that the Weimaraner, contrary to the bloodhound, is a 'hard' dog, which is not so. 'Hard' Weimaraners are very rare. The following statement made by Kleemann regarding the bloodhound appears to be the perfect description of the Weimaraner: 'The bloodhound is very timid and the slightest harsh treatment can spoil him for ever.' This is true of many of our dogs as I myself have already experienced, but he is exaggerating when he says the Bloodhound is timid.

Dr Kleemann and the author of the article in *Wild und Hund* have overlooked something very important which refutes the Great Dane theory. Besides speaking only of the physical appearance when comparing two breeds, I must also consider the inherited mental characteristics. From whence did the Weimaraner inherit his scenting qualities, his willingness for retrieving, his other hunting instincts, his intelligence? From the Great Dane or rather from the bloodhound or the *Brache*, the ancestor of the bloodhound? Is the latter not a greater probability?

Even though we know practically nothing about the origin of the Weimaraner, we do positively know that according to the afore-mentioned opinions regarding the *Deutsch Kurzhaar* and the Great Dane, these cannot be accepted as knowledge or as true facts, not even as a probability.

We are grateful to Dr Kleemann for his acknowledgement of the excellent hunting qualities of our Weimaraners.

4. The Deutsche Kurzhaar (German Short-haired Pointer)

An article entitled 'The Origin of the Weimaraner' appeared in *Deutsche Waidwerk* (19) on 11 August 1939. The author merely gave his initials, R.F., and it is assumed that this was Robert Friess, a Chief Forester, whose views were as follows:

The origin of this silver-grey dog has long been the subject of argument. Different theories attempt to explain this rare and odd colour. There exist the pointer theory, the Great Dane theory, the bloodhound theory, and all of them disregard the most important thing. The silver-grey or blue colour can originate from brown or blue through lack of pigment. The light eyes and the light coloured nose of the Weimaraner show that he has just a small amount of pigment and that the colour originated from brown dogs through fading of the colour. All German *Vorstehhunde* possess pointer blood to some extent, bearing in mind that the German-English cross-breeding forty or fifty years ago was regarded as being a general success. The breeders wanted to improve the nose of the setter and pointer, the *Hoch-wind-und Huehnernase* (high wind and bird nose), the speed and persistence, and the premature pointing - in which they were highly successful. They also required the addition of the *Spuernase* (tracing nose) which was a necessary qualification for tracking after the shot.

These were characteristics inherited from the *Brache* and *Schweisshund* which every *Vorstehhund* possesses because all long-eared hunting dogs in Europe and Asia are without exception descendants of the *Brache* – yes, the

Schweisshunde and *Leithunde* are pure descendants of the *Brache*. The old *Huehnerhunde* of German origin also have a little amount of the Great Dane, of the old *Hatzrueden*, of the *Saupacker*. All coarse-haired *Brachen* and *Vorstehhunde* have a small amount of the old coarse-haired shepherd dogs, the sheep-poodle. This old shepherd dog should not be confused with the modern shepherd dog, the *Schaeferspitz* who was only a herd-driving dog and has been transformed into his present shape through breeding. Even wolves were cross-bred into this breed for this reason. The usual coarse-haired, rarely stiff-haired and long stiff-haired shepherd dog, the purest breed of which exists in the Hungarian *Komondor* (Kuvasz) were kept for protecting the herd against wild animals and human robbers. These very sharp shepherd dogs were also used to seize bears and boars and to improve the sharpness of other hunting dogs; and their thick hair growth and indifference to all kinds of weather had given them their love for water. When we turn back to the origin of all breeds, we come across all kinds of cross-breeds and last of all, the wolf.

The pointer theory is just as correct as the bloodhound and Great Dane theories, but concerning the Weimaraner and his colour, they are all incorrect. For example, the blue Great Dane, the 'Bismarck Dane' originated from black Great Danes. Today these colours are not wanted by the breeders. The colour is a faded black, the real blue Danes still have black noses and very often dark eyes. This colour never occurs among Weimaraners. The usual and preferred Weimaraner colour is light grey with a very slight brown hue, the so-called 'old silver' colour. The nose and eyes are light coloured. This proves the origin of brown, i.e. coffee-brown coloured dogs who originated from black dogs through lack of pigment. Black is the richest colour and only red has the same strength; both can produce brown. Both colours seem to have the same amount of pigment and are closely related in other aspects.

Therefore it is no surprise that when brown pure-breds, for example, German long-hairs are crossed with dark red dogs with black noses such as the Irish Setters, the results are mostly pure black hounds. Through this the faded brown pigment is strengthened and transformed into black again. In England the Irish Setter is often crossed with the black and red Gordon Setter when his colour is too light and his nose becomes red. It is an old rule regarding the breeding of red *Dachshunde* that the breeding of red-coloured dogs together will finally result in yellow-coloured dogs with red noses. They are then strengthened in colour with black/red dogs. If the yellow is allowed to continue fading, the light yellow, whitish-yellow and finally white with a slight yellow tint is produced as in Spitz, Pomeranians and Eskimo dogs. Similarly, pure brown breeding finally results in silver-brown and grey dogs. First light brown, yellow, and yes, even whitish-yellow eyes are produced. Then probably supported through lack of Vitamin D, silver-grey dogs

14

(Weimaraner colours) are brought about within all breeds which had been purely bred brown. This is still happening. Very often these plain coloured dogs are secretly and immediately destroyed. Under the above circumstances, brown bred with brown *Dobermanns* often produce grey ones; coffee-brown *Dachshunde* frequently gave birth to silver-grey dogs with a yellow hue. I have already seen that German Short-hairs as well as German long-hairs produce silver-grey.

At present there exists no German Short-hair breed which is bred brown with brown; the above may prove to occur occasionally but mostly these 'colour errors' are destroyed secretly. That pure-brown German long-hair breeds have produced Weimaraner-coloured dogs is proved by the pictures of the above mentioned hounds with the colour of the Weimaraner which were illustrated a short time ago in the hunting press. Here one could assume that this was the return of some former Weimaraner cross-breeding. However, this is contradicted by another example, the Weimaraner-coloured German *Wachtelhunde* (Pointer-Spaniel) the origin of which I can trace back to the first stud-dog. There is positively no Weimaraner blood in this breed. This Weimaraner colour was brought about through a mutation.

Finally pure brown inheriting breeds were brought about which produced neither spots nor yellow tint, instead 100 per cent pure brown. They traced back nine brown stud-dogs, the tenth one was white-brown with a yellow tint. As the hounds of a gamekeeper were not permitted to be spotted in colour because of the Forest and Game Protection Service, they were eliminated.

Suddenly Weimaraner colours appeared among the pure brown thoroughbred *Wachtelhund* breeds. This happened during the war and the following period in which they were given only vegetables, lacking vitamins and fat. The first case could have been a mistake, but as this appeared to repeat itself in other pure brown bred breeds, it became clear that this was due to lack of pigment, a fading of the brown colour, therefore a mutation. This led back to the fact that the parents, grandparents, etc. must have been given poor food lacking vitamins. When it was possible to give the dogs their normal and correct food (fat, meat, etc.) only one silver-grey puppy came into this world within 15 years. During this following period after the war, about six or more were produced within only three or four years. Recent scientific experiments in America have revealed that this fading of black or brown turning into blue or grey is due to the lack of Vitamin D. This grey colour can be artificially produced when Vitamin D is withdrawn. There is no doubt that the Weimaraner colour originates from a mutation within the brown, shorthair breed. If these Weimaraner-coloured *Wachtelhunde* had been continually paired, a beautiful silver-grey breed could have been brought about. However, suitable as this colour may be for a *Puerschhund* (dog for deer and buck hunting), it is not the correct colour and is even dangerous for a

Stoeberhund (dog for small game hunting). This is the reason that they were eliminated even though several of these beautiful and efficient, small, silver-grey long-haired dogs had been raised.

Regarding the origin of the Weimaraner, the old expert Karl Brandt states that the Grand Duke Karl August of Weimar had paired a German Short-haired bitch with a pointer at the end of the eighteenth century, which resulted in a grey hound. This fact and clever breeding have brought about the existence of the Weimaraners. That, undoubtedly, was just one case, in which by chance a silver-grey short-hair was produced. But surely there must have been others before that? In 1631 Van Dyck painted a portrait of Prinz Rupprecht von der Pfalz with a Weimaraner-coloured short-haired *Huehner-hund*. Strebel, who is the best judge and researcher in regard to the origin of all dog breeds, is of the opinion that 'it is daring to draw the pointer into the question of the Weimaraner'. Strebel's opinion is that the blue is a faded black. I think that the silver-grey is a faded brown and suppose that I have given sufficient proof. The brown colour often seems to shimmer through the grey. Unfortunately I cannot agree with Major Herber that the colour of the Weimaraner originates from grey bloodhounds, *Schweisshunde* or *Brachen*. All *Brachen* of Europe and Asia, i.e. all long-eared pure *Brachen* have only two colours, either black with a red tint, or yellow with or without black hair tips. The third colour of the *Brache* – white – is no colour, just an achromatism which can be brought into existence through a certain breeding. First white toes, then a white chest and white tip of the tail appeared.

The Weimaraner simply originated from pure-bred brown short-haired *Vorstehhunde*; the colour of the Weimaraner is a faded or degenerated brown. The eyes, the nose and the nails are automatically drawn into this degeneration although the aforementioned *Brachen* and terriers can still have dark, even black eyes, noses and nails as they still possess black pigment.

If the Weimaraner of today, as all his owners and followers assert, is especially reliable in scenting and is, therefore, qualified for work after the shot, it is due to the fact that the breed was very soon separated from the old German Short-hair who also had a small amount of *Schweisshund, Brachen,* and even Great Dane blood. In younger years I myself have only once hunted with a Weimaraner-coloured German long-hair of brown parents.

The Weimaraner, therefore, was not such a complete victim of the 'great and important refreshing of blood' with the modern English Pointer, the expert in bird hunting. People who can still remember the heavy, sure-scenting, loud-hunting, old brown German Short-hair and who had hunted with this dog, who was not very good in the fields but excelled in woodland, and was a sharp, protective, game-keeper's dog, do not require further details. Forty years ago they had seen their own breed drowning in Pointer blood.

Let us be grateful that such a peculiar but efficient family has saved itself through long years and has served the German Forestry Service with its loyalty.

The last origin of all breeds trails back into the darkness and none of them leapt out of Noah's Ark in their present shape and colour.

Major Herber's reply to R.F. appeared in *Deutsche Waidwerk* (22), dated 1 September 1939:

Perhaps it would have been more correct to put a question mark after the title of R.F.'s article in No. 19 of this magazine dated 11 August 1939, as was done with all other attempts to prove its origin. After reading the article published in the *Hunting Press* in October 1938, there is no doubt that the German Shorthair could not be the ancestor of the Weimaraner.

As I have achieved the title 'father of the Weimaraner' after seventeen years of activity for the grey breed, which is acknowledged by R.F., I suppose I may express my opinion which I have reached during this period. I am not stating that this is a confirmed assertion, only a possibility. The reader may judge for himself if this possibility can be accepted as a probability.

As the Weimaraner was not found in old literature, he did not exist as a breed. However, such short-haired light-grey dogs could possibly have existed in small numbers in that period (also R.F.'s opinion), but they were unknown or disregarded by these sporting writers. In their opinion they were the worthless results of cross-breedings. But as it has been proved that two black animals can produce grey ones, it seems best to look for black ancestors in the old period. There was one black breed, the St Hubertus *Brachen* among the dogs used for hunting in the old days. As the characteristics of both breeds are almost the same, it is possible that the Weimaraner is a mutation within the *Brache* breed, which is more-or-less the ancestor of all *Vorstehhunde*. At the time, a breeder appeared to like these grey mutations and paired them so that gradually these dogs appeared in larger numbers here in Thuringen. As this grey dog was not identical with any other *Vorstehhund* breed, particularly not the German Shorthair, the Weimaraner was accepted as a breed by the Delegate Commission. The Delegate Commission would surely have named this grey dog a grey German Shorthair if they could have proved any connection between the two breeds.

Our hon. member, Herr Winztingerode auf Adelsborn, has known the Weimaraner since 1869 and asserts that they gave voice on trail, which indicated an inheritance from the *Brache* and not from the German Shorthair; furthermore, that black parents produced greys.

Why does R.F. describe the indirect descent from the German Shorthair, which is not true? If R.F. can produce grey dogs from brown German Shorthairs by withdrawing vitamins, then he can do the same with black ones; therefore, this is no proof for stating that the Weimaraner originates from German Shorthairs. R.F. says the Weimaraner colour is simply a degenerated brown – yes, that would be very simple if it were true, but it is not. If you can show me one brown spot on a Weimaraner, I will have to destroy the complete Weimaraner pedigree. The Weimaraner is a grey-reddish-yellow shimmering colour which we incorrectly call 'deer-grey'. Now and then there are Weimaraners with a reddish-yellow hue or markings on the jowls and legs such as the *Brachen* had, but never brown or a tint of the same. Brown was not wanted by the *Brache* breeders. Has the Weimaraner inherited these reddish-yellow markings from the German Shorthair? R.F. goes on: 'The eyes, nose and nails are automatically drawn into this degeneration'. Naturally they are if this theory of degeneration was correct. Half of my Weimaraners have dark nails; just a few possess light nails. The noses are according to the breed standard, of a dark flesh colour, never light coloured, and the eyes which suit the colour of the Weimaraner's coat have nothing to do with the German Shorthair.

Now the long-haired Weimaraner. We know that pure brown long-haired breeds can possess Weimaraner colours but this does not occur here. We have no brown German Longhairs and we do not intend to borrow any. Our long-haired Weimaraners have been bred from short-haired ones, which has been proved. We, therefore, protest against the expression 'German Longhairs with Weimaraner colour' – they are just as much not German Longhairs as our short-haired Weimaraners are not German Shorthairs. As they are being listed as long-haired Weimaraners, every registered long-haired *Vorstehhund* is a long-haired Weimaraner, since they are grey German long-haired pointers, they are not permitted to be registered. We did not intend to establish a new breed with the long-haired Weimaraner, we have only gratefully acknowledged and accepted this gift of nature which we had formerly stupidly rejected. Who can reproach us for this action, as there are also short, long and rough-haired *Dachshunde* and Fox Terriers.

In conclusion R.F. mentions the hunting qualities of the Weimaraner, the best of which are scenting, retrieving and his sharpness. However, this does not prove that the Weimaraner originates from the *Brache* or from the German Shorthairs. Every other breed can claim these characteristics as its own. I have hunted with the German long-haired and German Short-haired dogs (*Graeff-Bingen*) as well as with both kinds of Setter and I value them highly. I know exactly which breed I would prefer for one certain hunting district and which I would prefer for the other. I have erected a monument for my dear and loyal *Tell-Bingen* in the grounds of the *Ruhleben bei Spandau* shooting school. I am no fanatical follower of one breed and my efforts in this case are purely essential. It is not necessary to name three chief witnesses after giving the above corrections, but nevertheless I am giving the names of three eminent dog-experts: Karl Brandt, Dr Kleemann and von Otto. Karl Brandt says that 'even if the Weimaraner were painted a brown colour, one could instantly recognise him as a Weimaraner'. Dr Kleemann, Hon. Chairman and the outstanding expert on German Shorthairs, assumes that the Weimaraner originated from the Great Dane and speaks of R.F. and his theory only in the words 'some people say'. He certainly knows of no reason to deny us descendants and he should know best. When von Otto and I trained Weimaraners at the World Exhibition in Frankfurt in 1935, a man came to our training stand and politely asked the following question: 'If the colour were not as it is, would you believe the Weimaraner to be a *Deutsche Kurzhaar*?' Von Otto, always prepared to give information even during the busiest moments, replied: 'Certainly there exists a similarity, but just look closely – the colour is not so important. Look at the shape of the head, the longer fangs of all 17 dogs here, the jowl muscles, the different, longer and slightly pointed ears, the longer back . . .' I did not hear everything von Otto said, but he continued the discussion. The questioner, who had listened attentively, then asked: 'Are they German dogs?' Von Otto replied: 'Yes, probably of very old origin but we do not know very much about them. They certainly do not originate from the *Deutsche Kurzhaar*.' In 1925 in Dusseldorf where von Otto and I trained 13 Weimaraners he had already expressed the same opinion. He was one of the few judges who knew and valued our breed.

R.F. writes further: 'The Weimaraner was not such a complete victim of the "blood refreshening process". Otherwise he would not have been able to keep his spotless grey coat and would not have remained the only German Short-haired pointer breed which has not mingled with other breeds.'

In conclusion, I ask R.F. to accept my statements as being truly fundamental and I thank him for his efforts in attempting to develop a clear statement regarding the origin of our noble, beautiful grey dogs. However, I as well as Karl Brandt, Dr Kleemann and von Otto, could not agree with his opinion.

Karl Brandt had some interesting things to say about the Weimaraner too. He published a reader's letter in one of his numerous articles; this was from a Herr Münch who owned an estate in Blankenhein in Thuringen and who said:

About the origin of the Weimaraners around here, there were about 60 dogs which stemmed from my breeding alone, and the first of these dogs were bred by a Herr Weitzenberg in the late 1860s. He had bought a bitch in Danzig and had her mated with a rather grey dog *Griffon aus Köttersdorf* who sometimes produced long-haired puppies. Since the beginning of the 1870s Kämmergutspachter Egendorf and my father were breeding grey Weimaraners in our area.

Another of Brandt's articles referred to a field trial held at Sandersleben in April 1899 in which eleven dogs took part and which, in his words, 'failed lamentably'. This was blamed on unfavourable weather conditions on the days of the trial, and also on bad breeding, but it was mainly due to the fact that the old Weimaraner strains simply happened to be bred by shoot owners whose particular ground did not suit the working capabilities of the dogs – in that the dog did not need to have great searching powers as the huntsman was able to get his game easily. In some types of shoot a good searching dog was of no advantage at all and, in fact, the usefulness of the dog relied on other virtues. It was clear that the Weimaraner of those days compared unfavourably in field trials with other breeds, especially with the German Shorthair. In order to comprehend the abundance of game on those shooting grounds where the trial was held, there is an interesting result of a private shoot held the day after the disastrous Sandersleben trial. Brandt writes: 'We shot to eight guns and in a few hours had shot 32 hares, 193 rabbits, 8 cock pheasants, 51 hen pheasants, 1 corncrake, 1 cock-sparrow and 1 tom-cat!'

Brandt also remarked that the Weimaraner has a very characteristic tail such as no other shooting dog has and that if one dyed them artificially brown they would still be recognised by their tails! 'It is not the most beautiful part of their bodies as up to a third of its length up to a "nick" it is barrel or drum shaped and only from then on where it is normally docked it begins to taper. Immediately before this "nick" it is normally covered with longer, bristly hair, and the tail is also very often extraordinarily strong even in dogs that have a very noble, dry face.' According to the opinion of Wittekop who was another notable Weimaraner breeder of his time, the tail therefore looks best slightly short-docked. This peculiarity of the tail is as true today as it was then and is especially more noticeable now that the tendency is to leave the tail slightly longer.

As to the colour, Brandt says that in 1899 he obtained information from Pitschke that 'he had never seen a Weimaraner that did not have any white in him. Silver grey and white were colours in the breed which always occurred together. He would even consider it a breed characteristic as most Weimaraners were white behind the front paws.'

20

For many years, until her death in the late 1970s, Mrs Helen Schulze of Canada was the liaison between the Weimaraner Club of America and Europe. She was an Honorary Board Member of the German Weimaraner Club and their liaison with the American and Canadian clubs. The following short history was compiled by Mrs Schulze from material authorised by the German Weimaraner Club:

The saga of the Weimaraner reaches back as far as 1631. Although they existed before that time, no special attention was given to the gray dog which appeared on the large estates of the ruling classes. Before the year 1700 no German was permitted to keep pointing dogs; this was considered the privilege of the ruling landowners. The gray dog was an ideal hunting companion. He was known as the Weimar Pointer and so it was natural that the city of Weimar, and the country around, should be the origin of the investigation into the history of the gray dog. This began in the late 1800s. The Duke of Weimar was drawn into the investigation since there was adequate proof that the Duke and his relations had kept Weimaraners for their hunting pleasure for generations. However, they were not responsible for having developed the Weimaraner as a breed. Van Dyck's painting of Prince Rupprecht von der Pfalz with a Weimaraner-type hunting dog gave us our first touch of the history of this dog. By today's standards this was as close as a dog can come to be considered the Weimaraner of today. Gemalde von Ondry* painted the favoured hunting companion of the French King Ludwig XV (1715–74), showing 'Blanche' as a typical Weimaraner with all the characteristics we still look for. Other Ondry (*Oudry*) paintings are still to be seen today in the castle of the Comte de Sade in France.

Lord Witzingerode Knorr-Adelsborn and his family gave proof that the Weimaraner was the breed used on his estates as far back as 1864. His holdings are all around the cities of Halle, Weimar and Eisenach.

The new history of the Weimaraner began around 1870. In 1881 the first 'pure-bred' Weimaraner litter was born in Sandersleben in the kennels of Amtsrat Pitschke. He is credited with being the first breeder of the pure Weimaraner and this was the first registered litter of the Weimaraner breed. In 1883, the Treptow Dog Show made special mention and awarded a special prize to the Weimaraner as a 'heavy pointer with good musculature, a fine silver gray coat, and of great elegance'.

---

* This is an error: *Gemälde* is the German word for a painting or picture, and the painter in question is without doubt Jean-Baptiste Oudry (1686–1755) who, in 1736, was made Inspector-General of the Gobelins tapestry factory and designed a series of tapestries from 1736 to 1749 depicting the hunts of Louis XV. He was also commissioned to paint the hounds of the royal pack, and was appointed official painter of royal hunts.

The first Weimaraner Club was founded in 1897 in Halle Weimar. There was not much activity until 1922 when Major Herber took over as President.

The next extract is from an article entitled 'Keep your Dog Clean' published in the May 1952 Weimaraner Club of America Magazine. The author, Victor Moench, states that he was born about 25 miles from Weimar and entered the forestry service 50 miles southeast from Weimar, where part of his forestry training was with dogs and where he came into close contact with many of the Weimaraner-owning aristocrats.

Weimaraners in 1631 were called *Huehnerhund*. This word exactly translated means chicken dog or as we say here, bird dog. This covered any dog who would point birds and did not specify a special breed. All bird dogs today are still called *Huehnerhund* or *Vorstehhund*. No doubt the dog was a Weimaraner-like dog. There were no pure-bred Weimaraners at that time in Germany. There were no German pure-bred dogs (*Huehnerhund* or *Vorstehhund*). Diezel mentioned the importation of English Pointers in the early 1800s by a group of men formed for the sole purpose of producing a pure-bred bird dog in Germany but he knew that this specialist would not be the ideal German hunting dog (Diezel – page 68–69 *Erfahrungen aus dem Gebiete der Niederjagd*). I have a picture taken in 1862 of my father at 2 years of age sitting next to my grandfather's *Huehnerhund*. This was a rather large white and liver, long-coated dog. We never could find out whether it represented any breed. It was a *Huehnerhund* and that's all and came from Weimar. I suppose we now identify this too, as a Weimaraner. My grandfather was chief forester and chief hunter (*leibjaeger*) to the Duke of Sachsen Coburg Gotha. None of his sons in their youth knew anything about Weimaraners or German Shorthairs as they are today, and all were hunters. The Dukes entertained each other at hunts in their respective territories and Gotha is 25 miles from Weimar.

Diezel was born in 1779 in Sachsen Meiningen which is 50 miles southwest of Sachsen Weimar Eisenach. He hunted all over Germany, Austria and Hungary and does not mention one German pure bred bird dog as we know them today but does mention plenty of other pure breeds. Those dogs were probably in the formulative state because due to the wars and revolutions of 1848, the bigger game such as deer, bear and boar was depleted and if the boys wanted to play they had to concentrate more on birds, much to their chagrin. Therefore, they had to have a better *Huehnerhund* and *Vorstehhund* and that was the reason for pure bred German Pointers and Weimaraners, which were utility dogs, as the German hunter needed a dog who was good on feathers and fur – an all-round hunter and not a specialist like our English Pointer or Setter. This we now have and let's keep it that way.

If all the stories keep on we shall hear next that King Tut of Egypt hunted with Weimaraners.

3

Germany and Austria in the Twentieth Century

From 1924 onwards the breeding of Weimaraners in Germany is completely documented. Some figures of interest are given by Dr Werner Petri who states:

The number of entries vary considerably in the different years. In 1924 14 litters consisting of 76 puppies were registered. Up to 1936 the annual number of litters vary between 8 and 19, and the number of registered whelps between 44 and 105. In the first years especially the overall number of registrations differs considerably from the number of registered whelps because in those days many older dogs were subsequently registered. The years 1937 and 1938 were record years with 20 and 21 registered litters, and 109 and 112 registered whelps. After that the numbers dropped considerably, but then reached a new high in 1944 with 24 litters and 127 whelps. In 1945 though only 3 litters and 10 whelps were registered.

He goes on to make mention of the two dogs registered in 1928 which Howard Knight of the USA took out of Germany as foundation stock for America and which proved to be sterile. Dr Petri also notes the stock Knight subsequently acquired during 1937 and 1938, and also that during 1939 one of Knight's litters was entered in the German register with 1:1 whelps. Dr Petri says: 'The political circumstances of the time are also reflected in the breeding register. For instance in 1933 the dog Ponto aus der Grute was registered as being owned by His Excellency Hermann Goering. For the first time, and also the last time, in 1939 the Weimaraners bred in Austria were registered in the German register of pedigrees; 17 litters, 87 whelps as opposed to 14 litters, 80 whelps in Germany. 3 whelps of this year were exported to Czechoslovakia.'

The official recognition of the long-haired variety occurred in 1935 due to a long-haired puppy being born. So in 1935 the agreed breed standard adopted by the German and Austrian Clubs acknowledged the fact that long-haired variants could occur. In 1936 a long-haired

Weimaraner dog was registered for the first time in the German breeding register, namely the dog Illo von Hipkendahl (No. 1468). There was no indication of either parent being long-haired and unfortunately the grandparents were born before 1924 so the tracing of the pedigree was impossible. Further details of this dog are to be found in the chapter on long-hairs. Here is the 1935 standard:

27 APRIL 1935. AGREED BREED STANDARD ADOPTED BY THE GERMAN AND AUSTRIAN WEIMARANER CLUBS, AT FRANKFURT ON THE MAIN

Breeding Characteristics of the Weimaraner Pointer

This breed is the only Short-haired Pointer breed of Germany which succeeded in remaining unmixed (uncrossed).

GENERAL APPEARANCE
Altogether noble appearance; beautiful shape; sinewy; intelligent expression. Medium sized, height between 56–74 cm (22–29 inches). Bitch a little smaller (lower) than dog.

HEAD
In accordance with the size of the body, more often narrow than broad; dog a little broader than bitch. In the centre of the head a small groove, occipital bone protruding slightly. Corner teeth long without being pointed. Back of the nose (muzzle) straight; often slightly arched, never sagging upwards (dished). Extremely small gap (stop) in front of the forehead; lips hanging over moderately; small mouth wrinkle. Cheek muscles distinctly marked, because attached at the back. Dry head.

LEATHER
(Lopears.) Broad, rounded off in a point, slightly turned when at attention; when put forward, at approximately same level as corner of mouth; high and narrow attached.

NOSE
Dark flesh coloured turning to purple and gradually into grey.

EYES
Colour of amber, with intelligent expression.

BACK
A somewhat longish back, as long as it shows no downward inclination, is characteristic of the breed; not to be regarded as faulty.

TAIL
When not cropped, long, hanging down almost vertically, point bent slightly backwards. Thickness of tail in accordance with shape of body.

LEGS
Sinewy; upper arm well angled; pastern almost straight, paws well closed.

COAT
Soft to the touch; denser than with other short-haired breeds; underside (brisket) slightly less thick. Coarser hair is not faulty.

COLOUR
Silver-, deer-, or mouse-grey; head and leather mostly a little lighter; white markings in small measure, mostly on the chest, are neither ugly nor faulty since also characteristic of the breed. Neither is the reddish-yellow shade on the head or legs, which nowadays occurs seldom, to be regarded as a fault; however a Weimaraner with reddish-yellow colouring should not receive more than 'good' when tested for his shape. If outstanding for hunting purposes he should not be excluded from breeding. Along the middle of the back there is often a dark eel-stripe.

NOTICE
Very occasionally there are some long-haired Weimaraners. They have a right to be listed, provided their origin can be traced back undeniably until the fourth generation. One should strive to raise such long-haired Weimaraners. Approximately four vertebra only should be cropped from the tail.

The division of Germany in 1945 meant that few litters were registered and many bloodlines completely died out. Also at this time many puppies apparently died from distemper. Of course, after 1945 many American servicemen returned home with Weimaraners and this further depleted the German stock, to such an extent that at a meeting in 1951 the decision was reached to limit a breeder to selling no more than half the litter to foreigners.

After 1945 the Weimaraner devotees gathered together again and gradually the registrations began to rise until in 1975 there were 190 puppies registered for that year. It was on 13 October 1951 that the new club was formed and rules passed concerning guidelines for

Classic 'totverbeller' barking at discovery of dead game. Jessie vom Wasserschloss, bred and owned by Dr Werner Petri, Germany.

breeding, registration, sales and trials. There were also five *Landesgruppen* (state groups) established for Niedersachsen, Bayern, Schleswig-Holstein, Südwest, and Nordrhein-Westfalen.

The Committee had problems to iron out in the mid-1960s which must have been difficult, to say the least. One concerned the type of coat on the Weimaraner and as you will see from the FCI Breed Standard in Appendix I there are three types approved: (a) short, (b) 'stockhaarig', and (c) long. Of the 'stockhaarig' type, Dr Petri writes:

Concerning the hair variety question, three points aroused considerable passion. Firstly it was the question of allowing the cross breeding between the long and the short haired Weimaraner. Furthermore, the desirability of breeding '*stockhaarig*' was discussed, and finally the question that was put to the club from abroad about the admission of wire-haired Weimaraners had to be discussed and answered.

Gildo von der Teutonenburg bred by Josef Lohre, Germany. Owned by Josef Jurgen, Holland. As a defence dog has reached Sch.H.I, II, III.

After discussion on International level (*Weimaraner News* 4/64 page 13) at first it was agreed to allow the mating between long-haired bitches and '*stockhaarig*' dogs and, in exceptional cases, also short-haired dogs in order to secure the existence of the long-haired Weimaraners. But by 1965 any crossing between long and short-haired Weimaraners was forbidden, although the crossing of '*stockhaarig*' dogs was the exception to the rule. In *Weimaraner News* 3/58, Breedwarden Limpert had already earlier drawn attention to the '*stockhaarig*' Weimaraner and had considered it the most suitable kind of hair for the breed. In practice, though, this hair variant remains unimportant as it only results from crossing long and short-haired dogs and therefore occurs very rarely.

During 1974 a request from Czechoslovakia for the recognition of the wire-haired Weimaraner was refused on the grounds that obvious violation of the pure-breeding regulations must take place to achieve this particular type of coat, and this could never be condoned. Photographs presented with their request showed wire-haired dogs of light colour, some with a distinct beard after the style of the German Shorthair/*Pudelpointer* crosses.

The Executive Committee had in the early 1960s another great problem to contend with. This concerned the deliberate cross breeding with pointers in an effort by some breeders to 'improve' the Weimaraner. This was done without the prior knowledge of the Commitee. Obviously the matter eventually came to light and then there were heated discussions after which a separate breed register was opened and 'reliable' breeders were permitted to carry out controlled experimental matings. Over an eight year period about 60 whelps were registered, but this did not prove to be a successful venture and was considered detrimental to the breed due to particular faults persistently recurring. This experiment, which was called 'regeneration breeding', was closed on 9 September 1974. Only one good thing came out of all this, and that was the further proof that the distinctive grey colour of the Weimaraner is a recessive factor. Provided all those who participated in this cross breeding were strictly honourable there is no reason to suspect that the present-day pure-bred Weimaraner has any of this tainted blood in him.

As will be seen from the FCI Standard in Appendix I the German requirements are more detailed than the standard followed in Great Britain and, coupled with stringent breeding regulations, it covers all aspects considered essential for the evaluation of a dog's suitability for breeding.

Dog shows as we know them are frowned on by many Germans, who believe that the days when one showed dogs to gain recognition of the breed are long since over and the only dogs fit for shows nowadays are the 'luxury' breeds. Their prime object in breeding Weimaraners is to produce good working gundogs. But that is not to say that they are uninterested in whether or not their dogs conform physically to the standard – far from it. All the dogs used for breeding must pass *formwert* (conformation) and *haarwert* (coat tests) as well as show their ability in the field. There are now a few special club shows, usually held during the summer, where dogs can be judged for conformation and coat, and at these shows the markings are 'Excellent', 'Very Good', 'Good', 'Poor' or 'Fail'. The dog must gain the minimum mark of 'Good' in both tests to pass. When their field ability is tested and also found to be satisfactory and provided they conform to certain other regulations, they can then be selected as eligible for future breeding.

The most important of the field tests is the *Herbstzuchprufung*, or HZP, which is the Autumn Rating Test held in the Autumn following the dog's year of birth. At this time they are also tested for *Mannscharfe* (aggressiveness to man) where the rating is from 0 to 4 and for a pass the mark must be at least 2. Following the HZP the dogs are judged for conformation and coat if this has not been carried out previously at one of the special shows. Similarly, the VJP, or Spring Rating Test is for dogs whelped in the previous year, plus three months.

Basically, the requirements for breeding dogs are that both parents must be registered in the Club Breed Register, both must pass at least 'Good'/'Good' in the *formwert* and *haarwert* tests, and both must have passed in the HZP or a similar test and the club's internal *Mannscharfe* proving test. With male dogs it is also desirable that they pass the *Schutzhundprüfung* (guard dog trial). At least one parent must have proof of *Raubzeugscharfe* (sharpness on vermin) and particular value is given to the passing of the *Verlorenbringen* (retriever/tracking) and *Bringtreuprufung* (retrieving) trial, plus a proof of enthusiasm for water work. Also desirable is *Spurlaut* (the giving of tongue on trail). Both parents should also have been X-rayed for hip dysplasia and proved clear or borderline.

Faults are listed which would exclude a dog from breeding and if he had shown one or more fault his pedigree would then be rubber-stamped with 'Breeding prohibited' by the breed warden or the keeper of the breed register. The faults are: nervousness or shyness; gun-shy

Present-day field triallers in Germany before the V.J.P. Trial. (Photo: M. Holzel)

or water-shy; malformations of any kind; serious dental faults; serious illnesses such as epilepsy; cryptorchid or monorchid dogs; entropian or ectropian; hip dysplasia; obvious brown colouring; overlarge white chest markings as well as white paws.

Suitable dogs and bitches are only allowed to be used for breeding when they are at least 18 months of age. The highest age for breeding is 10 years for dogs and eight years for bitches. In one calendar year the bitch may only have one litter and there is *no* exception to this rule. The litters must be born between 1 October and 15 May – preferably between 1 November and 31 March – but in exceptional cases and with advance permission, up to 30 June. The most desirable number in the litter is to be not more than six healthy puppies and the birth must be notified to the breed warden within fourteen days so that he can inspect and tattoo the puppies. If a foster mother is required this must be authorised by the breed warden.

Six weeks before the required mating of his bitch, the breeder must contact his *Landesgruppen* who in turn contacts the breed warden who

31

will recommend a suitable stud dog – both must approve or the breeding will be forbidden. Every year after the results of the HZP are known, the *Bundeszuchtwart* adds to the list of dogs suitable for mating. This list is sent on to the *Landesgruppenzuchtwarte* who will issue any recommendations or warnings beforehand.

In West Germany today there are approximately 500 club members and the estimated number of dogs is 1,400 short-haired and 100 long-haired. The percentage of long-haired Weimaraners in Austria is very much higher. There are estimated to be about 60 Weimaraners in East Germany but trade between East and West is forbidden.

AUSTRIA

Forester-Engineer Otto von Stockmayer for many years hunted over German Short-haired Pointers until in 1913 he imported into Lower Austria the bitch Adda von Artlande (1055L), a kennel sister to Major Herber's Held von Artlande. This bitch, in his opinion far surpassed any dog he had previously hunted with; she was fast, with excellent nose, good in water, had great stamina and was sharp on predators. Employed, as he was, by Prince Hans von Ratibor on the Grafenegg Estates, he not surprisingly convinced the Prince of the breed's capabilities. In 1921 when the Prince himself imported a pair from Germany, only Weimaraners were thereafter worked on the estate. Perhaps one of the best known early breeders in Austria apart from von Stockmayer and the Prince was the Countess Maria Stubenberg of Walkersdorf of the von Diendorf kennel name, which along with Grafenegg, von der Ruine Wasse (Fors. Fridau), von Eisenhut (A. Obenaus) and von Hollabrunnen (R. Weislein) can be seen nine or ten generations back in many of our present-day pedigrees.

The *Osterreichischer Weimaraner-Verein* was founded in 1924 with the Prince as its first chairman. The first breed warden was Öberförster Georg Stühlinger who was a great trainer and who died in 1978 at the grand age of 90 after achieving many honours in the breed. When Prince Hans von Ratibor died in 1948 at the age of 66 at Schloss Grafenegg in Lower Austria, Förstrat Otto Stockmayer took over as chairman and was later made honorary president. Today, the Austrian

Weimaraner Club has a membership of 160 and there are an estimated 200 Weimaraners in the country, a high proportion of which are the long-haired variety (see below, Ch. 6).

The breeding regulations are similar to those of the German Weimaraner Club with minor differences. The minimum breeding age for both bitches and stud dogs is 18 months, and ends at seven years for bitches and nine years for dogs, and each bitch is only allowed one successful litter per year. The desirable number of puppies in a litter is not more than six, but if more are kept then the registration fee is increased to double for puppies number seven and eight, and to treble for the ninth puppy upwards. Similar working and conformation qualifications are required and also freedom from hip dysplasia and other hereditary defects etc.

The Austrian Weimaraner Club holds special field trials for Weimaraners only, but as there is only one *Prufungsordnung* (standard examination) from the Austrian *Jagdgebrauchshunde-Verband* (Kennel Club for Hunting Dogs) for all pointing dogs they also accept a few other breeds if the owner or handler is a club member. The letters 'AK' after the marking of the award card signifies that the dog is of a different breed; e.g. I Preis a, b or c for Weimaraners, or I Preis AK a, b or c for the others. In Austria it is an accepted fact that Weimaraners are slower workers than other breeds and they are judged accordingly, which is not the case in the UK, where all the hunt-point-retrieve breeds compete on equal terms. The Austrians call it *rassegerecht Richten* which very loosely translated means that each breed is judged fairly on its known ability.

4

British History of the Weimaraner

FOREWORD BY COLONEL ERIC RICHARDSON

. . . I had certainly known Bob Petty a very long time and the difficulty now is to try and pick out the little bits that I have stored away in my mind that would be of interest to you without boring you with a lot of details about Bob Petty and the sort of life that he and I had together. It is also impossible to do this without mentioning the Army, because this is how we met. I cannot remember the year exactly but I suppose it was about 1947 or 1948 when I was in the Tank Corps and Bob Petty was the Signals representative in the British Army of the Rhine in a department called 'G Research and Development'. In that position he was, I suppose, one of the most technically capable men in the whole of the Rhine Army. Indeed, for the whole of the latter part of the War anyway, he had been Eisenhower's 'red line' operator – which means that whenever Eisenhower made a call or received one, Bob Petty was on hand to deal with it. And on the subject of Eisenhower's telephone conversations with Churchill, Roosevelt, Patten or Montgomery there was no better authority than Bob Petty; in fact, *if* one could ever get him to talk on this subject he was undoubtedly a spell-binder!

Anyway, it was during a meeting in Bad Oeynhausen where the British Army of the Rhine had its headquarters in those days that I first met Bob Petty at a meeting to do with a piece of new equipment. By that time Bob Petty was not dealing with matters affecting the Royal Corps of Signals, he was back to what was, I suppose, his original trade dealing with the technical aspects of small arms and small arm ballistics in which, there is no doubt about it, he was one of the world's experts and he was fulfilling a Grade II appointment in the British Army of the Rhine at that time. I cannot remember exactly what I was doing at one of these meetings – I suspect not a lot! However, this is where I first met Bob Petty during a lunch-time session where I happened to mention to somebody – and Bob was on the edge of the conversation – that I had been wild boar shooting the night before. Bob approached me afterwards and we started discussing wild boar shooting from which it soon became quite clear that Bob Petty was not only passionately fond of wild boar shooting but that he was also without any doubt one of the finest shots in the British Army of the Rhine. I think the figures speak for themselves – by the time we both left the British Army of the Rhine Bob Petty's bag of 66 wild boar was untouched by any other soldier, officer or any other British person in Germany. It was certainly a figure that I never came more than about 50 per cent within reach of.

It also became clear after a time that we both had two other interests: one was an absolute passion for guns of all sorts, and the other was an intense love of dogs – particularly gundogs. The guns will be of no concern to you, but undoubtedly Bob Petty was not only a collector but also one of the most knowledgeable men that I've ever met on the subject of guns, particularly rifles. He wasn't one of the world's best game shots, but with a rifle at that time he certainly was fairly deadly!

We kept in touch after this first meeting and got to know each other very much better some time later, probably a year later, when I took up an appointment near Celle on the Lüneburger Heide. It wasn't a particularly big command but one of the aspects of the job was that the unit, because of its peculiar location on the Lüneburger Heide, had with it something in the order of 76,000 acres of shooting and 12 miles of river. There weren't many pig on the shoot but there were a few and Bob and I began to meet each other more frequently for duck shooting and then later wild boar on the Lüneburger Heide. Bob was then transferred to a place called Münsterlager where he commanded a signal unit which comprised chiefly of German ex-prisoners of war and a few senior signals officers and where most of his work was connected with the telephone cables across the Lüneburger Heide to the various British units.

I had by this time acquired – for 3 lbs of coffee – an extraordinary animal known as a German Pudelpointer. I say extraordinary because it really looked like a brown sheep with long curly hair. Its origins, I found out later, go back almost as far as shooting; it was the original Poodle, and the peculiar cut which the Standard Poodle has, known as the 'Parisian' cut was, I discovered, nothing more or less than the way the old Baltic wildfowlers used to clip their dogs in order to keep the joints warm and reduce the mass of hair to enable them to swim. Bob Petty had at that time a black Labrador – one of the most evil-looking dogs I think I have ever seen; there was much of Bill Sykes' bull terrier about the head, but Bob was fond of it and it had a good nose and if it believed that things should not only be well killed by the time it came back to Bob, well at least they were dead!

Our first major outing together was to the Baltic coast to a place called Aügustfen which the Eighth Hussars had command over at that time and Bob and I set off from there for four or five days shooting. Aügustfen turned out to be a vast sheet of water-flooded fields with little islands of manure heaps sticking out of the water and flooded fields right to the sea, and here Bob and I struggled along the flooded lanes attempting for I suppose the best part of three days to get among the wild geese of which there were plenty, but were virtually unapproachable. However, on the third morning we were both out and I was lying on my back on a manure heap surrounded by flood water when dawn came, clear and blue without a cloud in the sky – and no geese. Just as I was about to give up, at nine o'clock the geese started to come in and to cut a long story short, I shot 11 geese in 45 minutes. I walked back carrying this some almost hundredweight of gooseflesh of which I was heartily sick by the time I got to the pub where Bob and I met up. Bob at that time had I think got a similar number of geese and we were discussing our good fortune with a chap called Atkinson-Wills who was in the Eighth Hussars when I noticed a somewhat elderly man standing on the outskirts wearing a camou- flaged jacket whom I took to be a German beater of some sort until a well-educated languid voice behind me said: 'Young man, you shot very well this morning – you'll be very lucky if you ever do that again as long as you live.' Atkinson-Wills then apologised and introduced us. The man who had spoken to me turned out to be J. K. Stanford, the man I suppose I had known all my life through reading his articles in *The Field* and for whom I had the greatest possible respect, but never expected to meet under circumstances like this. He was, of course, quite right – I never again shot more than two geese at one time, let alone 11. I had at that time undoubtedly the ideal dog for wildfowling; my dear old Asta the German Pudelpointer was magnifi- cent; she retrieved every goose on that occasion, and on one particularly good night in a very high wind she retrieved 45 duck for me in about an hour and a half – she really was the most superb water dog.

A wildfowling day to remember – Eric Richardson and 'Asta'.

When we had gone back, Bob, whom I met some weeks later, had been down to the American zone where he had come across two American Air Force officers who had obtained some dogs called Weimaraners and Bob, with this enormous enthusiasm for anything to do with dogs and guns, seemed to become obsessed with the wish to get one or two or more of these 'Grey Ghosts'. I must admit I was fairly lukewarm at the time as I was perfectly happy with this superb old dog of mine (she wasn't old then but that is how I have come to think of her) and showed little or no interest.

However, in time Bob became more and more determined to get a Weimaraner and had by this time gone into the history of the breed and produced some astonishing facts and figures. So much so, that he

37

began to talk of going over the border into East Germany, where obviously the Weimar Republic was, to get one or two puppies. This, at the time, was an extremely dangerous thing to do and, in the event, he managed to get hold of somebody to come from the Eastern zone into the Western zone – the part of the Lüneburger Heide that we were in at that time was not all that far away from the Eastern zone. And he rang up very excited one day to say that he had made contact with a German *Förstmeister*, not only having made contact but that the *Förstmeister* having crossed the border had certainly no wish to go back. He was an authority on the Weimaraner and had brought one or two dogs with him. Furthermore he knew of a source of supply of Weimaraners in the Eastern zone and for the usual 'goodies' (or payment) he would be prepared, and so would his friends, to get the dogs across the border. In those days marks, either East or West, were of little value – by and large the incentives were some sort of food, mainly coffee beans because they were so negotiable – and this is how Bob Petty started to get hold of one or two dogs from the Eastern zone.

The first bitch he got was undoubtedly a beautiful bitch, the one that he kept I suppose the longest; this was the one he brought to England and who died at the full old age of 12 or 14 (Cobra von Boberstrand), a lovely old bitch. The dogs that followed were not in my view of the highest quality. It was extremely difficult to obtain a dog that was of the right colour, that is the light silver cigarette-box grey, and that had all the other desirable features – little round tight, cat-like feet and the strong, square muzzle of the retriever and the big nose of the pointer, with fine bones. You could often get a good colour and have appalling feet or chest, or a sway-back. There always seemed, to me, to be something wrong with them and frequently the dogs, I suppose due to the various breeds which had gone into producing the grey colour, would sometimes throw a thoroughly mousey or brown puppy or two in a litter; the silver grey was by no means consistent. Undoubtedly, a good one was a very nice dog and a very good pet and a nice dog to have about the house, which is more than can be said for some of the German Short-haired Pointers at the time, and particularly the *Drahthaar* (wire-hair) which had enormous character and strength and drive but who lived entirely for hunting and who regarded any time spent other than hunting as absolutely wasted. The Weimaraner was a reasonably quiet dog by comparison – not as quiet as the *Vizsla* nor as nice-natured but certainly better than some of the German Short-haired Pointers.

Förstmeister Fehse was by this time being paid by and employed by Bob full time not only to obtain the dogs when he was able to do so, but also to train Bob's dogs of various breeds, but increasingly Weimaraners. I had my doubts about some of the requirements of the German Trials and it seemed to me that at times in an attempt to produce a dog for all seasons one was missing the finer parts of one or other of the dog's ability. It seemed to be extremely difficult to produce a really soft-mouthed retriever while requiring the dog at the same time to kill a cat or a fox to pass its field trial. However, this is how the Germans have produced the finest rough-shooting dogs in the world; there is no doubt that at the end of the day one had a wonderful all-round dog. Herr Fehse was without doubt a very hard man, perhaps because of the way he had been brought up in Weimar, but it was how he had got his dogs to field trial championship level and it is how he had been taught and brought up to train and use his dogs, but it was frequently against the better judgement of Bob and myself. However, it produced results and if the dogs were somewhat frightened of him at the end of their training period, well, it was probably no bad thing.

At that particular time I seem to recall that the main claim to fame of the Weimaraner was its extraordinary ability to follow wounded deer or pig for enormous distances and with very little scent. I remember one particular legend that was built up of the stag that was shot in the morning, wounded, and followed all day – a stake was stuck in the ground when darkness stopped the chase – during the night it snowed 2 inches and the following morning the dog picked up the scent through the snow. Frankly, I'm not sure that it wasn't slightly overdone! Certainly, I never found the Weimaraner to be any better at following the scent of wounded boar or wounded deer than any other dog at the time trained for this purpose and undoubtedly the *Drahthaar* was a dog which put up the most enormous competition to any other type of breed. I personally some years later at a place called Lachenhaus, which had been the old Kaiser's shoot, saw a German Bloodhound do things with trails which I would not have believed possible and certainly I never saw a Weimaraner that could compete with some of the bloodhound strain that I saw down on the old Kaiser's shoot during the time I was a guest of the Army Commander there. I remember one particular occasion when I was staying with a young Förstmeister down in Lachenhaus when in the morning before we left to go and choose a stag, he was meticulous to ensure that his bloodhound was properly tied up and unable to get out of the house while we were out. Well, we had a bit of luck that morning and I shot an eight-pointer stag about 3 kilometres away from the Förstmeister's house. Having cleaned the stag, we walked back to the house; he asked me to wash up outside so there would be as little scent as possible for the dog to get hold of. Nevertheless the moment we walked into the room, the bloodhound nearly went mad and to cut a long story short, in the end it went straight through the window and tore across the open fields towards the forest. We went out as quickly as we could to my jeep and raced to where we had left the stag. When we got there, three kilometres away, the dog was there by the side of the stag and had clearly picked the scent up on the wind 3 kilometres away and gone absolutely straight across country. I never saw a Weimaraner who could do that.

You must think it rather odd that I should be telling most of my story which is probably slightly against the Weimaraner. This is unfortunate really because it is not what I intended, it is merely to put the breed into perspective; there was so much rubbish talked about them during the early days and certainly when we got the dogs over here there was this idiotic sort of legend that set the breed off on entirely the wrong lines and the wrong course.

Bob Petty stayed at Münsterlager until he was posted home to England at about the same time as I was. I had been in the Celle region for about three and a half years and during this time Bob had acquired about eight Weimaraners and I had five. He brought eight Weimaraners home to England and I brought five. Now there is no doubt about it that had we been able to find dogs easily, some of those dogs would not have been brought home. I certainly had two with distressingly long hare-feet, and the dear old bitch I had, a wonderful gundog, had decidedly snipey features and in moments of repose she would certainly let her back sag like an old mare. No, there's no doubt that of the five dogs I brought, two I think in all fairness ought to have been put down. I think Bob had a slightly better selection but, here again, we had what we could find and we brought them home. One thing was absolutely certain at that time there were no other Weimaraners in the United Kingdom.

Bob was posted to command a Signal Unit in Bampton, near Oxford, and I went to Tewkesbury in Gloucestershire although I actually lived just outside Cheltenham. I had at that time a house most suitable for dogs, with 83 acres, six loose boxes and quite a big garden area and as near perfection for keeping dogs as you could imagine. After about six or seven months the dogs came out of quarantine and I picked them up at Cheltenham Station and took them back; they were all in fairly good condition. I also had at that time a boxer and dear old Asta the German Pudelpointer. As I was away most of the day, it was also soon obvious that we had a great many too many dogs and my wife who had the house and two children found seven dogs at home quite a handful. In the end I decided to sell a big dog called Casar (Casar von Bolkewehr) to a chap called T. V. Redston who lived down the road. I mention his name because he really was a tremendous support in those days; he was a man with a lot of money and he wanted a 'Grey Ghost' dog, and I let him have one. But Casar was a handful by any standards. Casar was the sort of dog that Herr Fehse ought to have had to train. Casar only understood a man like Fehse, and the gentle treatment meted out by T. V. Redston would not have kept Casar under control for more than about 24 hours. Anyway, to cut it short, he could not control Casar and I took him back. Two of the dogs I eventually put down, as it was quite clear that my instincts in Germany were right and the dogs were really not fit to breed from if one wished to produce really top-grade high-class dogs.

I had a bitch called Anka (Anka vom Suntel). I kept Anka although she was not perhaps the best possible breeding specimen, but she was undoubtedly sharp and I think one of the reasons that persuaded me to keep her was the first time I took her out shooting. I had about four hundred acres not too far away and one night when I was out duck shooting, I could not get her away from a willow tree. Eventually I let her go and she scrambled up this small stumpy leaning willow tree and out of the top came a fox, instantly followed by Anka. The fox jumped the wrong side, into the water, and Anka jumped after it and after about 10 minutes she killed the fox in the water. As we had lost something in the order of 30 chickens some time previously from fox, I really hadn't the heart to get rid of Anka after that! She was a very, very sharp little dog indeed, but of course like many of her type she did like to ensure that any game she brought to you was dead, and she hadn't the glorious soft mouth of the Pudelpointer.

Bob, by this time, was getting himself more organised and although the conditions under which he kept his dogs were not initially to his liking, eventually he got more land at Bampton on which he could shoot and he began to get more and more people interested in the breed and began to take an interest in the field trials. At that time one had, of course, to run against retrievers or pointers and the dogs you ran against – the Labradors – were the very best of the retrievers, and the pointers that one ran against at places like J. Arthur Rank's at Sutton Scotney were the cream of the English Pointers, and it soon became apparent that it is unreasonable to ask a dual-purpose dog to run against a dog who has a single purpose in life, because it will always win. There was never any doubt in my mind that the Weimaraner or the Vizsla or the German Short-haired pointer would never be a better retriever than a Labrador and a better pointer than, let us say, one of J. Arthur Rank's pointers. But it would do something that certainly no other dog that I'd ever met in England would do – it would retrieve very well from land and water and it would also point, and frequently instinctively pointed magnificently, but of course it lacked the speed of the pointer and setter. However strong they were on point and however well they moved I've never yet seen a Vizsla or Weimaraner that was as fast as a good English pointer. One or two German Short-haired Pointers that I had in later years were very, very fast indeed, but again they were never in the same league as J. Arthur Rank's on the day.

Looking back, I suppose one of the saddest things to happen to the breed in this country was when the press got hold of this gimmicky expression 'The Grey Ghost'. This led to an intense interest in the breed and to the production of one of the most damning articles that has ever been produced. Bob rang me up one day and asked me if I would take part in a demonstration he had been asked to lay on for a chap called MacDonald Hastings. I cannot remember what part Bob took in it but I know that MacDonald Hastings came down to Cheltenham where I lived; I was away at the time and he interviewed my wife and took a number of photographs of the dogs we had at the time, and obtained as much information as he could. He then went off and wrote what I suppose he thought was a thoroughly complimentary, interesting and exciting article. But the effect of it was that he made the dog out to be the wonder dog of the age, the dog that would do everything except cook the meals, and laid great emphasis on its value. I think at that time, the odd puppy we had obtained about £80 for, and undoubtedly the back-street dealers (from South Wales I remember one came) saw this as a way of making a fortune. I think neither Bob nor I were quite prepared for the effect that this article would have on the breed. Certainly it had never occurred to me that people would buy puppies in order to breed them on cinder patches in the backs of council houses without the dogs ever seeing a green field let alone pointing or ranging free and certainly never hearing a gun go off. I think it was after two puppies had gone that we realised that these dogs were likely to get into the wrong hands and I certainly never sold a puppy to anyone without adequate proof that they were going to keep the dog under the right conditions and bring it up in a way to which the breed had been prepared.

However, the damage was done and certainly from that time on many of the dogs got into the hands of people who bred from them like rabbits; the bitches were covered the first time they came on heat without ever being trained, and from then on produced puppies as fast as they could produce them, and of course the breed suffered enormously. Some of the most evil-looking dogs I'd ever seen were produced at around this time. There is no doubt that the breed at that time was in a state where the greatest possible care should have been taken and any dog that failed to measure up even after nine months to the high standards of the dog's ancestors should have been put down. But of course they never were, or I never heard of a dog being put down. I do remember that one of the very few puppies I sold went to a gamekeeper in Scotland and after a year he told me the dog would not point so I took the dog back and I think that unless one behaves in this way with a new breed then the dog and the breed is never going to get off the ground.

I think it was also at around this time that Bob decided to introduce the Weimaraner Club. He was having some small success with the field trials but very little really and this was, of course, before the time of the specialised field trials although the German Short-haired Pointers were just beginning to get moving, and I think it was about then that Bob really began to take a serious interest in the field trial side and also into the formation of a club. I, unfortunately, was not able to go along with him; first of all because I do not think I am really a field-trial man, but also because at that time I was then posted to Hong Kong and of course it is quite impossible to take dogs to the Far East. I cleared out all the Weimaraners that were any good, and those that were unlikely to produce top grade specimens I had put down. I don't think I had contact with Bob other than correspondence as a friend rather than on the subject of Weimaraners until I came back from Hong Kong (and none of my dogs were left of course), and I am sure there are many people far more knowledgeable on what happened to Weimaraners and the Weimaraner Club from that time on. One thing

I must make clear is that whatever the Weimaraner Club is in the United Kingdom today is due entirely to Bob's tenacity and determination, and certainly although I was with him when the dogs were first brought in and indeed brought almost as many dogs as Bob did into this country, I never had Bob's driving enthusiasm for the breed.

I remember one of the things J. K. Stanford once said. He said: 'Any man really is only entitled to one supreme gundog in his lifetime', and I think probably my views of the Weimaraner to some extent were spoiled by this fact. I did have a supreme gundog in my lifetime – unfortunately it was a German Pudelpointer and not a Weimaraner!

Eric Richardson (Colonel)
August 1981

DOCUMENTED BRITISH HISTORY

Although the breed had been established in the USA since 1938, it was not until 1952 that the first Weimaraners arrived in Britain – the bitch Cobra von Boberstrand and the dog Bando von Fohr arrived from Germany on 7 March 1952. This pair was followed by six others imported by Major R. H. Petty, three of which were registered with the Kennel Club – the Germans Hella aus der Helmeute and Cid von Bolkewehr and the Austrian bitch Vita von der Haraska. At about the same time Major Eric Richardson's five Weimaraners arrived, only two of which were registered here – Anka vom Suntel and Cid's litter-brother Casar von Bolkewehr. These 13 Weimaraners had all been trained and trialed by Herr Fehse in Germany before their arrival in England. A further German pair were brought in by Mrs Olga Malet who was returning to Britain after a tour of duty in Germany with the US Air Force – an in-whelp bitch Babette von der Katzbach and a dog Arco von der Kolfurter Heide.

Of these first 15 imports only nine were actually registered and used for breeding, the remainder not being considered by Petty and Richardson to be of good enough quality. These nine therefore formed the foundation on which the breed would grow and a little later were supplemented with stock from the USA. It was during these very early years that Major Petty took over Mrs Malet's remaining stock as she

Ian Petty leads out Cobra and Bando after their stay in quarantine.
These were the very first pair of Weimaraners to set foot on British soil.

was for various reasons unable to continue her interest in the breed after contributing the Ipley 'A' and 'B' litters, and he also of course took over some of Major Richardson's stock when he was posted to Hong Kong.

This breed, new to Britain, naturally caused a great deal of interest and Major Petty found himself constantly answering enormous piles of correspondence, standing under hot television lights, and attending various functions up and down the country in his highly successful promotional drive. It was perhaps almost inevitable that the breed would find itself in odd pockets of the country being commercialised by unscrupulous, uncaring puppy farms and the following highly romanticised newspaper article in the *Daily Express* of 4 August 1953 could not have helped a great deal although no doubt written with the best will in the world. The author, MacDonald Hastings, later became a founder member of the Weimaraner Club.

IT HAPPENED BY NIGHT – THE GREY GHOST WAS SMUGGLED OVER THE FRONTIER.*
And here it is – a NEW DOG . . .

Not since Sherlock Holmes tracked down the Hound of the Baskervilles has there been such a story. After five years, the hunt for the elusive Grey Ghost has been brought to a successful conclusion. Only now, as Doctor Watson would say, can the adventure be told of an affair which might have had international consequences and involves at least one of the old ruling families of Middle Europe. The Grey Ghost is here. Cobra von Boberstrand, smuggled out of the Russian zone of Germany, is safe in Hatherleigh, North Devon.

THE LEGEND

It all began immediately after the war when Major Bob Petty and Major Eric Richardson, brother officers in the Army of Occupation in Germany, heard talk of a breed of working gun-dog, unknown in Britain. The dog, it was claimed, would do pretty well anything except cook the dinner and put the baby to bed. Its name was the Weimaraner because, for hundreds of years, the rulers of the German Grand Duchy of Weimar had used the Grey Ghosts as their personal hunting dogs. The romantic legend was that in the first place, they came to Weimar as part of the dowry of a Russian princess. Subsequently the Grand Dukes allowed nobody to own them except the foresters on their own estates. But, soon after the War, the Americans had

* Courtesy Express Newspapers plc.

Strawbridge 'B' puppies – the first to bear this famous affix.

obtained a breeding couple. Petty and Richardson knew that there was already a Weimaraner Club, with over 4,000 members, in Connecticut. American enthusiasts claimed that the Grey Ghost was a 'bird-dog, a retriever, a coon dog, rabbit dog, house pet, watch-dog, guard-dog, obedience champion and show dog all rolled into one'. But, privately, the two British officers believed that America had already spoiled the strain by breeding for the show-bench instead of the field. They wanted to lay hands on the real stuff inside Germany. Eric Richardson was acting as game warden in the Hamburg area. Bob Petty was a Royal Signals Officer. Between them they reckoned to get the buzz if ever a Grey Ghost showed. They hunted for two years. During that time, an American broadcast an offer of 2,000 dollars for a breeding couple. But nobody took him up.

FIRST LUCK

According to reports, there were about 40 Weimaraners in the Western zone. All the rest were behind the Iron Curtain. Wherever they travelled Bob Petty and Eric Richardson asked if anybody had seen a dog about the size of an English pointer, and much the same shape, with a coat of an unusual shade of silver-blue, and a flesh-coloured nose, shading to near violet or grey. Bob

47

Petty struck lucky first. A German gamekeeper said darkly that he knew of one in Magdeburg in the Russian zone. It cost Bob Petty 1,000 marks (about £80). And Cobra von Boberstrand, an eight-month old bitch, was smuggled across the Russian frontier by night. From that time, it was easy. As soon as the gamekeepers saw that the British officer had got a Weimaraner of his own, they took him into their confidence. Before they left Germany, Petty and Richardson each had a couple.

The other day Eric Richardson's Grey Ghosts were released from quarantine. They're with him now at the Royal Army Ordnance depot, at Aschurch, Tewkesbury. And in Hatherleigh, North Devon, Cobra von Boberstrand has presented Major and Mrs Petty with nine puppies, her second litter.

PERFECT

There are now fifteen full grown Weimaraners in the country. A club has been formed, under the presidency of Major-General Maurice Lea-Cox. Soon it is hoped to find the 25 members necessary for the registration of the Weimaraner with the Kennel Club. The coming of the Grey Ghost to Britain probably means the end of the long quest for the perfect one-man gun-dog. The Weimaraner finds game and points without training. He'll retrieve from land and water and he'll quarter the ground like a spaniel. He's steady to hand and his intelligence is said to be above average, even for a pointer. My own guess is that within five years the Grey Ghost will be one of the most sought after sporting dogs in the country.

MacDonald Hastings

The Weimaraner made its first appearance at Crufts in 1953 in the 'Any Variety Gundog' classes judged by Mr W. Worfolk. The 25 exhibits were made up of 12 Weimaraners, 1 Munsterlander, 7 Bearded Collies, 4 German Short-haired Pointers and 1 German Long-haired Setter. Col J. A. Brooks' bitch Heidi von Reiningen who was an American import, won second prize in the Novice class and third prize in the Open class. Another of Col Brooks' entries, Spitfire, was entered for sale at £125. Mrs E. M. Petty entered Cobra, Vita and Bando. Five of Mrs Malet's first litter were entered under the names Xcel Apollo, Xcel Athene, etc., but obviously the Kennel Club did not approve this affix and they were later registered as Ipley Apollo, etc., a prefix behind many of today's pedigrees. It was at this 1953 Crufts Show that the inaugural meeting of the Club was held when formal approval was given to officers, and Major-General Lea-Cox was elected

Chairman. The founder members of the Weimaraner Club of Great Britain were registered at the Kennel Club on 17 November 1953. That list consisted of the following:

Major-General Maurice Lea-Cox	Chairman	
Major R. H. Petty, TD	Secretary	Importers of the first Weimaraners
Mrs E. M. Petty	Treasurer	and owners of the *Strawbridge* affix
Mr Ian W. Petty		Major and Mrs Petty's son, currently shooting over a *Fleetapple* Weimaraner.
Lt Col Eric Richardson		Imported *Anka* and *Casar* etc., and owner of the *Monksway* affix.
Mr Frank Marland		Owned *Strawbridge Bando*. Judged the breed at the LKA in 1959.
Col J. A. Brooks and Mrs J. C. Brooks		Imported *Heidi v Reiningen* ex USA.
Mrs Olga Malet		Imported *Babette v d Katzbach*. Owner of the *Ipley* affix.
Mr P. R. A. Moxon		Sporting journalist, author and Field Trial judge.
Mr A. Hill and Mrs O. M. Hill and Miss P. A. Hill		Owned *Spitfire* which went to the USA.
Miss Marcia Bainbridge		Daughter of Mrs F. Bainbridge of the *Skyrose* affix. Marcia now owns Borzois, but her mother kept Weimaraners until quite recently.
Mr MacDonald Hastings		Journalist. Died in 1982.
Major R. M. MacGibbon		Owned and worked *Strawbridge Baron* in early field trials.
Mr James Robertson-Justice		Actor and film star.
Lt Col L. Morris		Shooting friend of Major Petty's who assisted with the early importations.
Dr A. McKenzie		Owned *Strawbridge Folly* in 1954 and has owned a Weimaraner as a shooting companion ever since. One of the very few founder members to stay with the breed, Dr McKenzie recently took delivery of two puppies by *Ragstone Ryuhlan*.
Col W. Ritchie		
Mrs J. Russell		
Mr F. Questry and Mrs L. H. Questry		
Mr G. K. King and Mr M. B. King		

Major and Mrs Petty very often supported exhibitions and shows with the entire entry coming from their Strawbridge Kennels in North Devon and they often had to drum up handlers from the ringside spectators. Major Petty always remembered one such show in 1955 at Blackpool when MacDonald Daly judged the entry of 16, most of which the Pettys had presented in the ring after a night-time journey made in two cars (one of which broke down), with over a dozen adult Weimaraners, a litter of puppies requiring hourly attention, plus a couple of Signalmen on 'temporary leave of absence'. Just for the record, the winner was Mr and Mrs L. Causeley's Strawbridge Carol, a win she repeated many times.

This same year, 1955, was a very busy one as apart from the exhibitions and shows, Weimaraners were being field-trialled at every available opportunity. The Kennel Club suggested that the decision to include Weimaraners in trials must be left to the individual Field Trial societies, and these were the Pointer and Setters clubs, there being no specialised hunt-point-retrieve clubs at that time. Thanks to the Yorkshire Gundog Club, Scottish Gundog Association, and other Pointer/Setter clubs, the breed had entries accepted at several trials during 1955 and 1956 but the results were not spectacular (see Appendix V, below). It was not until 1970 that the Weimaraner Club of Great Britain started running its own field trials.

1955 was also the first year that Weimaraners were granted separate classes at Crufts. The 18 exhibits were judged by Mrs May Pacey whose choice for best of breed was the bitch Strawbridge Carol, with Col J. A. Brooks' Thunderjet best dog. MacDonald Hastings wrote another newspaper article heralding this appearance of the breed at Crufts, entitled 'The Grey Ghost Goes on Show'. It was much like the previous article with some added 'information':

THE GREY GHOST GOES ON SHOW*

The Weimaraner, the jealously-guarded breed of German gundog, goes on show as a separate class for the first time this week at Cruft's Dog Show in London. The most talked of breed for years, it was introduced to Britain by two Army officers.

The Kaiser's War brought the Alsatian to Britain. Hitler's War has already given us the Boxer. Now two regular army officers, home from the Army of Occupation in Germany, have introduced the dog which the Germans regard as the supreme aristocrat of them all.

* Extracts courtesy Express Newspapers plc.

The Americans who prised five specimens out of Hitler just before the war, have christened the Weimaraner 'The Grey Ghost', in recognition of its haunting colour and silent, shadowy way of working. In Connecticut there's already a Weimaraner Club, with its own magazine, and over 4,000 members. The State of Wisconsin has adopted Weimaraners exclusively for police work. In New York, it's said to be the only breed of dog the police permit to walk on the sidewalks without a lead. But, primarily, the Weimaraner is a hunting dog, a pointer who finds and retrieves game from land and water and who, in its native Germany, is used to hunt fox, pull down deer and bay wild pigs. . . .

With the disappearance of the Grand Dukes, in 1918, their dogs almost disappeared too. In the years immediately before the war they were so uncommon that a Weimaraner was exhibited as a rarity in the Berlin Zoo. . . .

If you want a pup at the present time it will cost you about £50, if you can persuade one of the breeders to part with it. Even then you'll have to convince him that you mean to use your Weimaraner for the purpose he has been bred for – as a hunter – not an ornament.

MacDonald Hastings

In 1956 MacDonald Daly judged the Crufts entry of 17, and his best of breed winner was again Strawbridge Carol of whom he wrote 'Repeated the best of breed success she scored here last year, and under me at Blackpool in June. Won well, on her correct head, ear, legs and feet, loin, drive and movement. She is a bitch who doesn't like the handler to stand her up, and were she mine she would be trained to stand away from me on a loose lead in the way that Lloyd of Ware shows his Cockers. She will do the breed a lot of good as a matron.' A far-seeing man, MacDonald Daly! The best dog at Crufts that year was Mr G. F. Bowles' Arco of Monksway.

The first Breed Standard drawn up by the Weimaraner Club of Great Britain in the 1950s was basically the same as the approved 1963 Kennel Club Standard, apart from a scale of points which was not included in the approved version. The scale is quoted here just as a matter of interest:

Head	10	Hindlegs	15
Neck	5	Feet	10
Shoulders	10	Croup and Tail	10
Body	20	Colour and Coat	5
Forelegs	15	Total:	100

1963 Adopted and Approved Breed Standard

CHARACTERISTICS

In the case of the Weimaraner his hunting ability is the paramount concern and any fault of body or mind which detracts from this ability should be penalised. The dog should display a temperament that is keen, fearless and friendly, protective and obedient.

GENERAL APPEARANCE

A medium sized grey dog with light eyes, he should present a picture of great driving power, stamina, alertness and balance. Above all, the dog should indicate ability to work hard in the field. The walk is rather awkward. The trot should be effortless and ground-covering and should indicate smooth co-ordination. When seen from the rear, the hind feet should parallel the front feet. When seen from the side, the top line should remain strong and level.

HEAD AND SKULL

Moderately long and aristocratic, with moderate stop and slight median line extending back over the forehead. Rather prominent occipital bone and trumpets set well back, beginning at the back of the eye sockets. Measurement from the tip of the nose to stop to equal that from the stop to occipital bone. The flews should be moderately deep, enclosing a powerful jaw. Forehead perfectly straight, delicate at the nostrils. Skin tightly drawn. Neck clean cut and moderately long. Expression keen, kind and intelligent.

EYES

Round, in shades of light amber and hazel, set well enough apart to indicate good disposition and intelligence. When dilated under excitement the eyes may appear almost black.

EARS

Long and lobular, slightly folded and set high. The ear when drawn alongside the jaw should end approximately 1 inch from the point of the nose.

MOUTH

Well-set, strong and even teeth, well developed and proportionate to jaw with correct scissors bite, the upper teeth protruding slightly over the lower teeth but no more than one sixteenth of an inch. Complete dentition is greatly desired. Grey nose. Lips and gums of a pinkish flesh shade.

FOREQUARTERS

Forelegs straight and strong, with measurement from elbow to the ground equalling the distance from the elbow to the top of the withers.

52

BODY

The length of the body from the highest point of the withers to the root of the tail should equal the measurement from the highest point of the withers to the ground. The back set in a straight line should slope slightly from the withers. The chest should be well developed and deep, shoulders well laid and snug. Ribs well sprung and long. Abdomen firmly held, moderately tucked up flank. The brisket should drop to the elbow.

HINDQUARTERS

Well angulated with short stifles, and straight hocks well let down. Musculation well developed.

FEET

Firm and compact, webbed toes well arched, pads closed and thick. Nails short and grey or amber in colour. Dewclaws allowable only on dogs whelped prior to 1 March 1950 or adult dogs imported with claws on.

TAIL

Docked. At maturity it should measure approximately 6 inches with a tendency to be light rather than heavy and should be carried in a manner expressing confidence and sound temperament.

COAT

Short, smooth and sleek.

COLOUR

Shades of silver, mouse or roe grey usually blending to a lighter shade on the head and ears. Small white mark allowable on chest, but not on any other part of the body. White spots that have resulted from injuries shall not be penalised.

WEIGHT AND SIZE

Height at withers, dogs 23 to 25 inches, bitches 22 to 24 inches. Weight fully grown, dogs 55 to 65 lbs, bitches 45 to 55 lbs.

FAULTS:

VERY SERIOUS FAULTS

Coat any other colour than silver, mouse or roe grey. Eyes any other colour than light amber or hazel. Black or mottled mouth. Any other coat than short and sleek. Non-docked tail. Shyness or viciousness.

SERIOUS FAULTS

Poor gait. Very poor feet. Cowhocks. Faulty back, either roached or sway. Badly overshot or undershot. Snipey muzzle. Short ears. Yellow in white markings.

FAULTS
Doggy bitches. Bitchy dogs. Improper muscular condition. Badly affected
teeth. More than four teeth missing. Back too long or too short. Faulty coat
(other than seasonal). Neck too short, thick or throaty. Undersize. Low set
tail. Elbows in or out, feet turned in or out.

MINOR FAULTS
Tail too short or too long. Pink nose. Dewclaws on. Oversize should not be
considered a serious fault, providing correct structure and working ability is
in evidence.

In the following year, 1957, Mr F. Warner Hill judged a smaller
Crufts entry of 12 where the winners were Strawbridge Duke, who
was best of breed, with Strawbridge Carol best bitch. In 1958 Mr Joe
Braddon judged the 16 entered and found his best of breed in
Sandrock Ami and best bitch in Strawbridge Carol making it four
Crufts in a row for this bitch – a record not to be broken until 1974
when Champion Ragstone Ritter took his fifth consecutive Crufts CC.
1959 saw Mrs Gwen Broadley judge the 15 dogs and her choice for best
of breed was Dr Alex Mucklow's Sandrock Admiral, and the best
bitch an American in transit, Capt. H. F. Hoyt's Am. Ch. Von Agar's
Wachtell CD.

1960 saw a great step forward for the breed in the show-ring as it
was the first year the Kennel Club granted Challenge Certificates, four
sets in all, to be competed for at Crufts, Glasgow (SKC), Blackpool
and Birmingham. The breed's first two show champions emerged –
Mrs Rene Parsons judging at Blackpool crowned Mrs Barbara Douglas-
Redding's bitch Wolfox Silverglance, and at Birmingham Mr Stephen
Young crowned Mr Gerry Webb's dog Strawbridge Oliver, who went
on to become the first full champion in the breed when he qualified in
1961 at the German Short-haired Pointer Club trials at Hailes Castle in
Scotland.

In 1961 four sets of CCs were again allocated and in 1962 this was
doubled to eight. In 1963 there were nine, then for the next six years
there were 10 sets annually.

During May 1963 an initial field training class organised by the
Weimaraner Club was held at the Wheatsheaf Farm, Nuthurst,
Hockley Heath, Warwicks. This was under the supervision of Mrs
Louise Petrie-Hay and which 15 Weimaraners attended. After five
training sessions a Working Test was held on 8 September with eight

At Crufts 1965 Tony Burgoin chats to Bunny Roberts who is seen here with his bitch Ch. Theocsbury Abbie, known to all as 'Gail'. (Photo: Olle Rosenqvist)

dogs participating, the judge being Lt Col W. N. S. Donaldson. The winner of the Puppy class was Lotti Go-Lightly, owned and handled by Lt Col H. D. Tucker, the winner of the Novice class was Theocsbury Abbie, owned by Mr D. G. Roberts and handled by Mr J. N. Sowersby; and the winner of the Open class was Silver Trinket owned and handled by Mr H. G. Parsons.

In 1964 the first Junior Warrant was successfully completed at one of the Birmingham shows when under judge Mr Joe Braddon, Ragstone Remus took two first prizes. Bearing in mind the relatively small number of shows scheduling the breed and the very restricted number of classes at these shows, this was quite an achievement. Remus went on to take best of breed at Crufts in 1967 and 1968 and easily qualified for his full title at a GSP Club trial in 1968, and until 1982 remained the breed's foremost sire with seven champions to his credit although, compared to many other stud dogs, he sired surprisingly few litters. In 1982 the American imported dog Ch Kamsou Moonraker von Bismarck broke this record.

After 1971 the Challenge Certificate allocation was gradually increased until in 1983 there were 29 sets to be competed for. The allocation is now based on annual registration figures which have risen steadily from just 34 in 1953, to 735 in 1982. The grand total from 1953 until the end of 1982 is 6,765 — which probably represents a living population of around 5,000. Since the first year with CCs, 1960, to the end of September 1983, there have been 360 sets of CCs on offer. Only once has a CC been withheld and this was in 1974 at Paignton Championship Show when the judge Mr Dick Finch refused to award the CC in dogs. Up to the end of September 1983 there have been 92 champions made – 51 bitches and 41 dogs. Only two kennel affixes have won more than 50 CCs during this same period – Monroes with 56 and Ragstone with 115.

The Weimaraner Club of Great Britain annually runs one championship show; the first was held in 1973 and was judged by Mr L. C. James when the number of exhibits was 115; the latest in September 1983 attracted 193 exhibits. The Club also runs one or two open shows a year, several field trials (six in 1982/3 season), working tests for field and obedience, training classes for field and obedience, and occasional social functions. The 1983 Club membership number stands at over 1,400.

Imports into Britain from Germany, Austria and America

The German and Austrian Imports

1. *Cobra von Boberstrand*, J1b, J2, J1b, HZ2a, stm. Bitch, born 28.2.50.
   Breeder: Georg Laute, Germany. Imported by Major R. H. Petty 1952.
   Sire: Casar von der Finne, J1, J1, Sg, ss. (Later exported from Germany to the USA.)
   Dam: Alma von Boberstrand, Sg.

Cobra was the first Weimaraner to reach England along with Bando von Fohr. They arrived at the Hackbridge Quarantine Kennels on 7 March 1952. Cobra was in whelp at the time and her litter was born on 27 March 1952. Six of the puppies died in quarantine and the remaining two which were taken home by Major Petty died a little later, all from hardpad. Quarantine kennels in those days were not permitted to vaccinate against this killer disease. Cobra was mated again and her first successful litter in England was born on 22 December 1952 to Bando von Fohr – successful in that she whelped and the puppies survived – but in reality not a particularly significant litter apart from the dog Strawbridge Bando who is behind the Merse-side affix which produced Sh. Ch. Ballina of Merse-Side. Strawbridge Baron from the same litter has the distinction of being the first Weimaraner to gain entry to the Kennel Club Stud Book by reason of his second prize gained at the Yorkshire Gundog Club's trial on 13 April 1955 in the Novice Stake. Cobra's subsequent four litters were born on 18 August 1954 to Thunderjet, 13 May 1956 to Alex of Monksway, 17 July 1957 to Ipley Apollo, and 13 March 1958 to Sandrock Ami. These four litters were the Strawbridge F, J, O and S litters respectively out of which Franz went to Rhodesia, Fidget and Furst to Australia, Jake and June to the USA. Strawbridge Oliver

57

from the Apollo mating had the most early influence on the breed being used at stud 11 times, producing 79 registered progeny, many of which are to be found in present-day pedigrees. Before coming back to England, Major Petty had Cobra trained in Germany where, handled by Herr Fehse, she won prizes at the Club Youth Trial at Schaumburg/ Lippe on 21 April 1951 and at the Major Herber Memorial Trial held near Nienburg/Weser during October 1951.

2. *Bando von Fohr*. Dog, born 1.10.50.
>   Breeder: Frau Grawe-Duchene, Germany. Imported by Major R. H. Petty 1952.
>   Sire: Bodo v Reiningen. (Exported from Germany to the USA.)
>   Dam: Bona v Osteestrand.

Bando arrived with Cobra on 7 March 1952 and, like her, was trained and worked in Germany. Handled by Herr Fehse he was placed IIc at the Major Herber Memorial Trial in October 1951. He sired five litters, to Vita von der Haraska (Strawbridge E litter), Cobra von Boberstrand (Strawbridge B litter), Hella aus der Helmeute (Strawbridge G litter), Strawbridge Czarina (Strawbridge J litter) and Strawbridge Cobra (Goosefame litter).

3. *Vita von der Haraska*. Bitch, born 1.2.51.
>   Breeder: Baron A. St Bornemissza, Austria. Imported by Major R. H. Petty, 1952.
>   Sire: Sidi v Brunneckerhof.
>   Dam: Atta v Thayaschloss.

Vita had six litters. The first, to Cid von Bolkewehr, produced the Strawbridge C litter among which was Sh. Ch. Strawbridge Czarina and the CC winner Strawbridge Carol (many pedigrees and documents list this bitch as Coral which she should have been, but due to a Kennel Club error she became Carol – Coral and Carol were one and the same bitch) whose mating to Strawbridge Duke produced Sandrock Admiral and through him Sh. Ch. Wolfox Silverglance, Sh. Ch. Ace of Acomb, Sh. Ch. Monroes Dynamic, Ch. Ragstone Remus, Ch. Ragstone Ritter, etc. This bitch, therefore, had a most profound influence on the shape of the breed. Vita's second litter born 1.1.54 to Bando von Fohr produced the Strawbridge E litter which included Strawbridge Ermegard, the foundation bitch of Mrs F. Maddocks' Manana Kennels. Her third litter born 17.4.56 to Casar von Bolkewehr only produced one puppy, but a notable one as it turned out to be Strawbridge Irene, the only Weimaraner to win an Obedience CC. On 2.3.58 Vita whelped two Strawbridge R puppies to Strawbridge Duke, and her last two litters, both to Smokey included Strawbridge Lindex (dam of the Cloncurry field trial dogs) and Strawbridge Madam (dam of the Englas prefix).

4. *Cid von Bolkewehr*. Dog, born 19.4.51.
   Breeder: Melle Klinkenborg, Germany. Imported by Major R. H. Petty, 1952.
   Sire: Asso von Uplengen.
   Dam: Centa von der Burg.

At the German Youth Trials at Marklowe in April 1952, Cid was awarded III prize. He only sired one litter, namely the Strawbridge C litter out of Vita von der Haraska (see no. 3).

5. *Hella aus der Helmeute*. Bitch, born 17.11.50.
   Breeder: Helmut Limpert, Germany. Imported by Major R. H. Petty, 1952.
   Sire: Eggo Vierlinden.
   Dam: Dina v Bruchholz, J2, HZ2.

On 9.9.53 Hella's first litter was born to Ipley Apollo, the Strawbridge D litter of six. Some were bred from, but this line would have been dead without the potency of Strawbridge Duke who sired 15 litters and is to be found in a very high percentage of English pedigrees. Her second litter born 29.9.54 was to Bando von Fohr, the Strawbridge G litter from which Garnet went to Rhodesia, Gypsy and Graf to Australia. Her third and final litter was to Strawbridge Bruno and consisted of just one puppy born 26.5.56, Strawbridge Kate who was not bred from.

6. *Babette von der Katzbach*. Bitch, born 10.2.50.
   Breeder: Dr B. Scholz, Germany. Imported by Mrs O. Malet, 1952.
   Sire: Bodo von Reiningen. (Exported from Germany to the USA.)
   Dam: Benigna von der Teufelsposse.

Handled by Alberti, this bitch was placed IIIb at the Herber Memorial Trial in Germany in October 1951. She was imported in whelp to *Erich von Haimberg* (Bobo von Schwanebusch/Asta von Haimberg) a first-prize German trial winner. Her one and only litter was born on 26

March 1952 (one day before Cobra whelped), the Ipley A litter from which the most significant offspring was Ipley Apollo the sire of Strawbridge Duke, Manana Athene and Manana Adonis, Strawbridge Oliver and Strawbridge Vanessa, all of whom are behind many of the top winners in this country.

7. *Arco von der Kohlfurter Heide*. Dog, Born 2.2.50.
   Breeder: Frau Dr Hertha Schneider, Germany. Imported by Mrs O. Malet, 1952.
   Sire: Bodo v Haimberg.
   Dam: Dora v Schwanebusch.

Handled by Alberti, this dog was placed IIIa at the 1951 Major Herber Memorial Trial. He sired only one litter (to Strawbridge Duchess), none of which have registered progeny in this country. He changed hands a few times and eventually found his way to South Africa round about 1957 where he was fatally bitten by a cobra.

8. *Anka vom Suntel*. Bitch, born 28.8.51.
   Breeder: Karl Strube, Germany. Imported by Major E. Richardson, 1952.
   Sire: Bingo v Bruchholz.
   Dam: Dolly v Bruchholz. (II prize May 1950 Youth Trial, Niedersachen.

Anka had two litters, the first by Casar von Bolkewehr on 25.4.54 which produced seven puppies for the Monksway prefix. Out of these, Alex sired Wolfox Kentrish Kanonier, and Amber when mated to Strawbridge Duke produced Abbot of Monksway, the sire of champions Theocsbury Abbie and Archduke. Anka's second litter born 23.7.55 to Strawbridge Duke (after she was transferred into the Petty's ownership) produced the Strawbridge H litter, out of which Hans went to Portugal and the remainder were not bred.

9. *Casar von Bolkewehr*. Dog, born 19.4.51.
   Breeder: Melle Klinkenborg, Germany. Imported by Major E. Richardson, 1952.
   Sire: Asso von Uplengen.
   Dam: Centa von der Burg.

Litter-brother to *Cid* (no. 4), *Casar* was a first prize winner in April 1952 at the Youth Trial, Marklohe, Germany. He sired five litters in this country, the first out of Anka vom Suntel (no. 8), the second out of Col Brooks' Starfire, third out of the US import Heidi von Reiningen (no. 19) many of which went to the USA. His fourth litter out of Dr Macfarlane's Strawbridge Erica accounted for the Lochsloy prefix in Scotland. His last mating to Vita von der Haraska (no. 3) produced Strawbridge Irene CDx. Casar was a wilful, difficult dog to handle as will be seen from Major Richardson's foreword, above.

10. *Dea vom Steeg.* Bitch, born 22.11.53.
    Breeder: Kurt Rathert, Germany. Imported by Mr G. Jones circa 1954/5.
    Sire: Barras v Petersberg.
    Dam: Asta v Tannengrund.

Dea had three litters to Strawbridge Don resulting in a total of 12 puppies registered. Apparently only one was subsequently bred, namely the bitch Flor of Dnalemmor who was mated to Rolf of Rommeland, their seven puppies were not bred from. This line may not be completely dead as Flor and Rolf were exported to North Africa in 1957 and perhaps they were bred again. Fascinating names – try reversing Rolf's.

11. *Inka vom Weissen Kreuz*, J1, HZ3, Slt., Leistungszucht.
    Bitch, born 20.4.57.
    Breeder: Horst Budde, Germany. Imported by Lt Col W. N. S. Donaldson, 1959.
    Sire: Kuno aus der Helmeute, S.g., rs., ms., 'W', HZ2.
    Dam: Fanny von Reiningen, S.g., ms., slt., J3, HZ3.

Inka, a German field trial winner, unfortunately only had one litter. This was born 18.7.61 to Sandrock Admiral and proved to be most influential on the breed as it was the Derrybeg A litter of which Derrybeg Argus sired Ch. Ragstone Remus and through him many big winners both in the show-ring and in the shooting field.

12. *Earl vom Gleiberg Armen.* Dog, born 9.5.58.
    Breeder: H. Volkard, Germany. Imported by Mrs. C. J. Armenaki circa 1962.
    Sire: Alf von Kinzigtal.
    Dam: Iba von Haimberg.

This dog sired one litter to Wolfox Moonshall Rosette 21.4.62, but there were only two puppies, one of these was Wolfox Silver Sceptre who in turn whelped one puppy. This line is probably dead.

*Asta von gut
Blaustauden.*

13. *Dinna vom Morebach*. Bitch, born 21.3.69.
  Breeder: Franz Nemetz, Austria. Imported by Mrs E. L. Fearn 1969.
  Sire: Axel vom Wehrturm, FS Bierbaum 30.4.66 Ic.
  Dam: Cilli von Tattendorf, VGP.1, F Preis, WIEN 67, S.g.

Known to all as Sleepy, *Dinna* was a big bitch of immense charm and
breed type, very pale in colour. Mated to Ch. Ragstone Remus she
produced her one and only litter on 3.12.72. With Remus's grand-
mother being the German Inka vom Weissen Kreuz, these offspring
were full of good German and Austrian bloodlines and proved themselves well in the field as well as in the show-ring where three of them
gained their titles, namely Sh. Ch. Gunther, Sh. Ch. Ludmilla and
Ch. Wotan – all of Ragstone as were the entire litter of 11. To date

Gunther holds the breed record for CCs won by a male Weimaraner and both he and Wotan are championship show group winners. 'Sleepy' died in December 1981 at the age of 12¾.

14. *Asta von gut Blaustauden.* Long-haired Bitch, born 2.3.73.
   Breeder: Rev. Foster Rudolph Trost. Imported from Austria by Mrs Ann Janson, 1973.
   Sire: Blitz von Schloss Wildberg.
   Dam: Candy von Grand Village.

Asta was the first long-haired import to be bred from in this country and her two litters to the long-haired dog Dino von der Hagardburg (no. 15) produced 11 registered puppies. One of these made breed history by being the first long-haired Weimaraner to win a CC. This was the dog born 27.3.75 Aruni Dinwiddi from Seicer who won his first CC at Paignton in 1978 and his second at Bournemouth in the same year. He was not used at stud until 1982.

'Sleepy' – Dinna vom Morebach. (Photo: M. Gough)

15. *Dino von der Hagardburg.* Long-haired Dog, born 8.1.74.
    Breeder: Winfred Seidl. Imported from Austria by Mrs Ann Janson, 1974.
    Sire: Arno von der Hagardburg.
    Dam: Cora von der Hagardburg.

Dino's contribution to the breed from his two matings to Asta (no. 14) was the Aruni D from Seicer and Aruni E from Seicer puppies, all long-hairs of course. He also sired a short-haired litter out of Uhlan Champelle of Hawsvale who was a litter sister to the long-haired sport Mafia Man of Monroes, the Hawsvale I litter. He sired a long-haired litter out of Monroes Tatti Firebird who was the long-haired product of litter-mates Mafia Man (long) and Uhlan Fantasia (short); also a litter out of Torwood Hairy Firebird who was a long-haired bitch out of a mixed litter. Dino did not stay with Mrs Janson, and eventually lived and worked with Mr Geoff Simmons of the Baynard prefix in Yorkshire.

16. *Hasso von der Hagardburg.* Long-haired Dog, born 14.2.79.
    Breeder: Winfred Seidl. Imported from Austria by Mr and Mrs L. F. Smith, 1979.
    Sire: Iro vom Brunnwiesgut.
    Dam: Asta vom Auhofergut.

Currently siring litters mainly out of long-haired stock under the owner's Pondridge affix.

17. *Salto vom Zenthof.* Dog, born 10.4.81.
    Breeder: Heinz Reuper. Imported from West Germany by Mr and Mrs John Mayhew of Australia, 1981.
    Sire: Alan v Forst Horice, S.g./S.g., rgr., J68, H162, H172, ms4.
    Dam: Bianka v Welfenland, S.g./S.g., rgr., J60, H175, ms2.

Salto left quarantine during January 1982 and was then homed by Mrs Jane George when he was used lightly at stud before leaving for his new life in Australia.

18. *Ragstone Rudbeckia* (Richtkanonier of Ragstone/Sh. Ch. Ludmilla of Ragstone) returned from Holland late 1981 in whelp to the German-bred dog owned by Josef Jürgen of Kerkrade, Holland:
    Gildo von der Teutonenburg, S.g./S.g., SCH.H.I, SCH.H.II, SCH.H.III, VJP, HZP, VsWP.II, HD free. Dog, born 7.10.77.

Breeder: Josef Lohre, West Germany.
Sire: Apoll vom Annenhof, H3.
Dam: Jette vom Zenthof, +H143.

Owned by Mrs H. Cross, Rudbeckia whelped nine puppies in quarantine but unhappily lost all but one bitch (Roerag Rhula vom Ragstone) so it remains to be seen what, if any, influence Gildo has on the breed in the future.

The American Imports

19. *Heidi von Reiningen*. Bitch, born 31.1.51.
    Breeder: Dr O. J. Huck. Imported from the USA by Col J. A. Brooks, 1952.
    Sire: Bodo von Reiningen (German import).
    Dam: Fieldmaster's Sally Ann.

Heidi was imported in 1952, the first from America. She was in whelp to Int. Ch. Helmanhof's Storm Cloud CDx UD whose sire was the legendary Grafmar's Ador CD who gained his obedience title at six months and two days, and whose dam was Silver Blue Sue. Heidi's litter was born 29.7.52 – Shootingstar, Thunderstreak, Spitfire (or Starfire), Thunderbolt and, lastly Thunderjet who was best of sex in dogs at Crufts 1955 judged by the late May Pacey. Heidi's second and last litter was born in 1954 to Casar von Bolkewehr, all named after aircraft, seven in all.

20. *Schatzi von Waldenberg*. Bitch, born 24.1.52.
    Breeder: Mrs O. Montford. Imported from the USA by Mr and Mrs R. C. Wood.
    Sire: Grafmar's Rachmaninoff.
    Dam: Grafmar's Recompense.

This bitch whelped five puppies in 1956 to Strawbridge Bando, but the line has died out.

21. *Gretchen von Harrasburg*. Bitch, born 24.2.52.
    Breeder: E. A. Richardson. Imported from the USA by Capt. J. B. Everitt.
    Sire: Dick von der Harrasburg.
    Dam: Ella von Bruchholz.

'Smokey' pictured with Paula Webb.

Imported with the dog Gustav von Schweinfurt (no. 22), this pair bred together twice. Three puppies were registered from the first mating and only two from the second. The only progeny likely to crop up in our pedigrees is a dog from the first litter born 26.8.55, namely Smokey who sired three litters and was responsible for Wolfox's Sandrock Cha-Cha and Sandrock Coral. Smokey later went to the USA where he became Smokey von Franbrue.

22. *Gustav von Schweinfurt*. Dog, born 3.6.53.
    Breeder: Dr G. F. Dobler. Imported from the USA by Capt. J. B.
    Everitt.
    Sire: US Dual Ch. Palladian Perseus.
    Dam: Karmae's Silver Sally, CD.

See above, no. 21.

23. *Valhalla's Helmsman Arrow*. Dog, born 7.9.55.
    Breeder: J. Conley. Imported from the USA by Miss Rita Monkhouse,
    circa 1958.
    Sire: US Ch. Casar von Haussermann.
    Dam: Marward's Brenda.

'Fella' was only used six times although Miss Monkhouse (Cabaret) specifically imported him to widen the bloodlines. He is to be found behind some of the Cartford, Cabaret, and Andelyb's affixes, also those Ragstone lines carrying Ragstone Rasheba.

24. *Ragnor's Turk*. Dog, born 23.6.64.
    Breeder: Dr A. N. S. Abrey. Imported from Rhodesia by Mr Roy
    Syddall.
    Sire: Santa Barbara Yukon of Ragnor.
    Dam: Ragnor's Helga.

Included in this section as Turk was American on his sire's side. His dam was by Strawbridge Franz out of Strawbridge Garnet, both exported by Major Petty, so the pedigree contains seven of the original British imports: Vita, Cobra, Bando, Hella, Gustav, Gretchen and Heidi. Turk was a big, very bold, dark coloured dog who was only in this country for a short time before returning to Rhodesia. During his stay he sired one litter only and this was to Schoenfeldt Angelica who had two puppies. Only one was bred from; this was the CC winning Ragstone Renee who had a litter by Ch. Ragstone Ritter before she was exported to the USA.

25. *Flottheim's Kym*. Bitch, born 15.5.66.
    Breeder: Mr and Mrs P. Schubert. Imported from the USA by Mrs S.
    Worthing-Davies.
    Sire: US Ch. Flottheim's Goldey.
    Dam: Pat von der Heide.

Sixteen Kympenna's puppies from two litters by Sh. Ch. Monroes

Nexus are this bitch's American contribution. From the litter born 2.8.70, Mrs J. Matuszewska's Sh. Ch. Kympenna's Tristan has been the most influential being the sire of (to date) at least 42 litters and will, therefore, be found in a great many pedigrees.

26. *Igoe's Gray Lady*. Bitch, born 18.9.67.
    Breeder: Mr and Mrs P. Whitfield. Imported from the USA by Mr P. Lockhart.
    Sire: Kelchners Silver Knight.
    Dam: Liberty Lady.

Mated twice, once to Karl Rhu, next to Arlebroc Abbot. Unwittingly perhaps the cause of much controversy in the breed. Her litter born 19.11.71 to Abbot produced the bitch Gray Moonshadow of Duenna which, when mated to Ortega Opal Mint gave birth to a 'sport'. This 'sport' was the long-haired dog Mafia Man of Monroes and was the very first long-haired Weimaraner to be born in this country.

27. *Webbdant's Arabesque*, TDx. Bitch, born 13.5.72.
    Breeder: Mr and Mrs J. Webb. Imported from the USA by Mrs D. Brickl.
    Sire: Greypoint's Schultz II.
    Dam: US Ch. Webbdant's Tempo.

Mated to Sh. Ch. Gunther of Ragstone, she produced the Abbisline G litter on 9.10.76, one of which, Gabrielle, went to Canada where she obtained her Canadian championship title.

28. *Ch. Kamsou Moonraker von Bismarck*. Dog, born 14.10.75.
    Breeders: Kamsou Kennels. Imported from the USA by Mr and Mrs R. George, 1976.
    Sire: Am. Ch. Kam's Tempest.
    Dam: Am. Ch. Kam's Dusty Moonshine.

'Prosper' gained his show champion title quite soon after his release from quarantine, and completed his full title in the field in 1980. His quality in front, forechest and quarters outweighed his slightly feminine head, and his influence on the breed must be felt as he was used at stud fairly widely and produced many champion offspring. To Sh. Ch. Hansom Hirondelle he produced Ch. Denmo Blueberry Muffin, and Sh. Ch. Denmo Roadrunner, and to Sh. Ch. Ludmilla of Ragstone he produced Sh. Ch. Ragstone Ryuhlan (and New Zealand

Ch. R. Ryulla). A later mating to Hirondelle produced Sh. Ch.
Denmo Raspberry Highball, Sh. Ch. Denmo Side-Car, and Sh. Ch.
Denmo Prairie Oyster; and to Sh. Ch. Hansom Hobby Hawk the dog
Sh. Ch. Hansom Brandyman of Gunalt and bitch Sh. Ch. Hansom
Hospitality.

29. *Sh. Ch. Arimar's Rolf von der Reiteralm.* Dog, born 15.1.79.
   Breeders: J. Isabell and J. Morgan. Imported from the USA by Mr and
   Mrs J. Mayhew of Australia 1979.
   Sire: Am. and Can. Dual Ch. Ronamax Rufus v d Reiteralm, CD,
   SDX, RDX.
   Dam: Am. Ch. I've a Dream of Arimar, CD, NSD.

'Tank', after his release from quarantine was homed, trained and
handled to his show champion title by Jane George before he went on
to New Zealand in November 1980 and then to Australia in 1981. Like
his temporary stable-companion Moonraker, he also gained his UK
title quite quickly and his Australian owners were fortunate enough to
be in this country to witness his second and third CC wins. He sired
three litters whilst in England, the first to Jane George's Ch. Denmo
Blueberry Muffiin born 1.11.80 founding her Fineshade affix. 'Tank'
gained both his New Zealand and Australian titles.

30. *Graver Alder.* Bitch, born 25.10.74.
   Breeder: J. Lawson-Kennedy. Imported from the USA by Ms L.
   Kennedy-Maples.
   Sire: Greypoint's Sandman, TD.
   Dam: Kennedy's Liebchen-Ayr.

Whelped a litter 20.4.80 to Sh. Ch. Greyfilk Knightsman.

5

A Few Personal Views

Having been dominated for over twenty years by this fascinating, if often infuriating, breed, my own humble ha'porth of opinion as to its origin comes down squarely in favour of the *Schweisshunde* (bloodhound). He seems the only possible ancestor when both colour and working ability are considered. Hound traits were very much in evidence when we used to run half a dozen Weimaraners with the same number of Rhodesian Ridgebacks, especially when hare, rabbit or fox got up before the ringleaders could be gathered on to leashes! Then it was complete oblivion to the whistle or anything else as the pack streamed away into the distance giving tongue – and advertising the fact to the entire neighbourhood that Mrs B. was out of control again! Much to my shame. Well, no – let's be honest – to my secret pleasure, tinged with a nagging fear that they might be gone a bit longer than the original plan. It seemed so natural and they were so utterly joyous in voice and stride it was difficult not to share their joy, and perhaps feel a twinge of regret for those town-dogs pounding the pavement on a leash with just the odd tree to sniff and water. Properly under control, the Weimaraner is a fantastic tracking-dog and many are the tales of his prowess in this field.

On the subject of colour, the breed standard calls for a *grey* dog, and shades of grey do not include blue or tan, both of which can and do occur. Taking a colour photograph of a Weimaraner can have some surprising results and many is the time I have heard owners complaining about the quality of the printing – but I wonder? Mrs Bede-Maxwell wrote to me in 1974 and part of her letter was about this:

Here (in America) we have the continued attempt to legalise the blue Weimaraner which is now, by standard revision subject to judicial disqualification. For the life of me I can't see how the Weimaraner, admitted stem of the old *Schweisshunde*, could legally carry black. And in respect of that – an intriguing observation. There's a good silver-gray dog here who has had several nice wins under me and he was a Group winner under me this

70

autumn. Now the reason I mention this is because the day of the Group win, a colored picture was taken of his win, with the handler, myself, the trophy. It was late afternoon. Came the picture and this good *gray* dog came out a sort of tan-biscuity color all over. Now my dress, the handler's clothes, the grass etc., were all correct for color, but my gray dog was *tan*. I also have another color picture with him that was taken a couple of months earlier and he is properly his own visible *gray*! Now, what I've thought, pondering this, is that the late afternoon sun – which as I know can redden color pictures – had picked up the underlying pigmentation which is likely enough Weimaraner heritage – the *brown implicit in the hair*. I'm expressing this badly because in terms of discussing color inheritance, I've no great competence, I am not expert, nor student, though I have read most of the classic tomes. Anyway, what I'm trying to say is that this freak but very beautiful professionally taken picture, which rendered everything justly, and completely altered the dog's coat color, must have taken something that basically was not there for the human eye, but in some combination of light for time of day, drew out from the dog's coat some element that was deep within the construction of the hair. I do know that many Weimaraner coats do present what the Germans call a shimmer of brown; again of course the legacy of the *Schweisshunde* which were always some shadings of yellow to reddish brown.

It is obviously apparent that many newer owners offering their dogs at stud are unaware of the incidence of truly mismarked puppies and are, therefore, unable to give any advice to the bitch owner. By mismarked, I refer to that puppy or puppies in the litter displaying those inherited, characteristic bloodhound markings. Call them what you will – apricot points, ginger jobs, Dobe markings, etc., they all throw back to the *Schweisshunde* again. Genes, chromosomes and alleles are just terms coined by the experts to confuse me – and I suspect plenty of other ordinary folk too! I do know the experts can predict, by study of these odd words, what percentage of a given litter will be mismarked. I know too that old Mother Nature can throw her spanner in the works very effectively and make these predictions fly away in the face of reality. One such prediction by the gene experts was that a particular litter must contain at least 50 per cent of mismarked puppies. In the event, 10 perfectly clear puppies were whelped. To my simple mind, it must also follow that mismarked puppies can appear quite unexpectedly, but with experience it is comparatively easy to spot the mismarked puppy at birth (especially whilst still wet). The most dominantly marked location seems to be the underside of the tail which appears to be biscuit coloured. A *very*

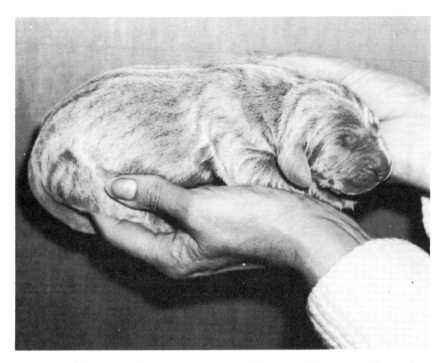

The distinctive stripes on a new-born Weimaraner disappear at about 10 days of age when the eyes open.

careful examination of the rest of the animal will result in observation of slightly different shading on the eyebrows, cheeks and inside legs. I have heard other breeders state that this is not always apparent at birth and only manifests itself several weeks later (when it is morally very difficult to put the puppy down). I cannot accept this as I feel that if the colour is missing at birth it will not suddenly appear later, but it certainly requires extremely careful inspection of the coat to recognise the slight shading.

In the American chapter you will find further mention of the blue Weimaraner. Although this colour variation does not apparently crop up (as far as I know) in this country, I thought it pertinent to include the subject in view of the fact that over recent years there have been several American imports and there must, therefore, be the possibility that blues will occur sooner or later. We must be prepared to act summarily. The German Weimaraner Club was most emphatic in its rejection of the Americans' desire to include blue as an accepted colour in their breed standard, and stated that no more exports would be allowed from Germany if such a thing happened. They also said that the amber colour of the eyes and the colour of the nails, both breed characteristics, would also be changed if blue was accepted.

I well recall a few Crufts ago, a lady from America was visiting and showing off colour slides of her 'Blue'. I happened to be talking to Mrs Hilda Pugh at the time, and that extremely forthright lady President of the Canadian Kennel Club very sharply rounded on the unfortunate American and pronounced loudly and acidly 'Should have been bucketed at birth!' Well, I feel the same and that goes for the 'ginger jobs' too. The striking grey colour of the Weimaraner is unique in the world of dogs and long may it remain so.

6

The Longhairs

As with the short-haired Weimaraner, no specific breed records appertaining to the long-haired Weimaraner in Germany in the very early days were kept, and little is known about them apart from fragments of information gleaned from various sources. It is known that long-haired dogs were exhibited at Hanover in 1879 and that Herr von Kalkstein-Koppeln had bred them since 1873. Also, long-haired Weimaraners were advertised for sale in *Jägerzeitung* – 10, 3.11.1889, where a four-year-old bitch, long-haired, Weimaraner-*Vorstehhund* was offered for 120 Mk in Sangershausen; and in 31, 16.1.1890, a litter of eight brown, black and silver-grey long-haired *Vorstehhunde* puppies.

What is documented is a litter born on 7 February 1933 bred by Josef Schaffer Kaufmann in Stranzendorf, North Austria, out of which Obmann Robert Pattay selected a puppy registered as Tell von Stranzendorf. This dog caused much comment when he was exhibited in Vienna in 1934 as he was obviously a long-haired specimen although not purchased as such. Major Herber was drawn into discussion and investigation and, as a result, at the German club's meeting in 1935 at Frankfurt/Main when several members confirmed that they had knowledge of other long-haired dogs in the past, the decision was reached to recognise the variant. When shortly afterwards the German and Austrian clubs jointly approved the new Standard for the Breed, it included the following statement: 'Very occasionally there are some long-haired Weimaraners. They have a right to be listed, provided their origin can be traced back undeniably until the fourth generation. One should strive to raise such long-haired Weimaraners.' It was also agreed that the tail should be docked at the fourth vertebra but after some time it was ruled that the dog should have a full tail. However, in the German standard of 1952 it called for the tail to be docked at 14 days at the second or third vertebra for long-hairs.

In 1936 the dog Illo von Hipkendahl (1468) was the first long-haired Weimaraner to be entered in the German breeding register although neither parent showed any evidence of long hair, and the grandparents being born before 1924 meant that the pedigree was untraceable.

World War II put an abrupt end to any large-scale breeding programme for the German long-hairs as many of the breeders and their dogs were never heard of again, presumed the casualties of war. The Austrians were slightly more fortunate and a few complete litters survived along with the Austrian stud-book which recorded the following long-hairs: Adel, Adda, Anka, Antje and Aura von Hirschgrund; Troll, Tell, Trick, Tanne, Terra, Teska and Toska von der Wastlhutte; Tel von Stranzendorf; Illo von Hipkendahl; Poldi z Mnisku; Satta von Brunneckerhof and Cora von Bornhof.

Cora von Bornhof had a mixed litter by the short-haired dog Bravo von Rossberg but all three long-haired dogs from the litter died before being used at stud. In May 1935 the long-haired bitch Donna von Diendorf was born from the short-haired parents Gift von Rundhof and Lia Grafenegg, the breeder being the Countess Stubenburg of Walkersburg Castle, Austria. Donna's litter-sister Dita appears in some British pedigrees. The 'T' von der Wastlhutte litter mentioned above was sired by Illo von Hipkendahl out of Robert Pattay's Poldi z Mnisku, a Czechoslovakian bitch he had acquired from Baron Kast. The von Hirschgrund litter was bred by Dr Ulrich Kluge and was sired by Robert Pattay's Illo von Hipkendahl out of Teska von der Wastlhutte (father/daughter). Prince Hans von Ratibor of the Schloss Grafenegg was also a notable breeder of long-hairs and they were trained and worked very successfully by Breed warden Forstrat Georg Stuhlinger.

At the present time the long-haired variant is not recognised in the USA although it has, of course, cropped up from time to time. Possibly one of the earliest owners of long-hairs was Miss Harding of New Jersey who campaigned vigorously to get recognition and acceptance of the variant but all to no avail. Her first Weimaraner was a short-hair obtained in 1940 from the Grafmar kennels of Margaret Horn and out of this bitch she retained Blythe Spirit who was subsequently mated to the famous German import Bert von der Harrasberg. From this, Miss Harding kept a dog Bayonet Farm Incandescence which, when bred to a bitch from Ohio Jimclaire's Silvergraus, produced Bayonet Farm Moonbeam. After checking with some other breeders as to the wisdom of the idea, she bred Moonbeam back to her sire Incandescence thinking that perhaps she might obtain a long-hair! And that is exactly what happened - four short-haired males and one long-haired female. Unfortunately her tail was docked as her long coat was not readily apparent at a couple of days of age. However, she was taken around wherever Miss Harding thought people might be interested and, in 1966 when this long-haired bitch Bayonet Farm Sea Urchin was four years old, contact was made with a long-haired male named Ann's Pretty Boy Mike and seven long-haired puppies, four male, three female, resulted. Miss Harding writes:

I tried to get people interested in the long-hairs but perhaps because I was not a hunting or a field trial person I got no response. I even took some to trials but since they were not entered, not being trained, I was advised not to even take them out of the car. They are so beautiful in motion, but my persuasion fell on deaf ears, and maybe once or twice on the wrong ears . . . I sold one puppy to a Canadian who had previously had a long-haired dog and had searched the country and found no others but mine. This was all very frustrating and disappointing for me, but I did have wonderful years with my beautiful dogs. Later, I bought one in Austria (Salzburg) and he died in 1981 aged 11 years. When he was nine years old I taught him to track and he took to it marvellously and we had two wonderful years tracking which I found a great sport.

This was Hasso von Brunnsweisgut bred by Hans Geishammer.

The first general sight in Britain of the long-haired variant came in the form of photographs in the Club's magazine *Weimaraner News* (11) during September 1965. This contained a report from Joan and Ken Fussell on their visit to the World Show at Brno, Czechoslovakia, during June 1965. The relevant part of their report reads:

Still in Vienna however, we had to wait 24 hours for our first sight of a long-haired Weimaraner but it was worth it; our expectations were completely fulfilled and we all said that the two we saw were as beautiful a sight as we had ever seen. The owner, Herr Blaunsteiner, had a dog and a bitch; the dog was a beautiful specimen, the bitch perhaps a little too fine but whereas the dog had just the suspicion of being a shade too dark, the bitch was the most perfect silver-grey, the colour of a 3 week old pup. How to describe them? Certainly the outline is Weimar, particularly the head where the long hair was not very apparent until one came to the ears. Here there was copious hair with a certain amount of feathering. Bodywise, the length of hair, etc. closely resembled that of a Flat-coated Retriever; tails are not docked and on

Hasso von Brunnsweisgut tracking in the snow with his American owner Laura Harding.

those we saw, there was a good deal of feathering starting halfway along and carrying to the tip. 'Billy' the dog was already a champion but was not taken to Brno – the Czech's loss we fear. It had been arranged that we spend a day in the field with these two dogs watching them work but torrential rain prevented our doing so and the following day we were due to leave for Brno.

Partly as a result of this brief word picture of the long-hairs and of seeing the Fussell's photographs and hearing their fuller comments, Ann Janson became intrigued with the possibility of importing a long-haired Weimaraner. She had also observed that her own short-haired dogs were somewhat unwilling to face gorse bushes and were slow to water and felt perhaps a dog with more furnishings might be keener – she had experience of her father's working Irish setter so was more than half way to accepting a long coat! Added to which was the (to Ann) distinct advantage that she thought she would not be required to dock the tails of new-born puppies. It took three years of letter-writing and negotiations with various Austrian breeders until one day she received a telegram from Herr Winfred Seidl notifying her of the availability of a bitch. Hot-foot, Ann and husband Roy, along with Joan Matuszewska, sped to Austria, met Herr Seidl and was introduced to Asta von Gut Blaustauden who was born on 2 March 1973, bred by the Rev. Foster Rudolf Trost, and came from the Hungarian/Czech border. They arranged to have her shipped home and then patiently waited until quarantine was completed and the first long-haired import could be seen and admired by all.

Meanwhile, whilst these lengthy negotiations were proceeding just before Asta was born, an unexpected happening set the breed in Britain by its ears. On 8 January 1973 a litter bred in Scotland by Mr J. Seymour contained a long-haired dog – the first to be recorded in Britain. It is only fair to say that the long-haired entry into Britain was not an auspicious one. This first arrival was a 'sport' born of short-haired parents and unfortunately he had several hereditary defects. This litter also contained one other puppy which was possibly long-haired but it did not survive; all the others were normal short-hairs. The sire was Ortega Opal Mint and the dam Grey Moonshadow of

Aruni Dinwiddi from Seicer the first long-haired Weimaraner to gain a CC in Britain. Bred and owned by Ann Janson.

Duenna who was out of an American imported bitch Igoes Gray Lady (see import section). This long-haired dog was subsequently acquired and registered by Joan Matuszewska as Mafia Man of Monroes. He was used at stud once only and this was on his short-haired litter-sister Uhlan Fantasia who produced five long-haired puppies out of a total of nine in July 1974. (Another short-haired bitch from the same litter, Uhlan Champelle of Hawsvale, was mated to the second long-haired import Dino von der Hagardburg and produced a litter of eight of which surprisingly *none* was long-haired.) Cmdr Val Hawes' research into Mafia Man's pedigree came up with the fact that on his sire's side six generations back is the dog Sidi von Brunneckerhof whose litter-sister Satta was long-haired. A further three generations back in Sidi's pedigree is the dog Gift von Rundhof who also appears in the same pedigree two generations back when he sired Dita von Diendorf whose litter-sister Donna was long-haired. It would appear to have taken about 35 years for this gene to eventually find its counterpart in a chromosome now paired with its own, from the dam. One of Major Petty's original imports, the bitch Vita von der Haraska, also has Sidi von Brunneckerhof as a sire.

The third long-haired Weimaraner to arrive in Britain was the dog Dino von der Hagardburg born 8 January 1974 who was a gift from Herr Seidl to Ann Janson. Dino sired two litters to Asta and one of the progeny made breed history when in 1978 the dog Aruni Dinwiddi from Seicer won two CCs. Dino was later transferred to Joan Matuszewska and finally to Geoff Simmons.

Mafia Man, Asta and Dino were, therefore, the foundation stock for the long-hairs in this country, together with the much more recent import in 1979 from Austria by Mr and Mrs L. Smith of the dog Hasso von der Hagardburg bred by Herr Seidl.

After lengthy negotiations between the Weimaraner Club and the Kennel Club, the January 1974 *Kennel Gazette* announced the following:

The Committee at its meeting on the 20th November agreed that the 'long-haired Weimaraner' may be recorded as such on registration certificates. At the present time there is no intention of establishing the 'long-haired Weimaraner' as a separate breed and the long haired specimens of the breed will, until further notice, be treated in exactly the same way as the Saluki, whereby the less common type of coat may be indicated on the registration certificate.

The Breed Standard was amended and approved by the Kennel Club on 2 June 1976.

However, not all went smoothly. At the 1977 AGM of the Weimaraner Club of Great Britain, Roy Janson reported that a long-haired dog offspring of the first two imported Austrian long-hairs had been put down on veterinary advice as he was believed to be suffering from hereditary epilepsy. As a consequence a number of siblings and puppies from a repeat mating were taken for electro-encephalograph readings and some were found to have abnormal readings indicative of a tendency to epilepsy. A meeting was held at which Dr M. B. Willis of the Kennel Club team investigating hereditary abnormalities gave his view on the subject. A summary of his talk and recommendations is quoted here and is the same report as circularised by the Weimaraner Club to its members:

In what is known as true or idiopathic epilepsy the fits are said to have a specific character and it is essential to have veterinary diagnosis as fits can also caused by encephalitis, brain damage, malfunction of the parathyroid gland, teething, parasites encysted in brain tissue etc. Veterinary diagnosis of the seizures suffered by the longhaired dog which was destroyed suggest that they were typical of idiopathic epilepsy. The exact mode of inheritance is not known but is thought to be polygenic and of a threshold character. Age of onset can range from 0–7 years but a substantial majority have a first fit at about two years of age. It has been noted that the higher the degree of inbreeding, the earlier the age of onset. Dr Willis suggested that whilst e.e.g. readings were in some cases a useful diagnostic tool, they were by no means infallible – he personally knew of a German Shepherd Dog that had a normal e.e.g. reading and which did in fact have epileptic fits. He recommended that dogs which had fits should under *no* circumstances be used for breeding. Siblings of such dogs should be used with caution. He recommended that longhaired dogs (for 'dogs' read 'dogs/bitches') should be mated to the best possible specimens of shorthaired dogs and that the primary aim should be to produce good Weimaraners irrespective of coat. In view of the epileptic factor breeders should be prepared to lose the long hair in the first generation. Short-haired offspring of such matings could be bred back to obtain long-haired dogs when necessary. Rigorous culling should be practised of unsound or untypical stock. There was no short cut by way of a breeding plan and we should be prepared to wait several generations for useful results. It might be useful not to breed from Austrian stock until the animals were over two years old, because, although this by no means guaranteed that the animals in question would never have a fit, at least it would lengthen the odds. It was most important that accurate records were kept by all breeders and that

Monroes Linnet bred by Joan Matuszewska and owned by Ola T. Walter of Sweden. By Dino von der Hagardburg ex Monroes Tatti Firebird. (Photo: Olle Rosenqvist)

breeders were completely honest about their findings, that information was pooled and that the progress of progeny was followed for several years and if possible for a lifetime. Owners of dogs with abnormal e.e.g.s but which had not presented with fits, should, if they bred from their dogs be prepared to tell clients that they wished to record the progress of the pups and would refund purchase price if the pup was epileptic.

Since that meeting, experimental matings have taken place between the two coats in an effort to stabilise the long-hairs, but little real headway has been made. Whether it is a wise move to mix up the genes in this way, no doubt time will tell but some breeders of the short-hairs are adamantly refusing to allow their stock to become part of this scheme as they feel that there are possibly enough problems to face already without the added burdens perhaps connected with the long-hairs. Dr Willis' recommendation would appear to be orientated purely towards improvement of the long-hairs regardless of the overall effect on the breed and certainly the detrimental effect it could have on any resultant short-haired progeny from the mixed matings. It is

81

understandable that some owners of long-haired stock might perhaps consider the risk worth taking, but the majority of owners of short-haired stock surely would not. It is unfortunately becoming more difficult to completely separate the coats, as novice owners of new stud dogs are very often quite unaware of the presence of long-haired ancestors in bitches brought for mating.

At the time of writing there have been approximately 100 long-hairs born in this country. The majority – 75 per cent – have been sired by the imports Dino and Hasso von der Hagardburg, with Aruni Dinwiddi from Seicer contributing one litter. The remaining 25 per cent are mainly the progeny of mixed coats. Despite the fairly large number of long-hairs in the country it was noticeable at the Weimaraner Club's 1983 Championship Show when ten-year anniversary rosettes were on offer to exhibits in the special long-hair class, of the five entered, only four were present, two of which were Ann Janson's veterans Asta and Dinwiddi.

One cannot but help feeling a certain amount of sympathy for the Jansons who must have been disappointed at the way this variant of the breed has progressed despite their valiant efforts to keep the two coats separate. There is a place for the long-haired Weimaraner and it is to be hoped that it will in time stand on its own merits – merits which include a willingness and unquestioned ability to work well in the field and, depending upon your viewpoint, nearly a full tail!

7

Field Trials and Working Trials

Field Trials

The first Weimaraners to show their paces in field trials in the early
1950s met with very limited success – they had to compete on level
terms with the Pointers and Setters until a few years later when they
were able to run in trials organised by the German Short-haired
Pointer Club. It was not until 1970 that the Weimaraner Club ran its
own trials, open to all the hunt-point-retrieve breeds. The breed's first
field trial winners were the bitches owned, trained and handled by
Colonel H. D. Tucker. In 1967 Lotti Go-Lightly won a GSP Novice
Stake and in 1972 her daughter Katie Go-Lightly won a Weimaraner
Club Novice Stake. 'Tommy' Tucker was one of the great characters
in our breed and his gentle handling and infinite patience with dogs
was something we rarely seem to see these days. He was courtesy
personified and was never too busy to help the novice with kindly
advice. His death in September 1975 was a great loss to the breed. His
'Training Notes' written in 1971 are full of sound advice and his
inherent gentleness and understanding of the breed is readily apparent
from the following extracts:

Training is an equal partnership between master and pupil. Master must
therefore also be of suitable material. He must always be good-humoured, be
willing to take endless trouble and never, never lose his temper. At the
Cavalry School in the horsed days we were told 'Before you hit a horse put a
smile on your face'. This means that punishment when necessary must be
calculated and sufficient to fit the crime and no more. If excessive it may put
the training back weeks or months or, in the case of a nervous pupil, may
ruin for life. I cannot think it is ever necessary to hit a Weimaraner. They are
too sensitive. To take by the scruff of the neck and give a mild shaking should
always be sufficient. The key of the door is – gentle – cheerful – firmness.

When voice is used, speak quietly, only loud enough for the dog to hear. There are two reasons for this. It ensures that Master is keeping his temper and in the shooting field a loud voice is a menace as it will scare all game in the vicinity; indeed it is best to use hand signals only in the field. If you did not start these lessons as a puppy, start now. It is never too late.

Hard Mouth I fear that Weimaraners have a reputation in many quarters for hard mouth. This is part fact and part prejudice though what proportion of each I am unable to say. Much can be done in training and there is good reason to believe that Weimaraners should be entered to game very cautiously indeed. First retrieves must be on dead birds with elastic bands to prevent the wings flapping about. It would be madness to start a Weimaraner on a runner. Having given plenty of retrieves on a dead, cold bird proceed as follows for the first retrieve with the gun. The dog is quartering and goes on point. Move up to him and order him to flush as you will have done many times without the gun. Shoot the bird and the dog will 'sit' as already trained to do. Unload, place the gun beside dog and leave him sitting; move to bird. Kneel down and take bird in both hands. Call dog. Stroke bird and dog for several minutes. The object is to impart to him that this is not a fierce creature to be attacked and bitten – on the contrary it is of value to Master and is to be treated gently. Allow him to sniff bird and finally allow him to take it in his mouth – but be sure you put part of your hand into his mouth with the bird. He will not bite your hand but if he does exert too much pressure your immediate protest will be a first class lesson to him to be gentle for it occurred at the very moment that he commited the crime. Give this lesson as often as opportunity offers and also with fur. Of course there are many dogs that are tender on dead birds but will bite and kill a runner. I can suggest no cure for these but I do know that some of them grow out of it.

Water It appears to be a characteristic of Weimaraners that they are scared of water when young and that they take to it readily when about three years old. The three years can obviously be reduced by very careful introduction to water for once they can be persuaded to enter it their fear vanishes. But we must have superlative patience. It is probably unwise to start on water training until a Weimaraner is a year old at least and perhaps more. The first step should obviously be to get your dog to follow you through very shallow water. Progress to slightly deeper water but not deep enough to swim. The more of this you do the better and the summer is the time to do it. Now you come to the real crunch of persuading your dog to swim. The method to choose should perhaps be influenced by the character of the dog. I have had experience of only two Weimaraners which is not enough to be authoritative. The method I have used is to draw the dog across deep water with a light rope attached to the collar. Thereafter they would swim across on command but much practice is necessary before they become good swimmers. The ultimate in water training is for a dog when swimming far out in a lake or river to turn towards Master when whistled and to change direction on hand signal.

The British field sportsman is a very conservative creature. He knows those breeds of dog that tradition has passed down to him and he is reluctant to accept, or is even hostile to, any new breed with which he is not acquainted. When you arrive therefore in the shooting field either as a gun or a humble 'picker-up', your Weimaraner will be eyed with suspicion until he has proved his worth. Do not therefore embarrass yourself or the breed by taking him out at all until you are confident of his steadiness and reliability.

The art of field-trialing and the training of dogs for field-trial competition is adequately covered in many excellent publications so will not be repeated or re-hashed here. I do think, however, that there is a world of difference between the working of the Weimaraner in field-trials where, unless the trial is confined to the breed, they compete on even terms with the other hunt-point-retrieve breeds often to their disadvantage, and the rough-shooter's dog at which work they seem to excel. A few questions relevant to this aspect have been asked and the answers given in the form of a written 'forum'. The 'panellists' are Mr John Gassman, one of the early importers into this country of the German Short-haired Pointer and a very experienced and respected field-trial judge; Mr Trevor Horsefield, successful owner of field-trialed Weimaraners who is now qualified to judge at field-trials; Mrs Louise Petrie-Hay of the 'Waidman' affix, breeder and trainer of Weimaraners, German Short-haired Pointers and Hungarian Vizslas, also a very experienced field-trial judge who gave many helpful training sessions in the Weimaraner Club's early days.

Weimaraners have not featured in field trial results as highly as the German Short-haired Pointers over the years. Admittedly, fewer actually compete but what in your opinion is the main cause for their apparent lack of success?

John Gassman: 'I have not had close contact with Weimaraners and for this reason I can only make general observations. First of all, if dogs are to be successful in field trials there are three things which should be right. Firstly they should have the right breeding; the breeder should be encouraged to breed dogs with a good nose and which are biddable. Secondly, the handler should be knowledgeable about what he is asked for in field trials and watch the finer points too. The handler should have confidence in his dog and learn from his failures and not be disappointed if he is not winning. Thirdly, luck plays a very big role. For instance, the dog may not have the opportunity to display its true ability, i.e. the opportunity for pointing is not always present at a field trial, also the circumstances may prevent the dog from making a stylish retrieve to show off its best ability.'

Trevor Horsefield: 'The reason that the Weimaraner has not featured in field trials is that it has been adopted by the pet market rather than the shooting fraternity. It has been used increasingly for showing as an entity in itself, and for obedience and police work. As a result of this puppies are seldom getting into the hands of experienced dog people to get the early start essential for field trial success. Inexperienced dogs coupled with inexperienced handlers will seldom succeed in the stylised trial sphere. In addition to this handicap the Weimaraner has also had to overcome much prejudice. Some prejudice has been ill-founded but some has been based on the performance of inexperienced and ill-equipped dogs and handlers in field trials. Inherent and basic differences prevail which give rise to further prejudice from judges weaned on and accustomed to alternative styles. However, having said all this, the Weimaraner's performance may not be excused if it enters a sphere of competition which demands certain parameters not suited to its training and inherent qualities. By experience I know that the Weimaraner must be controlled and where this is done by an inexperienced handler most, if not all, sparkle in the dogs may be controlled or conditioned out.'

Louise Petrie-Hay: 'Over the years the work of Weimaraners in trials has been poor until the last, say, three seasons. Originally, Tommy Tucker flew the flag successfully because his bitch worked as GSP judges liked – a fast hunter, a positive pointer, a good retriever, soft mouth and adequate in water. The other runners were slow, indecisive in their pointing, frequently hard-mouthed and failed in water. That is a fair assessment of the majority of Weimaraner entrants. But recently they have improved, probably with the increase of training classes and also with more owners of shooting Weimaraners becoming interested in trials and adapting their dog's work accordingly.'

Having judged field trials at which all the hunt-point-retrieve breeds have competed, what (if any) do you consider are the basic differences in work style?

John Gassman: 'There are no differences in work style of any of the pointing/retriever breeds.'

Trevor Horsefield: 'There is no doubt that to *some* extent the Weimaraner is the proverbial 'square peg' in the field trial world. The Weimaraner is derived from the St Hubert hound and from this has a strongly developed ground scenting ability. This, more than any other feature, gives the difference in work style. Totally orientated to ground scenting the Weimaraner works slowly and thoroughly over its beat. Unlikely to miss much the dog will leave a clean beat behind it. Despite this thoroughness the dog may not present as many birds as the faster GSP. This statement will depend much on the weather and scent conditions as it is often possible to see birds moving ahead of the Weimaraner whilst it "sweeps up" all the scent behind. Under these circumstances, the GSP will rush forward missing ground to hold the birds under cover which may then be pointed. Air scent versus ground scent is the obvious difference and I know from my experience of Weimaraner working deer that for tracking the wounded game the Weimaraner excels. This, however, is not the purpose or objective of the field trial day.'

Louise Petrie-Hay: 'Basically, the Weimaraner, I believe is *more* a *tracking* dog than a pointing dog. By this I mean that naturally as a puppy he is ground-scenting whereas as GSP puppy is naturally air-scenting. This is very noticeable when – as I have had – a bunch of mixed puppies are loose in a field. So – the Weimaraner has to be encouraged to air-scent and the GSP to ground-scent when training starts. Unless a Weimaraner can be taught to set his head high he cannot pick up air-scent at any distance – hence the position that a Weimaraner will only point when close to game because the scent is then lower on the ground and available to his lower nose. And naturally with a bird dog it is preferable to get advance notice of game with the consequent lack of disturbance and time to prepare to shoot. The Weimaraner appears generally to be a slower and more methodical ground coverer. This is advantageous in woodland and roots but a fearful bore where the ground is open and game is scarce – and at trials these are the conditions which usually prevail, so the Weimaraner is seen at a disadvantage.'

A greater percentage of Weimaraners are worked 'privately', picking-up, wildfowling or deerstalking as opposed to being worked in field trials. Do you think this type of work perhaps comes more naturally to the breed than the somewhat stylised field trials?

John Gassman: 'A field trial should be equal to a day's 'private' shooting so if somebody goes picking-up, wildfowling or deerstalking it should be a great help to him when competing in a field trial. In all these activities both handler and dog must complement each other.'

Trevor Horsefield: 'The Weimaraner with its slower steadier work style is ideally suited to the rough shooter. Close woodland cover is more suited to the breed than the open expanses and for good steady work, within gun range, the Weimaraner may be selected.'

Louise Petrie-Hay: 'Field trials are a specialised sport for gundog owners who enjoy competition and it is up to them to train their dogs for trials. Very, very few dogs can be successfully trialed and normally shot over – no one in their senses uses their field trial dog for serious rough shooting if he intends to get to the top in trials.'

After reading the origin theories and documented history of the breed in Germany, it seems unreasonable to expect the Weimaraner to work in the same style as the GSP. He was obviously never designed to do so. He has not the same amount of pointer blood in his veins and is far better suited to woodland work than to the GSP's strongpoint, the wide open spaces. However, with his undoubted capacity for learning there should be no reason why he could not be taught satisfactorily enough for him to compete on level terms in field trials against the other hunt-point-retrieve breeds.

It would seem that the breed slots neither into the pointer/setter group nor the hunt-point-retrieve group as far as field trials are concerned. Should they attempt to slot into the bloodhound trials group? Or have we the proverbial jack of all trades and master of none?

Working Trials

In 1956 Mrs S. M. Milward pioneered the way for the breed in this highly competitive field and trained and handled her bitch Strawbridge Irene CDx to a very high standard. 'Ike', as she was fondly known, had her first obedience win in Test A at Wimbledon Open Obedience Show in December 1956 at the age of eight months. At 11 months she won Novice and at 12 months Junior Stake; and a Certificate of Merit at one of the ASPADS Trials. Continuing her fine performance when winning Test B at 16 months, she went on to her CDx and the Junior Stake at SATS in 1957 at the age of 17 months. After a string of wins in Tests A, B and C and Certificates of Merit during 1957 and 1958, her ultimate glory was when she won the Obedience Challenge Certificate at Paignton Championship Show in July 1958. This win opened the door for competition at Crufts but tragically 'Ike' died on the eve of receiving her invitation. Mrs Milward had to wait nearly 20 years before she had the pleasure of seeing Weimaraners competing more actively in her field, but now the sport is flourishing although we still await the winning of another Obedience CC – a record that Mary and 'Ike' will have held for a very long time.

It was not until 1964 that the second obedience qualification came to the breed when Miss Kay Price piloted the sweet-natured dog Cartford Capricorn to his CDx. This was a noble effort as Kay had a mobility problem, was unable to walk fast, and also had to travel great distances from her Cornish home to compete. However, she was always cheerful and a popular figure when she successfully showed 'Adam' at the Championship shows winning two CCs with him.

About three years later Mrs Diana Oldershaw worked her first Weimaraner Gunmetal Guy to his CDx and UDx titles. She later qualified two bitches Waidman Giselle CDx and Gunmetal Emma CDx. At one Championship show, Guy had the distinction of being the only Weimaraner to display award cards over his bench gained in both the show-ring and the obedience-ring. Emma won two CCs and a Certificate of Merit at a field trial.

However, the real break-through came with the near explosion into the Weimaraner world of Mrs Val O'Keeffe (formerly Val Sutton). Diminutive in stature, but dynamic and dominant in her training, she has really brought this side of work into prominence over the years she has been connected with the breed. She has tirelessly poured her considerable energies into organising training classes, tests of work and instructional week-ends for the benefit of Weimaraner owners who perhaps not able to show or field-trial their dogs have found this type of work both interesting and rewarding. To date she has the distinction of owning the highest-titled Weimaraner in Fossana Bruno who is not only a field-qualified Show Champion but also adds CDx, UDx, WDx and TD after his name.

The first bitch to gain the WDx qualification was Mrs D. Shaw's good-looking Cristal of Bulow CDx, UDx, WDx. Owner trained and handled she was occasionally seen in the show-ring where she won one CC and a reserve CC. Her versatility won her the Weimaraner of the Year award in 1976; she was not bred from, and died aged seven in 1979. During 1983 Miss Cooke's Grinshill Rana Vanessa CDx, UDx, WDx, gained the first TDx title in the breed.

No other hunt-point-retrieve breed in this country can match the obedience records of the Weimaraner. However, whilst few would deny that work of any description is preferable to a life devoid of activity, one must never lose sight of the fact that the breed *is a gundog*. It cannot be argued that any breed of gundog is suited to the man-work required in the PD Stakes. Fortunately Weimaraner Police Dogs are few and for the breed's sake must remain few. Private individuals should on no account be tempted to train their dogs for the PD test of courage, search and escort, recall from criminal or the pursuit and detention of criminal exercises.

Weimaraners in Uniform

The Weimaraner is not widely used by the police, but the handful which have been successfully trained have worked extremely well. The Metropolitan Police have been offered quite a number over the years, but generally speaking, they have not kennelled too well. This is not surprising as it is, of course, a well-known fact that Weimaraners are not particularly amenable to kennel life. However, the six dogs trained and operated by the various police forces have been the exceptions – Gunmetal George, Monroes Thor, Greyhaven Boromir, Monroes A-Kaiser, Brett of Kenstaff, and Monroes Prangen.

Gunmetal George, born 21.6.69, bred by Mrs Diana Oldershaw, by Sh. Ch. Monroes Nexus out of Waidman Giselle CDx was the first grey police dog to command attention. After 14 weeks training at the Metropolitan Police Training School at Keston he passed out with a certificate for the best dog on the course and was then based at Richmond, Surrey, with his handler PC John Niblett. Newspapers and television programmes featured George quite regularly in the early days as the sole grey dog in a large squad of German Shepherds. He gained a Certificate of Merit at one of the SATS Trials and remained on duty until quite a good old age, although not always with his original handler.

Schutzhund-Prufung 'mannscharfe'. Demonstration of manwork in Germany.

Pride of the Police Force was Metpol Monroes Thor, UDx WDx PDx. Born 31.7.70 by Monroes Orest (Sh. Ch. Monroes Nexus/ Sh. Ch. Monroes Idyll) out of Monroes Pandora (Ch. Ragstone Remus/ Ch. Andelyb's Balch), bred by Mrs Joan Matuszewska. Handled and homed by PC Paul Dodd, Thor became a member of the Metropolitan Police Dog Demonstration Team in 1972. He took part in many demonstrations including the East of England and South of England Shows, Wembley and White City Stadiums, and Crufts Dog Show in 1976, 1977 and 1978. Like George, being one grey dog among so many German Shepherds he just had to stand out! In 1979 he appeared in the Royal Tournament at Earls Court, and the Tattoo to celebrate the 150th Anniversary of the Metropolitan Police at the Wembley Arena. He appeared on television in 'Blue Peter' and gave demonstrations in front of Her Majesty the Queen and also the Prime Minister. Thor was the first Weimaraner to qualify WDx and the first and, to date, the only Weimaraner to qualify PDx, also the first to obtain a Certificate of Merit in Tracking Dog. His awards in Kennel Club and Police Trials are too numerous to list. He was the winner in 1973 of the Frederika Shield for the best police dog in manwork tests. He won the Weimaraner of the Year Award in 1974. In 1978 he gained third place for the Black Knight Trophy awarded to the most outstanding dog and handler in the Metropolitan Police. Thor was always stationed at Richmond Police Station and together with his handler Paul Dodd averaged 80 arrests each year. Thor's last job before retirement was to locate the body of a murdered girl after a day-long mass search. He retired from active duty on 12 October 1980 at the age of 10 years 2½ months and now lives peacefully at home with Paul Dodd and his family.

Brett of Kenstaff, born 17.7.71, bred by Mrs E. A. Cullum, sired by Leightons Silver Prince (Druids Firedancer/Rosemarie of Whitsands) out of Manana Dorabest (Manana Halsall Sea Count/Manana Mandy's Pandora), was also known as Rooksbridge Brett although he was not registered as such. '*Blaze*' retired from active duty in 1978 after working with Sgt Norman Oliver in the Avon and Somerset Constabulary at Bristol.

Born 28.8.74, bred by Mr and Mrs A. H. J. Rapp, Greyhaven Boromir was sired by Sh. Ch. Abbeystag Oceanmist (Ch. Ragstone Ritter/Waidman Jemima) out of Gina Wildmoss (Ch. Ragstone Remus/ Cleo Wildmoss). 'Guidot' is stationed at Chiswick with his handler PC Kenneth Rowland in the Metropolitan Police.

Also with the Metropolitan Police and currently stationed at Chigwell is Metpol Monroes A-Kaiser handled by PC Dennis Walland. Kaiser was born 27.12.77, bred by Mrs Joan Matuszewska, by Monroes Yarrow (Sh. Ch. Kympenna's Tristan/Monroes Innisron Brunnhilde) out of Sh. Ch. Monroes Aequo (Sh. Ch. Monroes Nexus/Sh. Ch. Monroes Ubiquitous).

Working with PC Paul Dodd as Thor's replacement is Metpol Monroes Prangen. Born 23.8.79, bred by Mrs Joan Matuszewska by Waidman Hank (Sh. Ch. Kympenna's Tristan/Waidman Abbeystag Gytha) out of Monroes Matilda (Waidman Gog/Monroes Tamara), Prangen is based at Richmond Police Station. Active in working trials, this team have so far qualified CDx, UDx, WDx.

Metpol Monroes Thor locates the body of a missing person (R97438 British official photograph)

Metpol Monroes Thor and PC Paul Dodd.

At the time of writing the Royal Air Force Police have one Weimaraner under training. Bred by Mr and Mrs D. Rumfitt on 31.3.80, Jomijade Jupiter Ranger is by Sh. Ch. Fleetapple Wilmar (Ch. Wotan of Ragstone/Cannylad's Lady Hamilton of Fleetapple) out of Clampitt Ivory (Hawsvale Hermod/Monroes Birdsong). He is undergoing search dog training and his course reports are most satisfactory. After his passing-out in August 1982 his destination is undisclosed at present.

8

The Weimaraner in the USA and Canada

The United States

In October 1929 the first Weimaraners arrived in America. Howard Knight, an international sportsman had been to Germany, seen the remarkable capabilities of the breed and was eventually permitted to join the German Weimaraner Club. He succeeded in acquiring a pair of Weimaraners, Cosack von Kiebitztein and Lotte von Bangstede, which he hoped would be the foundation of the breed in the States. However, the Germans were apparently so jealous in keeping the breed strictly under control in their own country that both animals were found to be sterile. Howard Knight hunted with these two dogs for nine years and during that time became more convinced than ever that the Weimaraner was too good to be confined to one country only and, through Major Herber, he eventually obtained five more in 1938. These were the dog Mars aus der Wulfsreide born 25.4.38 (No. 1736), the bitch Aura von Gaiberg born 17.2.37 (No. 1680), and the litter-sisters Adda and Dorle von Schwarzenkamp born 9.3.34 (Igor Uefingen/Haida von Zeubachtal). The fifth was the dog Tasso aus der Grute but unfortunately he also proved to be sterile, but believed not deliberately so.

Soon after the outbreak of the World War II, Howard Knight turned over all his stock to Gus and Margaret Horn of the Grafmar Kennels, breeders of German Shepherds. Knight felt they could be trusted to do the best possible for the breed. During the War one other bitch arrived in the States from Austria, Suzanne von Aspern, but apart from her it was many years before further fresh blood became available.

Mars was the first Weimaraner dog to sire puppies in the USA and was used only four times before his early death; one litter each to Adda von Schwarzenkamp, Ch. Grafmar's Venus CD, Ch. Grafmar's Diana and Aura von Gaiberg.

96

Aura von Gaiberg CD was bred by Gastwirt Ludwig Gaul, sired by Feldmann (Arnold) 'SSS' out of Int. Ch. Cilly von Kreuzgrund, *Germ. Sgrn. CACIB*, and during her life-time produced four litters, three to Grafmar's Silver Knight (Mars/Adda) and one to Mars. She was the pioneer obedience worker of them all and won her CD degree in three straight shows in 1941 being the first Weimaraner to gain this title. In the following Spring her son Grafmar's Taurus completed all but his tracking test for the UD at under 10 months of age when he died from poisoning. Later, his CD record was broken by Grafmar's Ador (Mars/Adda) who gained his CD at six months and two days, a record that can be tied but not broken. Another of Aura's offspring was Ch. Grafmar's Diana (by Grafmar's Silver Knight) who was the breed's first champion bitch and was owned by Jack Baird. Diana was one of four champions and eight obedience title-holders in this litter which contained Ch. Grafmar's Kreuz the first champion, and Ch. Grafmar's Jupiter UDT the first dog to complete all obedience titles. Jupiter sired the National Field Champion Bitsu von Basha (out of Super Silver's Dusty) who, in turn, sired Crested Glade Warrior who had the honour of being the first Weimaraner to win the National German Pointing Dogs Championship.

A club was formed in 1941 and the first official meeting was in Boston on 21 February 1943, Howard Knight being elected president. Following the American Kennel Club's recognition, the breed made its first show appearance at Westminster in 1943. The following Breed Standard for Weimaraners adopted by the WCA was approved by the Board of Directors of the AKC at the meeting on 11 July 1944:

BREED STANDARD I

GENERAL APPEARANCE

Colour Gray (Silver, Bright, Dark, Yellow); the Dark Gray may be either ash or blue, often blending to a lighter shade on head and ears. A white star on the chest is allowable, but at no other place on the body. Any yellow tinge in such a star is a definite fault.

Look for individuality and class in carriage as an indication of character and breeding and indicated by the head, eye and stance. There should be every indication of a good hunting nose well balanced over a business-like muzzle with reasonably deep flews. There should be a strong clean neck gracefully joining muscular shoulders separated by a well-developed chest – all supported by staunch legs. The back should be moderate in length, strong, and straight over well-developed ribs. The hind quarters should slope gently over muscular legs with low stifles and firm feet. The whole should sum up to the maximum of power, speed, grace and endurance, absolutely sound fore and aft.

WEIGHT AND HEIGHT
Dogs 65 to 85 lbs; Bitches 55 to 75 lbs. Height at withers – Dogs 24 to 26 inches; Bitches 22 to 25 inches. Oversize should not be considered a too serious fault if conformation is correct and instinctive character is outstanding.

HEAD
Fine featured and aristocratic. Somewhat narrower than the Pointer, or at least giving that effect because of the long muzzle and rather prominent occipital bone and trumpets which are set well back but beginning at the back of the eye socket. The flews should be quite deep, enclosing a powerful jaw. The foreface should be perfectly straight, delicate at the nostrils, and the hair slightly darker than the hair on the body, with the skin tightly drawn.

EARS
General characteristics of the hound, slightly folded and placed rather high – soft coat.

EYES
Color – Blue-gray or amber, appearing amber to gray, dependant upon light – quite prominent when alert – and if the pupils are dilated the eyes may appear almost black. Should be set well enough apart to indicate good disposition and intelligence.

TEETH
Well set, strong and even. Must be well developed and proportionate to jaw with powerful scissors bite. Teeth undershot or overshot is a serious fault.

TAIL
Cropped to 1½ inches when a puppy (within three days). Approximately six inches at maturity – tendency to be light rather than heavy and carried expressively.

LEGS
Fore – straight, muscular and well-boned. Hind – muscular and evidence of driving power. Stifles well let down.

FEET
Firm, well arched and closed, giving evidence of ability to stand hard work and withstand bruises. Nails should be gray, black or amber.

GAIT

The walk is rather awkward, promptly to become a perfect rhythm at a trot and effortless ground covering grace on extended legs.

TEMPERAMENT

The breed is lively, fearless, kind and obedient. They are extremely sensitive and exceptionally smart and anxious to please. Any sign of weak nerves, shyness, or viciousness should be heavily penalised.

In October 1947 Jack Denton Scott as Gundog Editor of *Field and Stream* Magazine wrote an article entitled 'The Gray Ghost Arrives' which was, perhaps, one of the first to really arouse the general public's interest in the breed. At that time there were about 300 to 350 Weimaraners in America and few people had heard about them. Shortly after this article was published, Jack Denton Scott was approached by some Club members and was subsequently appointed the Club's Executive Secretary. He promoted the breed through his prolific writings in magazines such as *Argosy, Life, Look, Field and Stream, Pageant*, etc. His ultimate publicity production was a motion picture titled 'The Doggonedest Dog' which premiered at the Capitol Theatre on Broadway, New York City. Reprinted here is that first article:

THE GRAY GHOST ARRIVES*

Probably everyone in the gundog world has heard about the fabulous 'Gray Ghost', the Weimaraner, by this time. Since the American Kennel Club recognized the breed in 1942, there has been a great beating of drums, and the voice of the Weimaraner Club has been loud in the land. 'This dog, this Weimaraner,' they said, 'can run effortlessly beside an automobile traveling at the rate of 38 miles an hour, and pull ahead of the car and not even appear winded' . . . 'one saved the life of a man who had fallen into a stream and because of a bad arm couldn't arise' . . . 'what other dog would jump a bridge rail and make a 30 foot drop to retrieve a duck without command?' . . . 'two of the best known dog men in this country said that the Weimaraner was the most beautiful dog they had ever seen on point' . . . 'and nose! say, a young Weimaraner found a child that had been missing for days. They got the bloodhounds beat 60 ways from Sunday' . . . 'one of the judges in obedience trials made the remark that the Weimaraner should be given a

* Courtesy *Field and Stream* magazine.

99

handicap, because they always came out top dog in the trials' . . . 'the Weimaraner doesn't have to be trained to hunt birds. Their bloodlines are so excellent and their forebears bred so purely for the last 137 years, that they are just natural born hunters.'

All this sounded very pretty, and quite likely fine embroidered malarkey – prejudice and partiality reared their flat heads, and this writer took it all in, but still thought, 'There just ain't no such animal!'

But the reports continued; so for the good of gundogdom, and my own peace of mind, I decided to investigate this breed, this Weimaraner, this super-dog – the hunting dog of the future.

Norman Rinehart, who has the fine Feldstrom Kennels in La Porte, Indiana, sold me a Weimaraner, name of Heinrich, Baron von Feldstrom, as likely a looking gun dog as I had ever seen. Quite to my amazement, I yard broke this pup in five days, taught him to retrieve in two weeks. He is still in his puppyhood and too young, from my way of thinking, to field train as a gun dog. That will come later. I corresponded with Norman Rinehart of the Feldstrom Kennels, and he told me he had first heard of the Weimaraner from a German friend of his. B.W. (before Weimaraners) Rinehart had liked, and was quite fanatic on the German Shorthair pointer, but after he had finally located and purchased a Weimaraner, he no longer talked at length of the Shorthair. Rinehart told me proudly of their great nose, soft mouths, and their silent, catlike movements afield. Rinehart is a very honest man, and as fine a dog man as I have ever met.

I searched further for factual evidence to substantiate the amazing statements I had heard about the breed.

Here are some of the facts: the breed came into existence in 1810 as the result of the long-nurtured desire of the lords of the Court of Weimar for an individualized, highly personalized, all purpose hunting dog. Undoubtedly conceit and vanity had much to do with the Weimaraner's noble and distinctive appearance. The Weimar aristocracy wanted a dog whose appearance matched his ability: a dog that would grace their castles, a dog as noble as they thought themselves to be.

All records point to the Red *Schweisshunde* as the basic blood used in manufacturing the Weimaraner. This undoubtedly accounts for the great nose of the dog. Unlike nearly every other breed, the Weimaraner of today hasn't changed from the Weimaraner of 1810. This is phenomenal in dog breeding. Although the Germans keep the Weimaraner shrouded in mystery, it is known that the main basic stock in the numerous experiments that led to the Weimaraner, was the majority of Germany's hunting breeds, and many of the utility breeds. Recall them, the best of them, and you may know 50 per cent of the Weimaraner's make-up.

Breeders of the Weimaraner never kenneled the dog; he was a bedside and hearthside fellow. A club was formed, ruled by stern breed wardens.

Breeders could not trade, give away, sell Weimaraners without their consent. Never were there over 1,000 dogs in existence.

In Germany the Weimaraner first worked out on wolves, wild boar, deer, bear, and most other species of big game. For practical purposes, namely to help lay a better table, the Weimaraner was finally used on birds. Both upland game and water fowl. They were fast, had a natural style, flashy point, and were unmatched at soft-mouthed retrieving.

Tales of the prowess of the dog reached America and the ears of international sportsman Howard Knight. He went, scoffingly, to Germany to view the wonder dogs, returned biting his nails and trying to devise some system of getting a few of them to this country. He finally succeeded in getting a dog and a bitch over here. They went over so solidly, he returned to Germany and convinced the breed wardens that America should have enough stock for a 10-year breeding program. This was extremely difficult to sell the Germans, and the Weimaraner Club. They had perfected this dog, kept all others but the fortunate few of Weimar out, destroyed all inferior specimens of the breed, now they didn't want the Americans to destroy their genealogical triumph. But Knight sold them, and today America has about 200 Weimaraners. The Weimaraner Club of America was formed with Howard Knight as president, and observes the stringent rules of the German club.

All prospective members are severely investigated; the club demands that the Weimaraner be a gun dog, not destroyed on the show bench like many other American and English breeds have been; all breeding is controlled; standard is strictly adhered to; and, although we don't have the gimlet-eyed breed wardens in this country, the Weimaraner Club of America has up to this point, done an excellent job against tremendous odds.

One rainy day not too many months ago, the aforementioned Jack Baird was walking on his land in Wappinger's Falls, New York, when he slipped and fell, twisting his left arm under him. His other arm was in a sling, and he had fallen in the deep brook which snakes through his property. He couldn't get up, was weak from an illness, and rapidly drowning. His Weimaraner bitch, Diana, stood watching him for a moment. Then, quickly sensing his danger, moved over to Jack, worked herself under his left arm until he could hoist himself out of the water on her strong back, and slowly dragged him from the stream.

Called 'Gray Ghosts', not because of their color which is a silver gray, but because of their quick catlike stealth afield, the Weimaraner hits the scales at 85 lbs, and is a deceptive mover. He treads much like a big jungle cat and is sleekly muscled and proportioned. Full description will not be given here.

Lee Baldock, well-known trainer who has 12,000 acres in Woodland, California, with game and water fowl in abundance upon which to break his dogs, has at this writing several Weimaraners of the Lampkins' in training. Baldock is a setter and pointer man, a Chesapeake and Labrador plugger from away back. He gives a dog a 10 day workout and, if he isn't perfectly satisfied in that length of time, asks the owner to take him back. He was doubtful at first about the Weimaraner, had never seen one work. Last week he wrote me a letter, 'They're birdy these Weimaraners,' he said. 'Have wonderful noses, are fast and sure in the field, and I feel sure will make an astounding mark in this country.' More he couldn't say. He's only had the dogs a short time.

Ken Brown of Pittsfield, Mass., has a Ghost, Grafmar's SOS, called Tammy, and was recently called in by Chief of Police Frank Cone, to help in searching for a 2½-year-old boy who was missing. Tammy found the boy in a river. It was that simple. After all other means failed the Weimaraner was called in and trailed the boy in a matter of hours. Several law agencies are using the 'Gray Ghosts' and believe they have better noses than the bloodhound. A prominent member of a German family in this country recently made the statement that given a couple of Weimaraners and a little time he could find any missing man. He wanted especially to be given cases bloodhounds had failed on. He had no takers.

Grafmar's Ador won his CD at six months of age. CD for the uninitiated means Companion Dog and is an exacting obedience test given by the American Kennel Club. Pups are never given the final test and most mature dogs have a rough time getting their CD. A Weimaraner pup has established the world's record in obedience.

Another Ghost named Lance owned by Art Brown of Minnesota jumped a bridge rail and leaped 30 feet below into swift water to retrieve a duck. This without the urge of command.

Morgan Jorgenson says that the Gray Ghosts have the softest mouths of any retriever. A. I. Pruett, a man who has spent thousands having his dogs trained, swears that his Weimaraner trained himself and was as finished a bird dog in 15 months as any of his other dogs were in three years. Doctors Karl Stingily and B. K. Shafer of the Stingily Clinic, Meridan, Mass., tell all that the Weimaraner is the best pheasant, duck, goose dog known to man.

Stephen J. Chamberlin, an avowed pointer man, bought a Weimaraner on the say-so of Margaret Horn of Grafmar fame, and wrote the following, 'I was told because of their heritage and the 137 years of purebred breeding and training, a Weimaraner would hunt and point without so much as a snitch of training. I pooh-poohed this, bought a pup, called him Rex and waited until he was about a year and a half old, being careful never to let him smell any kind of a bird. Last season I put him in the car, drove along until I came to a likely looking alder run, stopped and got out. Fifty yards from the road this Weimaraner came to a beauty of a point. I thought it an accident or something, walked up, and wham! out goes a woodcock. I was lucky and shot him. Almost unconsciously I said, "Dead bird!" and damn' if that gray miracle of a ghost didn't retrieve that bird! All this without any training.

Howard Knight, the president of the Weimaraner Club, has told some pretty tall ones about the "Gray Ghosts" in the past. But he is not a damn' liar. Everything anyone says about these dogs is true.'

Ad infinitum. I have a folder-full of documented feats of the Weimaraners. I take no stand on them in writing. These are merely facts.

C. Ross Hamilton, a well-known judge in many obedience trials, said at a recent trial, 'The only fair way to show these Weimaraners is to handicap them five points and give the other dogs a chance.' Mr Hamilton is not a Weimaraner owner.

It seems that on all fronts the 'Gray Ghosts' have arrived. It looks like they're here to stay.

In 1949 an amended standard was drawn up and was published in the Club magazine in February 1950. Although it was not approved by the AKC, some breeders jumped on the bandwagon and with such an open standard to guide them, dogs of all shapes, sizes, colours and coats began to appear in quantity. The controversial points were the clauses on height and colour, and as for coat texture, this received not a mention. The whole standard is reprinted here as apart from those clauses mentioned, many other parts of it are interesting:

FIRST REVISED STANDARD 1949

GENERAL APPEARANCE
A medium sized gray dog with light eyes he presents a picture of alert beauty, balance, nobility and above all, the ability to work in the field. Any indication of clumsiness, soft living or weakness, mental or physical, should be penalized.

HEIGHT
Height at withers – Dogs 24 to 29 inches – Bitches 22 to 26 inches. In measuring, a perpendicular line should be taken from the floor to the highest point of the wither. Oversize should not be considered a fault providing correct structure and working ability is in evidence. However, a dog over the standard height would naturally bow to one within the standard, all things being equal.

HEAD
Long and aristocratic with moderate stop and slight median line extending back over the forehead. Rather prominent occipital bone and trumpets which are set well back, beginning at the back of the eye sockets. The flews should be deep, enclosing a powerful jaw, foreface perfectly straight, delicate at

US Ch. Gwinner's Pinwheel, bred, owned and handled by Tony Gwinner. Born 22.7.59 by Am. Can. Ch. Johnson's Arco v d Auger ex Am. Ch. Cati v d Gretchenhof. Judge Orton Korbel.

nostrils, skin tightly drawn. Neck cut clean, never short, thick or throaty. Expression kind, keen, intelligent.

(a) *Ears* – Hound ears, slightly folded. Set high.

(b) *Eyes* – Light gray to amber with intelligent expressions. When excited pupils may appear almost black.

104

(c) *Teeth* – Well set, strong and even. Must be well developed and proportionate to jaw with correct scissors bite, i.e. the upper teeth protruding slightly over the lower teeth. When the upper teeth protrude more than approximately a sixteenth of an inch the dog is overshot and this is a minor to serious fault dependent upon amount. Conversely, when the under teeth are in front of the upper teeth the dog is undershot, which again depending upon seriousness, should be considered a serious to a very serious fault and always a disqualification in breeding. More than four missing teeth are a very serious fault. Complete dentition is greatly to be desired. Faults of dentition which are acquired, i.e. discolored, distemper or worn teeth should be considered minor faults and penalized according to their seriousness.

(d) *Nose* – Dark color, never pink.

BODY

The Weimaraner should be longer than high, approximately as 10 is to nine. The body should give the impression of lithe strength, back strong and sloping very slightly from withers, croup long and gradually sloping (too level or too flat a croup prevents proper functioning of the hindquarters). Free gait and endurance are transmitted through a strong back neither roached nor soft. The latter (sway back) is by far the greater fault. Forechest should be well developed with no sense of hollowness, shoulder well laid on and tight. Chest deep and capacious with ample room for lungs and heart, ribs well sprung and long neither barrel-shaped nor too flat. Abdomen firmly held and not paunchy, moderately tucked up flank.

COLOR

All shades of gray to taupe often blending to a lighter shade on head and ears. White markings on the chest and toes is allowable but at no other place on body. Dogs with albino characteristics are to be disqualified. Any yellow tinge in the white markings is a definite fault. Yellow or brown spots or markings are a disqualification.

LEGS

(a) *Forelegs* – Should be straight and strong, developed in proportion to the size of the dog. There should be no looseness of elbows. Results of rickets or sponginess should be penalized. The forelegs should be spaced neither too wide nor too close. The pastern should slope slightly which contributes to the ease and elasticity of gait.

(b) *Feet* – Firm, compact, toes well arched, pads thick and strong, nails short and strong. The feet are vastly important to the working ability and endurance of the dog and the thin, spread or hare foot is very undesirable. Feet east and west should also be penalized. Nails gray, black or amber.

Usually pictured with the never-to-be-forgotten 'Trigger', Roy Rogers swaps him for a different four-legged friend.

(c) *Dewclaws* – May become a hindrance in the field, therefore all dewclaws must be removed within three days of birth from both fore and hind legs. Dewclaws on dogs whelped after 1 March 1950 shall be considered a serious fault. Dogs whelped prior to 1 March 1950 having dewclaws are not to be penalized.

(d) *Metacarpus (the so-called hock)* – This is the fulcrum upon which much of the forward movement and endurance of the dog depends and it should be short, cleancut and of great strength. Cowhocks are a very serious fault, penalization depending upon the acuteness of the fault.

106

TAIL
Should be cropped generally to 1¼ to 1½ inches within three days of birth. Approximately six inches at maturity, tendency to be light rather than heavy. Should be carried in a manner to express confidence and sound temperament.

GAIT
The walk is rather awkward. The trot should be effortless ground-covering, smooth and co-ordinating giving promise of great endurance.

TEMPERAMENT
The perfect Weimaraner temperament is keen, fearless, kind but protective and naturally obedient. Injustice is never forgotten. When confidence is gained there is a sympathetic bond between dog and master which is beyond price. A dog which shows weak nerves, shyness or viciousness should be disqualified. (Viciousness should not be confused with protectiveness toward owner or owner's property.) Any dog which is weak-nerved, shy or vicious should never be bred and for the good of the breed should be put humanely to sleep.

AGE FOR BREEDING
This is a slow maturing breed and a long-lived one. Bitches should not be bred nor dogs used at stud until fully matured – usually at about two years.

JUDGING
It is suggested that the German system of judging in motion be adopted as far as is practicable. The strong, well-knit, sound, strong-backed free-moving dog is the one which will work all day in the field. This is the purpose for which the Weimaraner is bred. Faults and virtues may be evaluated on this basis of general appearance and movement much more readily in the opinion of this committee than on any point by point system. Excessive posing is discouraged.

The year 1950 saw the first Weimaraner National Field Trial which was won by Leon Arpin's Nat. Fld. Ch. Ricki of Rocklege (Ch. Decker's Misty Marvel/Silver Blue Lark), a great working dog who sired many field winners. One of Ricki's most well-known sons was Dual Ch. Palladian Perseus who in 1954 won the inaugural WCA National Open Championship recognised by 'American Field', thus becoming the breed's first dual champion.

But the 1950s and 1960s were difficult years for the truly dedicated American breeders despite the exciting successes of the breed in various spheres. They had to cope with indiscriminate breeding and exploitation, and somehow bring the breed back to sanity. That they managed to do so says much for the excellent bloodlines of the original imports, plus later dominant imports – notably the dogs Alto von Harrasburg (Arno von Bruckberg/Asta von Bruckberg) and the famous champions Bert, Burt and Boddy von der Harrasburg bred by Max Baumler, by Sieger Arco Van Der Filzen 'V', out of Siegerin Asta von Bruckberg 'V', rs, ms, sil, W, sss, spurl, tot. Burt was owned by Franz Sachse and his excellent conformation made him a best in show dog, but he also hunted well for his master retrieving birds from the water in the Alaskan snow. He sired about nineteen champions and several outstanding field performers too. Bert, owned by Mr and Mrs Elvin Deal, was said to be one of the greatest Weimaraners who ever lived, and certainly his record is impressive – he became champion in seven shows including Winners Dog at Westminster at 11 months old; he was the first Weimaraner to win an Open All-Aged Stake against Pointers and Setters, and was named to the 1955 Sports Afield All-American Team. He had 17 Field Trial wins and ran in his last Pointer/Setter trial at 11 years of age being placed third. He sired 21 champions and, like Burt, many field winners.

The Weimaraner was the twentieth most popular dog in America in 1963, but after that registrations began to level off. In 1965 a more sensible Breed Standard was drawn up, adopted and approved by the AKC. It is practically the same as the current Standard dated 31 December 1972 printed here. The 1965 wording, where different, is printed in italics under the relevant sections.

BREED STANDARD, 31 DECEMBER 1972
(1965 wording printed in italics)

GENERAL APPEARANCE
A medium sized gray dog, with fine aristocratic features. He should present a picture of grace, speed, stamina, alertness and balance. Above all, the dog's conformation must indicate the ability to work with great speed and endurance in the field.

HEIGHT
Height at the withers: Dogs 25 inches to 27 inches; Bitches 23 inches to 25 inches. One inch over or under the specified height of each sex is allowable but should be penalized. Dogs measuring less than 24 inches or more than 28 inches and bitches measuring less than 22 inches or more than 26 inches shall be disqualified.

HEAD
Moderately long and aristocratic, with moderate stop and slight median line extending back over the forehead. Rather prominent occipital bone and trumpets well set back, beginning at the back of the eye sockets. Measurement from tip of nose to stop equal that from stop to occipital bone. The flews should be straight, delicate at the nostrils. Skin tightly drawn. Neck clean-cut and moderately long. Expression kind, keen and intelligent.

EARS
Long and lobular, slightly folded and set high. The ear when drawn snugly alongside the jaw should end approximately two inches from the point of the nose.

EYES
In shades of light amber, gray or blue-gray, set well enough apart to indicate good disposition and intelligence. When dilated under excitement the eyes may appear almost black.

TEETH
Well set, strong and even, well-developed and proportionate to jaw with correct scissors bite, the upper teeth protruding slightly over the lower teeth, but not more than one-sixteenth of an inch. Complete dentition is greatly to be desired.

NOSE
Gray.

LIPS AND GUMS
Pinkish flesh shades.

BODY
The back should be moderate in length, set in a straight line, strong and should slope slightly from the withers. The chest should be well developed and deep with shoulders well laid back. Ribs well sprung and long. Abdomen firmly held; moderately tucked up flank. The brisket should extend to the elbow.

COAT AND COLOR
Short, smooth and sleek, solid color in shades of mouse-gray to silver gray, usually blending to lighter shades on the head and ears. A small white marking on the chest is permitted, but should be penalized on any other portion of the body. White spots resulting from an injury should not be penalized. A distinctly long coat is a disqualification. A distinctly blue or

109

black coat is a disqualification. *(1965 Standard omitted last two disqualification clauses.)*

LEGS
Forelegs straight and strong, with the measurement from the elbow to the ground approximately equaling the distance from the elbow to the top of the withers.
Hindquarters: Well angulated stifles and straight hocks. Musculation well developed.
Feet: Firm and compact, webbed, toes well arched, pads thick and closed, nails short and gray or amber in color.
Dewclaws should be removed.

TAIL
Docked. At maturity it should measure approximately six inches with a tendency to be light rather than heavy and should be carried in a manner expressing confidence and sound temperament. A non-docked tail should be penalized.

GAIT
The gait should be effortless and should indicate smooth co-ordination. When seen from the rear, the hind feet should be parallel to the front feet. When viewed from the side, the top line should remain strong and level.

TEMPERAMENT
The temperament should be friendly, fearless, alert and obedient.

MINOR FAULTS
Tail too short or too long. Pink nose.

MAJOR FAULTS
Doggy bitches. Bitchy dogs. Improper muscular condition. Badly affected teeth. More than four teeth missing. Back too long or too short. Faulty coat. Neck too short, thick or throaty. Low set tail. Elbows in or out. Feet east and west. Poor gait. Poor feet. Cow hocks. Faulty back, either roached or sway. Badly overshot or undershot bite. Snipy muzzle. Short ears.

VERY SERIOUS FAULTS
White, other than a spot on the chest. Eyes, other than gray, blue-gray or light amber. Black mottled mouth. Non-docked tail. Dogs exhibiting strong fear, shyness and extreme nervousness.

US Ch. Debar's Platinum Specter bred by C. Paul Berry Jr, owned by Homer L. Carr. Born 21.4.51 by Ch. Deal's Sporting Sure Aim ex Ch. Grafmar's Dilly Dally.

DISQUALIFICATIONS

Deviation in height of more than 1 inch from standard either way. A distinctly long coat. A distinctly blue or black coat is a disqualification. *(1965 Standard stated under this heading: oversize or undersize. A distinctly long coat.)*

Before the WCA's revision of the standard which disqualified blue Weimaraners there was a great deal of argument for and against this decision, and some quotable items appeared in club magazines. Whilst in Great Britain we do not yet have this particular colour problem, several points are of interest in view of the fact that more stock is arriving from the USA into Britain. During 1969 Rita Ashby wrote:

Occupied Germany was in a complete state of disaster after the war and pure bred dogs suffered greatly. Thus it was, in the little town of Gaiberg, Germany, that Ludwig Gaul found himself at the end of the war, once a renowned breeder, left with only two old dogs. Food was at a premium, medical supplies were impossible to get, and the future of Germany's finely and carefully bred Weimaraners faced impending doom. A kindly and interested American offered to obtain the necessary food and supplies to subsidize Mr Gaul in a last, seemingly frantic effort to save his line. So Ludwig Gaul bred his two old dogs together – 10 year old Bodo von Gaiberg and 13 year old Int. Ch. Cilly von Kreuzgrund and from this mating of mother-to-son came a complete mutation, a thing only rarely seen in the science of genetics, a blue Weimaraner. This blue puppy was called Casar von Gaiberg. Stationed in Germany with the army in the late 1940s, Captain Harry Holt, an avid dog fancier, was intently searching about for a good sound Weimaraner to send back to a friend in the United States. When he came upon Casar he purchased him and Casar came to live with W. A. Olson in Minneapolis. Casar came from one of Germany's most regal Weimaraner families. His grandsire, Nelson von Bangstede, was given the highest award in European dogdom in 1935, that of World Champion. Nelson von Bangstede's daughter and Casar's dam was Cilly von Kreuzgrund, herself an International Champion. Cilly was also the dam of Casar's half-sister Aura von Gaiberg, one of the original Weimaraners brought to America by Howard Knight and one of the most distinguished members of the American foundation stock.

At the WCA Board Meeting on 5 December 1969 it was stated that during the five year period since 1952 to 1957, 150 blue Weimaraners were registered. Mrs Helen Schulze wrote:

Since 1920, my family has owned Weimaraners in Germany. Since 1953 I have attended 11 times the Fall Field Trials of the German Weimaraner

Club. The German Club accepted me as your voting representative to their Board. I also attend Board and Membership meetings. I have visited every kennel in Germany and I know that there is no blue dog anywhere. Mouse gray is not blue. Everything darker than mouse gray is disqualified for breeding. Everything not gray is destroyed.

Jack Denton Scott wrote of a stud dog used frequently who had ears like a Dalmatian, black gums and mouth like a Chow, was small and not Weimaraner-shaped, and whose colour was startling and looked as though a bottle of purple-black ink had been poured over him. In his book *The Weimaraner* he wrote:

What the owner of the blue-black stud had studiedly failed to mention was that his dog was the result of terribly close breeding, in-breeding, and on his German papers was the printed warning to closely watch the offspring if the dog was ever used, and, in the opinion of the Germans, the dog should *never* be used. This was also warned vocally in Germany in the house of Mr Fritz Kullmer at Fulda, in the presence of an Army officer friend of mine, mentioned to the very Army officer who brought the blue-black misfit to America.

The breeding of this *blue* Weimaraner is also mentioned in Dr Werner Petri's book *Der Weimaraner Vorstehhund*. In the German Weimaraner Breed Register an entry was made in 1949 of a single birth litter consisting of the dog Casar von Gaiberg with the typed remark: 'Casar has, according to a notification received on 20 June 1949 from Kullmer, the following peculiarities: black tinge over his entire back, ears more than short, and the colour of the eyes not pure amber.' Following that is a handwritten remark which expresses doubt about the reliability of the breeder and concludes: 'Verdict – unsuitable for breeding as it is probably in-bred or Doberman-crossed.'

There seems little doubt that this unfortunate dog was the ancestor of all the so-called 'blues' about which there has been such controversy.

Field Trials held in the States vary considerably from what we are accustomed to in Britain. The dogs are divided by age into three classes: Puppy (basically aged up to 12 or 15 months), Derby (up to two years old) and All Age (over two years). Younger dogs can compete in the higher classes if their handler is confident enough of their ability. Competition is further divided into Amateur and Open; the former open to dogs handled by an amateur only, and the latter with no restrictions.

A course is laid out which should take the dogs half an hour to negotiate. The first 22 minutes of the course is called the 'back field' and the last eight minutes is called the 'bird field'. Alternatively, the whole 30 minutes may be the 'back field' with only dogs in contention being called to a 'bird field'. The dogs are run in braces in an order determined by lot. At the starting line are two dogs followed by their two handlers (either on foot or more usually on horseback) and following them two mounted judges and a marshall followed by the gallery of spectators (again, either on foot or mounted).

In the 'back field' the dogs are judged on their method of hunting. Wild game is used wherever possible, but in some barren areas birds are released or planted throughout the course; lightly in the 'back field' but more plentifully in the 'bird field'. If the dog finds a bird in the 'back field', the bird is shot at with a blank, but if found in the 'bird field' then it is shot to enable steadiness and retrieving ability of the dog to be noted. When the 'bird field' is reached, mounted handlers must now walk and the dog given the opportunity to demonstrate bird finding ability etc.

The All Age dog should find his bird, point and hold steady until the handler is required to flush it. When the dog comes on point, his brace-mate should, if in the vicinity, back him. When the handler of the pointing dog flushes or causes the bird to fly, it will be shot and the dog sent to retrieve, during which time the backing dog must remain stationary.

The Derby dog is merely required to indicate his inherent ability to hunt, point (a flash point lasting merely seconds will suffice), flush and chase it out of sight if he wishes. He is not penalised for chasing fur or feather or for failing to honour his brace-mate's point – which are all disqualifications for the All Age dog. He must just show consistent effort and a reasonable amount of intelligence in where he hunts.

Puppies are judged for future promise and are not generally shot over unless both handlers in the brace agree. He should run and hunt with energy, hopefully make a flash point, use his nose and work at a reasonable distance from his handler without lagging behind.

Each brace runs for one hour. To be eligible for entry in one of the AF or AFTCA Trials the dog must have qualified at a regional trial recognised by the American Field, and the American Field Trial Club of America, who award the field championships. The qualification is a first, second or third placing, plus a Weimaraner Club water proficiency certificate. The winner of the championship can be named

'Champion' if the judges feel the performance was of championship calibre, but they are entitled to withhold the award if they consider it otherwise.

American Kennel Club championships are won in a similar way to bench championships in that each winning dog earns points dependent on the number of entries, and a total of 10 points must be collected including at least one major win of 3 points or more. If, in the opinion of the judges the winning performance was not good enough, the first place can be withheld resulting in no points being awarded.

The Weimaraner Club of America has a method of field and retriever ratings to test the aptitude of young dogs and the biddability of those dogs who have received further training, and this is an excellent programme. The ratings are divided into two separate classifications; one covering pointing and upland bird-field work and the other covering retrieving. There are also Versatility ratings and a Bench Register of Merit (BROM). Many dogs arrive in Britain from the States with an array of letters after their names which has tended to confuse the novice as we have no similar system. A short explanation follows:

NSD *Novice Shooting Dog* – The purpose of this rating is to determine whether young or untrained, inexperienced dogs have hunting aptitudes. They run on a pass or fail basis and must pass in all of the following categories: desire to hunt; boldness; initiative and search; indicating presence of game; reasonable obedience to handler's commands.

SD *Shooting Dog* – This rating is to establish that a dog of any age has definite hunting ability, bird sense, and shows some field training. Dogs must pass in the following: keen desire to hunt; boldness and independence; cover ground quickly in an attractive style; seek objectives; locate game; point; reasonable obedience to handler's commands.

SDX *Shooting Dog Excellent* – This is the top award and dogs qualifying must be finished, fully broken bird dogs. Their field work should show the class and style expected of top Weimaraners.

NRD *Novice Retrieving Dog* – Land retrieve single bird from 20 to 40 yards within five minutes. Water retrieve single bird with a minimum swim of 20 yards within five minutes.

RD *Retrieving Dog* – Land retrieve 2 birds, wide spaced within 10 minutes. Water retrieve 2 birds, wide spaced within 10 minutes.

Am. Can. Ch. Gwinner's Sportwheel owned and handled by Tony Gwinner. Judge Derek Rayne.

RDX *Retrieving Dog Excellent* – Dog must give finished performance. Land retrieve 2 birds, water retrieve 3 birds, blind retrieve single bird. Dog must be steady on line and enter the water immediately with eagerness.

BROM *Bench Register of Merit* – The WCA 'BROM' is primarily for the purpose of recognising those sires and dams which produce fine offspring. Points are awarded for the offspring's wins only. Briefly, for a sire to be eligible, eight of his progeny must achieve the AKC title of Champion. For a bitch to be eligible, four of her progeny must achieve the title of Champion.

V *Versatile* – 6 points must be obtained from 3 out of 5 groups.

VX *Versatile Excellent* – 9 points must be obtained from 3 out of 5 groups, and must include Bench Champion, Field Champion or Obedience Champion.

OFA *Orthopedic Foundation for Animals* – Certifies hip status by X-ray evaluation.

To obtain bench championship status, apart from being AKC registered, the dog must gain 15 championship points; 6 or more of these points must be 'majors' – i.e. 3, 4 or 5-point wins which must also be under two different judges. The actual number of points to be won at each show depends on the number of dogs present on the day and defeated by the winner in each sex. If however there are more points awarded to the dog winner and he is subsequently beaten for best of breed by the bitch winner, then she is awarded the same number of points as the dog winner and vice-versa.

The WCA has the highest number of Club members anywhere in the world standing at more than 2,400, and there are approximately 43 affiliated Weimaraner Clubs throughout the country.

The list of annual registrations published by the AKC for the breed also states the order of popularity. From 20th in 1963 it stood at 43rd in 1980. The figures relating to the 12-year period to 1980 are as follows:–

Year	Registrations	Order of Popularity
1969	6,290	28th out of 115
1970	6,898	
1971	7,615	
1972	7,246	
1973	7,208	
1974	6,961	
1975	6,244	
1976	6,243	
1977	5,519	
1978	5,004	
1979	4,605	
1980	4,714	43rd out of 125
	74,547	

117

CANADA

The first Canadian region of the Weimaraner Club of America was formed in Toronto on 19 June 1955; the elected officers being Mr Benjamin Schulze (Governor to the WCA) and Mrs Helen Schulze (secretary) of Niagara Falls, Mr H. Paton (president), Mr P. Tomlinson (first vice president), Mrs P. Tomlinson (treasurer), Mr B. Tomlinson (field trial chairman) and Mr B. Lomas (second vice president), all of Toronto. At that time there were estimated to be approximately 60 Weimaraners in Canada, mostly emanating from the States, although one of the earliest was a German-bred import Ajax von Reiningen owned by Mathew L. Sterzer who was a regional vice-president of the WCA. According to records it would appear that the first Weimaraner to be registered in Canada was in 1948 and was owned by Mr F. Bush, shortly followed by a pair owned by Mr Sterzer.

The first litter recorded was born on 2 September 1949, and was bred by Mr and Mrs Schulze. Sired by Grafmar's Citation out of Grafmar's Super Silver Dusty who was obtained from the Horn's kennel in Boston, this litter of seven included the dog Ch. Reinhard vom Heidehof. Later the Schulzes changed their affix Heidehof to the world-famous von der Harrasburg – perhaps a little confusing as this affix appears on many pedigrees and it is not always apparent (especially to newcomers in the breed) just where the stock originated. Mrs Helen Schulze was for many years (until her death in the mid-1970s) the link between the WCA and the German Weimaraner Club.

Today, the Weimaraner Association of Canada has a membership of about 60 with a roughly estimated population of 300 dogs. The nucleus is now in Ontario and the Club holds a specialist show once a year where entries rarely exceed 30. Serious exhibitors show in the United States where the competition is greater and a win carries more status. Not a great many Canadian dogs are field-trialled, but apparently quite a high proportion of owners take up obedience training. There are problems for dog-owners in Canada because of restrictions on exercise areas; for example, in Ottawa dogs are banned from parks, school-yards and most green-belt areas, therefore few large dogs are to be seen in town areas and the dedicated enthusiast is often forced to live many miles away from such civilisation.

Exports from Britain to Canada have not been numerous; only seven since 1957. The bitch owned by Mrs D. Brickl, Webbdant's Arabesque Am. CDx, TD, RD, NSD, came into Britain during 1975 and was mated in 1976 to Sh. Ch. Gunther of Ragstone. One of the resulting litter, Abbisline Gabrielle, went back to Canada where she gained her Canadian championship title for her owner Mrs Wendy McKay.

One of Canada's top show Weimaraners is the bitch Roschel's Fashion Impact, who is a Canadian and American Champion owned by Mr and Mrs Shoreman. Sired by Am. and Can. Ch. Colsidex Standing Ovation, out of Can. Ch. Rajah's May Magic v Reiteralm, 'Imp' is an eight times Best in Speciality Show winner at shows held in the U.S. and Canada and is a three times Best in All Breed Show winner in Canada. Bred by the Shoremans, and always amateur handled by Michael Shoreman, 'Imp' is the first Canadian bred Weimaraner in the history of the breed in Canada to achieve such awards.

9

The Weimaraner in France

The first club to be formed for the breed in France was founded in 1965 by the Comte de Sade and was named the *Club Français des Bracques de Weimar* with Germain de Brie as its President. At that time there were approximately 50 Weimaraners known to be in the country, but the growth of the club was slow and it was in fact disbanded in the mid-1970s. During Germain de Brie's Presidency, he wrote an article in *Revue du Chien* (5, 1973) already discussed in Chapter 2 above, in which he stated that the Weimaraner was a dog of French origin and one of France's oldest breeds, known in the late Middle Ages.

The first Weimaraner to be officially registered with the *Société Centrale Canine* was in 1954, although doubtless the breed existed already, particularly around the French/German borders. The first few registrations given here are listed in the *Livre des Origines Français (LOF)*:

1 Cara von Fohr. Bitch born 10/52, silver grey with no marks. Sire: Arp von Fohr. Dam: Bona von Osteestrand. Imported from Germany and registered 14.1.54 by Mlle Drouard of Paris.
2 Bessy von Buchwald. Bitch born 11.4.55. Sire: Girck von Harrasburg. Dam: Freya von Haimberg. Imported from Germany, owned by M. Ohl of Strasbourg. A member of the German Club, M. Ohl was in close touch with other French owners and was instrumental in bringing the breed to the public's notice.
3 Tony. Dog born 29.10.50 registered by M. Guichard. No further details.
4 Fausta. Bitch born 25.10.56 was the first to be bred in France but she died of Rabies 15.1.57. Bred by M. Gedon, by Tony out of Cara.
5 Fee von der Fanghütte. Dog born 18.3.56 registered 1960 by M. Saron of Paris. Sire: Marko. Dam: Luna.

6	Flint. Dog born 25.10.56 registered by M. Durand-Raucher. Fausta's littermate.
8	Arno. Dog – no further details.
11–16	3 dogs, 3 bitches born 10.8.61 by Arno (8).
17–21	4 dogs, 1 bitch born 30.3.62 by Arno (8) ex Luna.
24	Fox. Dog – no further details.
25	Nova. Bitch – no further details.
26–45	All progeny of Fox (24) and Nova (25) from several matings.

The dog Skool was born 7.2.69 from German parents, Igor von Steef and Lydia Chatterly owned by Lt Col Adams. He was used quite widely at stud on both French and German bred bitches and passed on beauty as well as working ability, and was considered to be an excellent sire.

The first two long-haired Weimaraner males to be registered, Irac and Inca, born 5.2.73 were from a mixed litter of eight, 5 dogs and 3 bitches, sired by Utah who is by Skool out of Isa.

The following statistics are extracted from the *Livre des Origines Françaises* where there are six types of Bracque listed: *Bracque d'Auvergne, Bracque français, Bracque St-Germain, Bracque allemand, Bracque de Weimar, Bracque hongrois*. The figures below apply to the Weimaraner, *Bracque de Weimar*:

Year	Births	LOF Confirmations*	LOF Refusals	Imports
1969	16	9		
1970	27	16		
1971	39	14		
1972	35	21		2
1973	33	19		5
1974	86	22	1	2
	1 L/C			
1975	153	63		12
1976	146	57		6
	1 L/C			
1977	180	50	1	6
	1 L/C			
1978	382	93	2	7
1979	262	160	2	6
1980	321	187	2	6
	2 L/C			

* A very brief explanation of 'LOF Confirmations' could perhaps be summed up in the present-day jargon 'quality control'. Basically, the dog must be confirmed by its breeder, and by a qualified specialist judge after it is 12 months of age, that it is of good enough quality to be bred from, and that there are no known genetic faults in its background.

Thought by many to be of Weimaraners, this statue is at Versailles.

The birth rate of about 3,000 per year of the *Bracque allemand* (German Short-haired Pointer) which alone represents about two-thirds of all LOF registrations has hardly changed over the past few years, whereas the Weimaraner and Vizsla, rarely seen 10 years ago, are progressing strongly.

During the course of 1976/1977 a number of people interested in the Weimaraner were concerned about the inactivity of the club and its apparent failure to further the interests of the breed in France. Under the leadership of André Harmand and Robert Rudloff, steps were taken to form a substitute club in order that the Weimaraner

122

could be effectively represented in the body of the official Kennel Club, *Société Centrale Canine*. A signed petition was presented to the President of the *SCC* who, with the approval of his Committee, decided on 27 January 1978 to proceed to disaffiliate the club's title and in the following December the new club was legally constituted and named the *Cercle des Amateurs du Bracque de Weimar*. Today the club has a membership of 500 and an estimated population of Weimaraners of between 1500 and 1800.

A well-illustrated article in *Figaro* on 23 February 1980 by Pierluigi Locchi highlighted the many talents of the breed, and touched on the supposed origins, from albinoism to beagles, bulldogs and of course the grey dogs of St Louis. This article, very readable, could perhaps lead to an upsurge in the popularity of the breed in France, as has happened elsewhere, but time will tell. Locchi makes mention of the breed's ability to hunt game under all conditions; strangle the lynx and wolf, hunt bear, roe-deer and fallow-deer, and track indefatigably. He also pointed out that it is a dog with formidable instincts which fact was manifested in a most extraordinary incident during May 1977 at l'Hotel du Duc de Brabant in Brussels. Apparently there was a fire in the hotel, and on the third floor was a family with their Weimaraner bitch. She was the last to be evacuated alive by the firemen and was saved because she had 'stretched out under the bed without trying to escape, keeping quite still so (it is thought) she could breathe as much oxygen as possible'. Formidable instinct – or sheer terror? Probably the best known public Weimaraner in France is the bitch Jugurtha which is owned by ex-President Giscard d'Estaing.

10

The Weimaraner in Holland

The first recorded gathering of Weimaraners in Holland was on 13 March 1966 at the *Jagerhuis* in the woods near Zeist where 45 dogs competed at a show. The results are worth mentioning, as they give one reason for the high influx of imported British and German stock which followed not long afterwards. Of the nine dogs aged under 18 months, five were assessed 'very good' and four 'good' although the judge was not wholly satisfied, as some were too nervous, some had heads which were too large, some had open feet and some were 'fear-biters'. Of the 15 dogs over the age of 18 months, four were 'excellent', nine 'very good' and two 'good' and although the judge thought these better than the youngsters, the same remarks applied to a lesser degree. There were seven bitches under 18 months old of which five were 'very good' and two 'good', and in this class the judge thought the quality generally better than that of the dogs. Fourteen bitches over 18 months old were considered by the judge to be the best entry; eight he marked 'excellent', three 'very good' and three 'good' and he thought that some of these were Weimaraners showing nobility, with good bone, compact feet, etc. The judge's general remarks do not appear to tie in with his assessment markings which would, on the face of it, seem high. However, in Holland four assessment marks are used: 'excellent', 'very good', 'good' and 'moderate' (although this last mark is seldom used so as not to offend the exhibitor!). 'Good' is regarded as the lowest mark and is usually reserved for the poorest specimen in the class. A dog cannot become a Dutch champion unless it has been judged over the age of 27 months and has been awarded four championship show wins under at least two different judges.

After this initial meeting in 1966, more owners started to get together although at the early shows no more than five or six Weimaraners were exhibited, as most of the owners disliked the idea of sitting around all day with their dogs in cages, particularly those owners who were fond of hunting with their Weimaraners, who found this pastime quite intolerable.

124

By the beginning of 1970 there were 154 Weimaraners registered with *De Raad van Beheer op Kynologisch Gebied in Nederland* (the Dutch Kennel Club), the earliest being recorded in 1957. Of these 154 only three were registered as imports to Holland – Kees Hoekzema's English-bred Acombdole Ami, the German-bred Hief aus der Greifenberg and Seppo von Altern Jesse. All the other registered dogs were born in Holland, the progeny of earlier imports not listed but doubtless from Germany and Austria. The 10 most famous kennel names in existence in 1970 were van het Kerkebosch, van de Blaircummer Tol, van het Strijkviertel, van het Menniste Koethuis, van de Ouwe Stee, of the Three Turnips, van het Ruygenbosch, van Noorderkoggen, van Slotzicht, van Lourenswolt and one kennel without a name from which Kees Hoekzema obtained his first Weimaraner 'Tunis', a Dutch Champion born 20.10.64 by Daan van het Kerkebosch out of Fiola van de Blaircummer Tol. It is thought that the oldest would be *van het*

Bonnie v d Weberhof mated to her full brother Alarcon v d Weberhof produced Cindy v d Weberhof owned by Kees Hoekzema.

Kerkebosch whose owner apparently stopped breeding in 1967. Most of the others mentioned seem to have died out although there are still one or two of the 'Old Guard' currently active in the breed. At the 1975 Club Match Kees Hoekzema recalls seeing the last bearer of the *van het Kerkebosch* kennel name, a bitch named 'Charlotte' then aged 16 years and indeed showing so well at that great age that the judge remarked that he wished all the dogs shown there were as well as this grand old lady. Ironically enough, she died just two months later.

Mr Borst was the gamekeeper and trainer for the *van het Kerkebosch* kennel and although he was literally on his death-bed during 1981 when the Hoekzemas visited him, his intellect was quite unimpaired and he remembered clearly the first Weimaraners to be seen in Holland which were in 1955 and which had been imported from Germany, soon to be followed by others from Austria and Germany. If there were earlier ones they were not registered and were therefore not traceable. Kees Hoekzema recalls that a rather old, expert judge, no

Dutch Ch. Acombdole Ami owned by Kees Hoekzema and bred by Dr Alex Mucklow was the first British Weimaraner to be exported to Holland (Photo: Jan Doornbusch)

Aymone of the Princes of Weimar by Dutch Ch. Acombdole Ami ex Cindy v d Weberhof.

longer alive said that he had seen a Weimaraner in the Hague during 1923 – which is quite possible because after the First World War many Germans came to the Hague as it was then the greatest seaside resort in Holland and as a reminder of that time there still exists today a Kurhaus. Basically though, it would appear that the breed has existed in Holland for about the same time as in Britain, since the mid-1950s.

Not to be forgotten was the Dutch-born Johan Carlquist who, before the Second World War, was a band-leader regularly to be heard on the radio. After the War ended he went to Spain to live where he was an impresario for bands from all over the world. Whilst in Spain he imported from Germany his first Weimaraners, the world-famous Alf von Forsthaus Dieberg and the bitch Nora von Haimberg. Later he moved to Germany where he had his kennel of some 15 dogs with the affix *von der Weberhof*. He always bred very closely and was said never to have sold his stock; he gave them away but always kept rights on them and after checking first that the puppies would be well looked

Jessie v h Strijkviertel by Dutch Ch. Acombdole Ami ex Goethe v h Kerkebosch bred by P. Stel, Holland and owned by A. & T. Fokine, Sweden. (Photo: Tony Angleryd, Västeras)

after, he would very often make spot checks to ascertain that things were to his liking. If they were not, then the dog would immediately be put in his car and driven off. Carlquist and his entire stock of Weimaraners were unhappily the victims of a very tragic end. Kees Hoekzema had a bitch from him, Cindy von der Weberhof, rather a small bitch, not of outstanding quality, but bred to Dutch Ch. Acombdole Ami she produced Aymone of the Princes of Weimar who won best in show at the 1975 Club Match.

On 24 May 1970 Kees Hoekzema instigated a meeting with other Weimaraner owners with the view to forming a club, and from the 18 founder members a board of seven was chosen with Mr van Sluis as President and Mr Hoekzema as Honorary Secretary and Treasurer. As soon as the membership reached 50 the Dutch Kennel Club officially recognised the *Vereniging de Weimarse Staande Hond*. As with the beginning in most other countries the breed progressed from the hands of the 'flowers of society' as Kees so poetically puts it and became more popular. During the five years that he was Club Secretary, in an attempt to improve the somewhat mediocre quality of the breed, he imported about 20 Weimaraners from Germany and up to 50 from Britain on behalf of other Club members. He became well-known in Britain and made many friends through his visits with his wife Magda to the Club's shows and also when he came personally to collect puppies. Sadly, there was dissension in the Dutch Club and it upset Kees greatly to think that his efforts and concern for the future well-being of the breed was being viewed unfavourably by some of his fellow-countrymen.

Of the British exports to Holland, several have gained their Dutch titles and many more are working extremely well for their enthusiastic hunting owners. Dutch Champions Monroes Supremo and Hawsvale Cherry Brandy bred by Mrs Joan Matuszewska and Mr Val Hawes respectively, have both produced many winners, particularly for the *Three Turnips* kennel of Mr Nierop. The Dutch Club has recently started field trialling and several training clubs now exist. The big event of each year is the club match when about 60 Weimaraners gather to compete. There are about 260 club members and the estimated number of dogs something in the region of 700 to 800.

11

The Weimaraner in Scandinavia

SWEDEN

During 1973 and 1974 four British-bred Weimaraners were exported to Sweden: Uhlan Katrina (Ortega Opal Mint/Gray Moonshadow of Duenna), Acombdole Caesar (Sh. Ch. Cannylad Olympus Daedalus/ Cannylad's Bimbo of Merse-Side), Roxford Astrid (Ragstone Rha/ Dangvord Daphne) and Ragstone Rhubasse (Ch. Ragstone Ritter/ Ragstone Rhossignol). The first three named were bred from, together with a Dutch bitch Jessie van der Streijkviertal (Neth. Ch. Acombdole Ami/Goethe van der Kerkebosch), a Norwegian dog Lord Silver-hufvud (Ch. Fantasic/Spetsi – whose grandparents Apollo Lad and Theocsbury Juno went from Britain to Norway), an Austrian bitch Petersbauers Asta (Zitto van der Murwitz/Cova von Kranichenstein – whose grandsire was Sh. Ch. Coninvale Paul of Acombdole), an American-bred dog from Finland, Tyson Samuel Ezekiel (Michels Blitz/Misty von Blau Augen), and a German-bred dog from Finland, Arco von Schloss Hachenburg.

Between 1974 and March 1981, this nucleus of Swedish Weimaraners consisting of a fair proportion of British bloodlines produced just 10 litters. The Swedish club estimated that possibly only one litter per year was likely to be born during the next few years to add to the approximate population of 60 dogs.

The Swedish Weimaraner Club *Svenska Weimaranerklubben* was founded in 1977. The chairman is Mona af Burēn, and the secretary is Agneta Kilborn, whose husband Lars has been kind enough to furnish the Swedish information. The Club's aims are to maintain a register of all Swedish Weimaraners, prevent commercial breeding or any unsuit-able matings, assist potential owners in the choice of stock, and aim towards breeding a versatile dog. The Club requires those dogs to be used for breeding to be typical of the breed, free from hip dysplasia and conforming to breed characteristics.

In Sweden the breed has a variety of work. For shooting purposes it is used mainly on pheasant, grouse, wild duck and small game, but also occasionally on elk. The Club's working dog branches use the Weimaraner for sleigh-pulling and as trackers and also pack-carriers. The breed competes against other gundogs in dog-sleigh racing, the usual distance being 30 km for dogs and 10 km for bitches with a weight of 30 kg including cargo for one dog, 50 kg for a brace of dogs, or 75 kg for a team of three followed by the dog's master ski-ing behind and attached by 5 m of rope. In 1981 the Weimaraner 'Dragos' (Tyson Samuel Ezekiel/Delight) bred by Åsa Löfberg was awarded the title Jämtland County Champion. There are also mountain races, the best known of which is the Åre-Draget which has a distance of about 100 km and is run over the mountains with a two-night stay in the snow under canvas.

Ragstone Rhubasse, by Ch. Ragstone Ritter ex Ragstone Rhossignol owned by Ola T. Walter, Sweden holds the record number of CACIBs in that country. (Photo: Ake Wintzell)

Canus Epona (owned by E. Johansson), Grey Magic (owned by A. & L. Kilborn) and Grey King (owned by M. af Buren) Sweden. (Photo: L. Kilborn)

The tracking branches have two sections – blood-tracking and man-tracking. The latter is somewhat similar to the British tracking tests in obedience trials. The blood track trail is over a distance of 600 m using about a third of a litre of blood. There are also guard and character tests to determine the dog's mental stability, plus a test to ensure the dog is not gun-shy. Pack-saddling is not competitive, but the Swedes maintain that a strong, muscular dog such as the Weimaraner makes a good pack-carrier and when trained will carry nearly one third of his own weight which is equivalent to the dog's feed during a week's hiking in the mountains.

As far as the show-ring is concerned, few Weimaraners gather together at the same shows due to the distances involved and it is seldom that there are more than three or four at the same show. An exception is the Nordic Winners Show where they muster as many as 14. The top winning CACIB winner in the breed is Ola T. Walter's bitch Ragstone Rhubasse.

THE WEIMARANER IN SCANDINAVIA

NORWAY

Britain's contribution to the Norwegian stock began in 1961 with the dog Cartford Saturn. In 1965 Apollo Lad and in 1968 his future mate Theocsbury Juno travelled out, and a few years after that Acombdole Czar and Kassandra of Ardlair. However the first Norwegian registrations were during 1968 and 1969 since when about 150 Weimaraners have been registered.

A club was formed in January 1981, the Secretary being Miss Eva Eriksen and today the *Norsk Weimaranerklubb* has about 60 members, few of whom have much opportunity to work or show their dogs.

FINLAND

There is no club for the breed in Finland, and according to the Finnish Kennel Club *Suomen Kennellitto* only two registrations have been made between 1977 and 1981, although it is known that in 1969 the bitch Ragstone Ryannie and in 1974 the dog Hawsvale Diplomat went out from Britain. There was also stock from Germany and the USA which made its way from Finland to Sweden. It is thought that there are perhaps only about 10 Weimaraners in the country.

DENMARK

The *Dansk Weimaraner Klub* was formed in 1961 and today has a membership of 145 made up from five regions around the country, each region working for the Club. The club runs three shows a year which generally attract between 15 and 20 entries and there are also about five shows a year under the auspices of the Danish Kennel Club which attract about 10 Weimaraners. The Danish club also runs a Field Trial each year which in April 1982 attracted an entry of three in the junior class and nine in the open class.

British Export Pedigrees to Denmark were issued to Sandrock Amanda (1957), Kingsholt Adam (1959), Theocsbury Friar (1966),

133

Abbeystag Galaxy (1970), Monroes Nonchalence (1968) and Rangatira Bandoline (1973). Four puppies were imported on 31 July 1961 from West Germany and there have also been imports from Holland. New Zealand also contributed in 1979 to the Danish stock with Ch. Waldheim Wild Cat who is a daughter of Australian Ch. Merrymar Valstorm.

There are estimated to be approximately 500 to 600 Weimaraners in Denmark at the present time. One notable dog is Danish Ch. Galan owned by Ib von Lunding – he won his fourth championship certificate in 1979 becoming the first ever Danish dog to attain full championship status as he was already the winner of a field trial and had passed the gundog retrieving test.

An interesting article written by Kristian Raunkjaer was published in *Jagt & Fisker* ('Hunting and Fishing') magazine in June 1981 in which he outlined the general history of the breed and also gave field training hints, saying that the breed would appear to be tailor-made for Denmark due to the hunting areas being not too large, with plenty of scope for the breed's natural ability in tracking. His account of his first encounter with the breed is reprinted here:

In conjunction with my work as a gamekeeper some years ago, it was my lot to train a Weimaraner for my then employer. At this time I had never seen a dog of this breed and I was very surprised when I was presented with this silver grey dog. It was a big, hefty male about 10 months old. I put him in the dog-run, but however strong or high the fencing was he managed to get out. One day he not only got out but also managed to get around the neighbourhood on his own and although we had been searching for him, we were unable to find him. After about two hours I suddenly heard a great deal of barking which came from the nearby forest, but it was only after about 15 minutes that I became really curious. I followed the sound and found the dog in the thick undergrowth where he was barking over a dead deer. This experience, and the problem of keeping him in the dog-run, proved to me that many Weimaraners are born with the ability to bark at the discovery of dead game (*'totverbellen'*) and also that they definitely do not like to be kept in a dog-run.

Curiously enough, although Sweden, Norway, Finland and Denmark are all part of Scandinavia, because of quarantine regulations the first three countries cannot exhibit in Denmark, or the Danish dogs exhibit in Sweden, Norway or Finland without subjecting their show stock to a spell in kennels.

12

The Weimaraner in Czechoslovakia

Czechoslovakia, formerly part of the Austrian Empire, became an independent Republic during 1918. Occupied by Germany in 1939 at the outbreak of World War II its independence was restored during 1944–45.

Weimaraners were first noted in Czechoslovakia during 1903 at a dog show held in Prague. It is also known that during the 1930s the

From Czechoslovakia comes this rare wire-haired Weimaraner owned by Josef Kalny. Jar z Jestrabich Hor, 'sg', 1st prize winner 'Herbstzuchtprufung', 2nd prize winner 'Volgebrauchzuchtprufung', 1st prize for sharpness on cats. (Photo: Robert Jakoubek)

breed was active, as records show that Baron Kast supplied the long-haired bitch Poldi z Mnisku to Robert Pattay in Austria.

A club was formed on 21 December 1966 under the presidency of Mr Robert Jakoubek with a membership of about 150 and named the *Klubové soutěži výmarských ohařů*. Today there are approximately 375 club members and about 500 Weimaraners with perhaps 25 breeders of short-haired dogs and seven breeders of the long-haired variety. There have also been a few wire-haired dogs which are recognised in Czechoslovakia and which are, therefore, allowed to compete at shows and trials, but they are not recognised in Germany although representation was made a few years ago in an effort to obtain official status. This refusal by the German club was because cross-breeding was obviously required to obtain the wiry coat, and all forms of cross-breeding had been strictly forbidden. It is not known exactly the ingredients of the wire-haired variant, but it is believed to contain Pudel-Pointer blood to some degree.

Practically all Weimaraners in Czechoslovakia are used primarily for hunting purposes and their field trial qualifications are noted thus: 'ZV', 'PZ', 'LZ', and 'VZ'. There is no test for man-sharpness as in Germany, but they do have a test for sharpness on cats. The coat colour would appear generally to be a somewhat darker shade of grey than is usual in Britain and most other countries.

13

The Weimaraner in Australia and New Zealand

AUSTRALIA

In 1955 Major Bob Petty sent out two pairs of Weimaraners from England to Australia – Strawbridge Furst and Fidget (Thunderjet/Cobra von Boberstrand), Strawbridge Graf and Gypsy (Bando von Fohr/Hella aus der Helmeute) all born in 1954. These arrived at about the same time as the first recorded import from the USA, the dog Regal Wunder Colombian Duke (US Ch. Rudolph aus der Wolfsriede/US Ch. Billous Azura Belle) who sired just one litter before being killed in a road accident. Duke was not brought in for any other reason than as a pet, as was the next dog from the USA, who accompanied his American student owner to Australia. However, this second dog, Fritz von Singen, had a greater impact on the breed's future as he was used at stud about five times, mainly on the British imported bitch Halsall Brown Pheasant (born 15.7.63 by Ch. Strawbridge Oliver out of Sandrock Coral) whose several litters, together with the Strawbridge stock already in residence, virtually founded the breed in Australia.

Fritz von Singen (Hans von Stedimar/The Lady Sachet von Gordon) although perhaps not a top specimen himself, gained his Australian championship status and sired some Weimaraners who rate well by world standards. The next known dog to arrive from America was imported by John and Rosemary Mayhew in 1981 – Arimar's Rolf von der Reiteralm (US Dual Ch. Ronamax Rufus Reiteralm CD/US Ch. I've a Dream of Arimar CD) who came via England and New Zealand where he gained championship titles before also annexing his Australian title, thus becoming Australia's only Weimaraner to sport these three titles – he is pictured number 74 in the Show Gallery, Appendix VIII.

German imports have been few. The first pair came with Mr G. Vize – the short-haired dog Arno vom Hoen Wald CM (born 20.2.72, Birk von Ried/Fee von Einkorn) and a long-haired bitch Pia aus der Greifenburg (born 11.4.72, Oka aus der Greifenburg/Amber von Schloss Freidrichstanneck) via England and New Zealand. Arno was retriever-trialled, not used widely at stud, but has left some outstanding stock: unfortunately he was poisoned in 1980. One of his grandsons from his mating with Pia is Australia's only Retrieving Champion, RT Ch. Spectral D'Artagnon CDx CM. The third German import was the bitch Astra vom Achtern Diek (Brix von Kaimbach/Bianka von Annenhof) who is owned by Mr Ted McKinley in New South Wales; she has had two litters and it is hoped that she may have her last litter by the next German import who arrived in 1982, the Mayhews' Salto von Zenthof (born 10.4.81, Alan von Forst Horice/Bianka von Welfenland) from England where he was used lightly at stud.

Aus. Ch. Halson Brown Pheasant had a false pregnancy when this lion cub was orphaned at birth in 1972 at Melbourne Zoo. She was offered the cub to foster which she did with great success and 'Arusha' grew into a fine lioness.

There have been at least 25 Weimaraners sent from England, the earliest being the previously mentioned Strawbridge Furst and Strawbridge Gypsy who were bred together once by Mr M. Sproul under his Lausder prefix, then under the Forestway prefix of Mr J. Forest. Strawbridge Fidget and Strawbridge Graf went to Dr Kristenson of Newcastle, New South Wales (and caused the writer a load of trouble as the English Kennel Club had them registered as being exported to East Africa!), and they were bred together by Mr M. J. Thomas under his Passau prefix and also gained their Australian championship titles. The typical pedigree set out overleaf shows clearly the extent to which these early British exports are to be found behind many breeding programmes:

Apart from Halsall Brown Pheasant, other British exports during the 1960s included Bruno of Monksway (Strawbridge Duke/Amber of Monksway, Moorland Sprite (Cartford Thundercloud/Moorland Gypsy), Acrise Amber (Moseby Greycoats/Englas Opal), Monroes Hannibal (Wolfox's Sandrock Cha-Cha/Manana Athene), Aust. Ch. Penny Silver Dawn (Sh. Ch. Ace of Acomb/Andelyb's Byth) and Derrybeg Anna (Sandrock Admiral/Inka vom Weissen Kreuz). Derrybeg Anna was mated to Marnisse Mercury, one of Regal Wunder Colombian Duke's progeny – Anna and Mercury were grandparents to Mr & Mrs Wally Finch's foundation bitch Weilock Lady Jane, start of the Milajun prefix.*

Halsall Brown Pheasant was owned by Mrs Frances Weatherley and lived to the good age of twelve years. Mr Gary Vize in the Weimaraner Club of Queensland's newsletter of July 1975 wrote the following tribute:

In seems less than justice that she should be remembered as running third in a Retrieving Trial in a snowstorm, and mothering a lion cub. This grand Weimaraner deserves better from us than these few flighty references to mark her passing. . . . Halsall Brown Pheasant will stand for all times as the pillar upon which Australian Weimaraners were built, and the breed could not have had a better beginning. Since she first set foot on our shores many imports have followed her, but surely none can compare with her, she was pure quality through and through. . . .

* Wally Finch writes: 'Milajun is the main character in an Aboriginal legend which explains the presence of a star in what we call the Orion constellation. When this star and another representing her husband appear, the dingos mate. Dingo pups equal good tucker to the Aborigines!'

Ghosty von Geigenburg
Australia to New Zealand

Ghosty Staubich

Naramona Greyghost

Greyghost Yampa

Passau Rollo

Waldlaken Princess

Naramona Greyghost

Strawbridge Graf	Bando von Fohr (Germany to UK)	
	Hella aus der Helmeute (Germany to UK)	
Strawbridge Fidget	Thunderjet (UK to USA)	Helmanhof's Storm Cloud (USA) Heidi v Reiningen (USA to UK in whelp)
	Cobra von Boberstrand (Germany to UK)	
Forestway Dieter	Strawbridge Furst	
	Strawbridge Gypsy	
Forestway Carla	Strawbridge Furst	
	Lausder Truda	Strawbridge Furst Strawbridge Gypsy
Forestway Dieter	Strawbridge Furst	
	Strawbridge Gypsy	
Forestway Carla	Strawbridge Furst	
	Lausder Truda	Strawbridge Furst Strawbridge Gypsy
Passau Heinrich	Strawbridge Graf	
	Strawbridge Fidget	
Halsall Brown Pheasant	Strawbridge Oliver	Ipley Apollo Cobra v Boberstrand (Germany to UK)
	Sandrock Coral	Smokey (von Branbrue) (UK to USA) Strawbridge Carol

140

It seems that every country has had the problem of over-active imaginations running rife in the press and certainly Australia had its share. Part of an article written during July 1969 in the Australian *Dog World* makes similar reading to articles circulated in Britain and the USA:

WEIMARANER – THE GREY GHOST

On cold, damp nights, when British soldiers lay soaked and shivering in their trenches on the battlefields of France during World War I many claimed that they had seen ghosts. They described the 'ghosts' as silvery shadows. But to the German troops, the shadows were not ghosts at all. They were solid, rugged Weimaraner dogs bearing flagons of rum around their necks. Was it the strange colouring of the dogs which prompted the German army to use them for this type of work? Or was it that the dogs were recognised for their high degree of loyalty and intelligence? Weimaraners were known as 'grey ghosts' as far back as 1757 when the Grand Duke Karl August of Thuringia, Germany, in the city of Weimar was said to be the first nobleman to breed them. No one who has seen the Weimaraner can fail to wonder at the manner in which the colouring of the dog changes with the light. In bright sunshine the Weimaraner is a silvery-mouse colour, but if the weather turns hot he becomes lilac and his grey nose turns mauve. On overcast days he becomes steel grey, and at night he turns into the grey ghost. . . . His webbed feet make him as at home in the water as he is on land. He has a short, dense coat which repels water. Beside the dog's wonderful hunting instinct he is known as a true companion. Weimaraners are especially good with children, being gentle and protective. . . . The Weimaraner is still a comparatively rare dog here. Perhaps they would not continue to be so rare if it were more widely known that they are rated second only to the German Shepherd in intelligence.

Few breeds in Australia enjoy representation by a club in each State and there are at present five Weimaraner clubs: Queensland, New South Wales, Victoria, South Australia and Western Australia. There are no Weimaraner clubs yet in the Australian Capital Territory, Tasmania or the Northern Territory, nor is there a national club, but there are regular exchanges of ideas and information between existing clubs, and many owners belong to more than one club. All the clubs encourage their members to show, trial and hunt with their Weimaraners and lay on practical demonstrations with helpful advice to newcomers at many functions throughout the year. There are approximately 550 club members all over the country but the total population of dogs is not easy to estimate. Annual registration figures are not to hand for the entire country, but Queensland's annual figures average 150 to 200 and probably New South Wales and Victoria's figures would be about the same if not more. A conservative national estimate might be 5,000.

Each year throughout the country the Agricultural and Industrial Societies of each county or shire hold fairs or shows to display the produce and skills of their particular area, and very often these incorporate a dog show as in Britain. The two largest and most important to the canine world are the 'Royals' held in Sydney and Melbourne. Perhaps these events are not in the same class when compared to Crufts or Westminster but they are still large-scale operations. In 1981 the Sydney 'Royal' attracted 5,222 entries which is an impressive figure considering the restrictions that must be imposed due to lack of available space. As with Crufts, the dogs must qualify for exhibition.

Between them the New South Wales and Victoria Clubs have made up something in the region of 120 Australian champions, with another 120 coming from the remainder of the country. From such a large number of champions, it is obviously difficult to single out more than a very few. Worthy of mention is Aust. Ch. Quailmaster Cloudy UD (Ch. Riverdrive Ace Carlo UD/Ch. Greymar Leibchen AOC, CM) the top winning show bitch who, although only having been bred from once, has produced top winning stock. She is one of six champions from the same litter, has qualified UD and also competed in retrieving trials. Aust. Ch. Ghostwind Claim to Fame (Ch. Monroes Zebedee/Ch. Quailmaster Nimbus) has won seven best in show awards (to date) and in 1981 was the winner of the 'Pal Top Dog' award in Western Australia, the first time in the country that a Weimaraner has won this award.

Show Procedure

Breeds are divided into six groups – toys, sporting terriers, gundogs, hounds, working dogs, and non-sporting. Breeds are divided into classes according to age and sex – Baby Puppy (3–6 months), Minor Puppy (6–9 months), Puppy (6–12 months), Junior (6–18 months), Intermediate (18–36 months), etc. Class winners compete against each other for best puppy in breed, Challenge Dog (i.e. best dog), Reserve

Challenge Dog, Challenge Bitch, Reserve Challenge Bitch, Best of Breed. Class winners also compete against other breeds for group awards in their class and the winners there compete against other group winners. Similarly Challenge winners compete against other Challenge winners from other breeds for Group Challenges and Show awards. Subject to the approval of the controlling body where the dog is domiciled, the title Australian Champion is awarded to dogs which win a total of 100 Challenge points. Only Challenge dogs and Challenge bitches win these points and then only at the judge's discretion. Five points plus one for every dog of the same breed and sex are awarded for each Challenge. Group and Show winners points are calculated the same way but no more than 25 points can be awarded at any one show. Points for Challenge of Group and Challenge of Breed, etc. are not accumulative. Puppies under six months of age are not eligible to compete for Challenges and are not counted in calculating points.

Obedience

On the obedience side, going on the numbers bred and trialled, the Weimaraner would rate as the top obedience dog in the country. The other (and obvious) top obedience dog is the German Shepherd but when one considers that the GSD registrations outnumber Weimaraners by at least 20 to 1, and that the number in obedience training is somewhere in the same ratio, the Weimaraner's record in obedience trials is nothing short of outstanding. Aust. Ch. Greymar Leibchen AOC, CM (Fritz von Singen/Halsall Brown Pheasant) was the first bitch of any breed to obtain the title Australian Obedience Champion (AOC). This consists of Utility Dog, Tracking Dog and Tracking Dog Excellent, and 'Izzie' held this record for many years. She also obtained a Certificate of Merit in retrieving trials which is only awarded for really excellent work. She has also produced more champions than any other Weimaraner, plus many fine working titled dogs, passing on to her progeny her all-round working ability.

Novice, Open and Utility are the classes in Obedience Trials. For each exercise in his class a dog is expected to earn at least 50 per cent to pass. In addition to passing each exercise dogs must earn at least 170 points out of a possible 200 to qualify. Three such qualifying scores awarded by at least two different judges are required in a class before a dog is eligible for the title associated with that particular class.

143

Tracking

Obedience clubs also stage Tracking Trials. Throughout the country, clubs which specialise in tracking can be counted on the fingers of one hand. As this is often regarded as a specialised field it is hardly surprising that there are few dogs actively competing. On the other hand more and more people are discovering that the techniques of training are not beyond their capabilities. Growing numbers actively competing is creating problems. The type of problems are mostly good. They are exposing a need for more trials and more judges. Dogs which are eligible to compete in Tracking Trials must have at least a Companion Dog title and a pass in the Seek Back and Scent Discrimination exercises in Utility class.

The exercises in Australian CD Stakes vary a little from the British stakes – they are heel on leash, stand for examination, heel free, stand stay, recall, one minute sit, three minute down. For the CDx – heel on leash, heel free, stand for examination, drop on recall, retrieve dumbbell on flat, retrieve dumbbell over obstacle, broad jump, three minute sit, five minute down. For the UD stake – seek back lost article, speak on command, or food refusal, scent discrimination, directed jumping, signal exercise, group examination, ten minute down. TD dogs have to complete two tracks at least one kilometer in length; one is of a person known to the dog and the other of a person unknown; both tracks have at least two 90° turns. TDx has six tracks, three of a known person and three of an unknown person. The award Australian Obedience Champion is the highest title which can be awarded. The fact that so few dogs hold this title indicates how difficult it is to achieve. It is only for dogs which already hold UD and TDx titles and probably only 20 dogs of all breeds have earned one.

Non Slip Retrieving Trials

It is quite possible that, apart from Germany, Australia may have the highest proportion of dogs engaged in some form of work on a variety of game. The first Field Trial Champion (in fact, the only one to date) is the dog Arnbrook Silver Gem (born 12.12.77, Kermann Kingsley Karn CDx/Denjaro Alumna CDx TD) bred and owned by Mr Fred Arnold of New South Wales, who gained his title against great odds from all other breeds. The first Weimaraner in the world to obtain the title of Retrieving Trial Champion is the dog Spectral D'Artagnon CDx

CM (Ghosty Silver Rock/Spectral Boadicea) a superb working dog who also has his CDx title. Retrieving trials are held in all states and in recent years the breed has gradually taken away the Labrador's stranglehold by establishing itself as one of the top three retrieving breeds in Australia. In Queensland it is apparently becoming common practice for Weimaraners to virtually scoop the pool at the big trials in the novice, restricted and all-aged stakes.

The purpose of a Non Slip Retrieving Trial is to test the retriever's ability to seek and retrieve 'fallen' game in field conditions which as close as possible emulate actual hunting. According to age and experience dogs compete in the following stakes: Puppy, Beginners, Derby, Novice, Restricted, All Age, Championship, Team and Brace. At the judge's discretion championship points may be awarded in Championship Stakes (first place 12 points, second place 6 points) and All Age Stakes (first place 6 points); the remaining classes do not carry points. Dogs must earn 12 points to become Aust. Retrieving Trial Champion. Other awards which may be gained are a Qualifying Certificate (QC) and a Certificate of Merit (CM) – neither are prizes but may be awarded at the judge's discretion. For the QC the dog must not be gunshy and must exhibit sufficient natural instinct to hunt, face cover and retrieve and be under reasonable control in any Stake. In the case of the CM dogs must complete all tests and must account themselves sufficiently well to warrant the award. Each of the stakes consists of three retrieves conducted on land and water (with the exception of Puppy Stakes which may have two retrieves). Game used is freshly killed for the Trial, and is generally pigeon, but quail, duck, snipe, rabbit, hare or pheasant may also be used.

Utility Field Trials

Stakes are Puppy, Derby, Novice, All-Aged, Championship, etc. Only one Championship Stake can be held each year in participating States except for the host State of the National Championship which may hold this in addition (this rule also applies to the aforementioned Non Slip Retrieving Trials). Championship points required for the title of Australian Field Trial Champion are 8 in number and are awarded as follows: Championship Stake 8 points for first, 4 for second; All-Aged 4 points for first, 2 for second; Novice 2 for first, 1 for second. Diplomas of Merit or Certificates of Merit are awarded under similar circumstances to those in the Non Slip Retrieving Trials.

The following description is by kind permission of Mr Geoff Redmond:

The ANKC Rule book defines a Field Trial as 'a meeting for the purpose of holding competitions for the work of dogs in the field and water'. To those of us who are enthusiasts of the 'Utility', 'All purpose' or 'versatile Gun Dogs' they mean a great deal more. The real purpose of a Field Trial is breed improvement. It is only through these trials that the outstanding dogs whose performances are best suited to perpetuate a breed are brought to the attention of all interested parties.

The Field Trial differs somewhat from the 'Natural Ability Test'. The Field Trial is to demonstrate the performance of properly trained Gun Dogs in the field. The performance should not differ from that in any ordinary day's shooting except that the work done should be in a more perfect way. It is important that these Trials are always conducted on natural wild game under natural hunting conditions. In fact the ANKC rules insist that Trials are not run on liberated or incapacitated game. It is only on natural game that the good dog is permitted to show his true virtues. His points are stauncher, his quartering more vigorous and his retrieving more determined. He is given the opportunity to 'road' a running bird in the bird's natural habitat. It is a true test of a dog's hunting ability in natural Australian hunting conditions.

The Trial is conducted with two rounds in the field and one in water. The water test can be held between, before or after the field rounds depending upon suitability of the trial site.

The dogs are awarded points on the following basis:

Ground Treatment   10 points each round. A dog should treat his ground in a thorough and methodical manner. A dog with a good nose will not potter on ground scents but will work his ground economically, working off body scents suspended in the air. He should quarter his ground taking every advantage from the natural conditions available, e.g.: wind direction, cover. When working into the wind a dog should cross in front of his handler and cast out 70–100 metres to the right or left. Good ground treatment is the foundation of a good trialling dog. All else is based upon it.

Pointing   15 points each round. A good dog should move in decisively on point without flushing the game. When pointing he should be staunch and upstanding although any pointing attitude is accepted but points are awarded accordingly. He should maintain contact with moving game. Any stickiness or lack of staunchness is penalised.

Steadiness   10 points each round. The dog should remain steady to any wild flushing or running game. He should be steady to shot and show no inclination to flush game. A dog will receive credit for honouring flushed game by remaining steady until sent on by his handler (standing, sitting or dropping).

146

Retrieve 15 points each round. The dog should mark the fall of the game; when ordered to retrieve should go straight to the game and bring immediately to the handler and deliver tenderly. Good marking and delivery are credited. Refusing to pick up game, breaking to shot and hard mouth are grounds for elimination.

Backing maximum 20 for trial. Upon one dog pointing game the other, providing he is suitably placed should instinctively adopt a pointing attitude. He should not creep or move in on the pointing dog.

Game Finding Ability 15 points each round. Some dogs for reasons such as nose and general experience are better game finders than others. Some show apparent 'bird sense' and can anticipate a bird's next move. Most trial judges are themselves experienced handlers and hunters. When scoring a dog on this aspect great care must be taken to allow for dogs who may have been disadvantaged by drawing a bad piece of ground. A judge will often when in doubt call a dog up again at a later time to give him more opportunity.

Style 10 points each round. This is seen in a well trained and well bred dog who covers his ground with his head held high, tail outstretched, moving in decisively on point and keen expression. Any lethargic action is contrary to good style.

Handling and Control 10 points each round. The good dog should require a minimum of handling, he should respond to each command. Quiet handling is credited and noisy handling is penalised as is ineffective handling. Chasing game is grounds for elimination.

Facing Cover 5 points each round. The dog should work and enter all cover (within reason). He should be penalised for avoiding thistley or uncomfortable cover (breeders should consider this with coat texture and pad cover).

Water Work 40 points. Keenness for water and strong swimming are major credits, any hesitation or dislike for water should be penalised. The water work should be conducted on similar lines to a Non Slip Retrieving Trial. A single marked retrieve from or across water. A blind retrieve from or across water (Championship Stakes only).

General Conduct of the Trial Prior to commencement of each round a draw is conducted. The dogs are drawn in pairs, one to wear a red collar the other a white. The dogs are sent off on equal terms. Handlers are permitted to work their dogs by voice, whistle or handsignals, but may be brought to order by the judge if he feels they are excessive or interfering with the other dog. Upon one dog finding game and indicating by pointing, the other dog *must not* be drawn across to take the point but must back of his own accord. The pointing dog must maintain contact with the game until the handler arrives and then flush on command. The handler (or Gun Steward if appointed), must then shoot the game. The dog should remain steady and then retrieve only on command. He should deliver tenderly to hand. The judge may instruct the handler of the backing dog to go to his dog prior to flush. The dogs are sent off again on equal terms.

The Weimaraner in UF Trials   Weimaraners have competed in UFTs since their inception in this country. The Weimaraner Club of NSW has conducted trials for six years and were instrumental in starting them up in NSW. To say that in this time the Weimaraner has fared poorly in trials is being kind. He has been criticised and maligned by judges and has been shown little respect by other competitors. Yet year after year some dedicated followers of the breed re-appear and trial their Weimaraners. The reason they come back baffles the owners of the GSPs. They cannot understand why the dog is not like the German Shorthaired Pointer. They feel he should work in exactly the same way, yet they never bother to find out why he does not. I have seen many Weimaraners appear at trials. Some have been bad specimens badly trained, others have been good specimens well trained. All have gone badly. The reason to me has become painfully obvious. Because they work slower and closer they cannot compete with the fast wide-ranging GSP. Usually most game is found before the Weimaraner gets near it. The only times I have seen Weimaraners go well in Trials is when they have been drawn together. The way the trials are conducted now the only way a Weimaraner can prove himself is if he is drawn with another Weimaraner or he outworks a GSP. For genetic reasons the latter is impossible. For no one can dispute that the German Shorthair is an outstanding *Trial* dog on upland game such as Quail. The future of the Weimaraner in Trials is dependent upon Weimaraner people trialling their dogs as trained Weimaraners and by strength of numbers educating trial judges that the Weimaraner isn't a poor GSP but a Weimaraner doing the same job in a different way. Then maybe one day we will see Weimaraner UFTs. After all we don't have to beat Irish Setters and Boxers to become show champions do we? It's not sour grapes on my part as I own both Weimaraners and GSPs and compete with both and judge both.

Mr Redmond's comments read in conjunction with Chapter 7 (*Field Trials and Working Trials*) bear witness to the fact that Weimaraner owners world-wide share similar opinions on field trials!

The following article *The Australian Hunting Scene* is very kindly contributed by Mr Wally Finch:

About 14½ million Australians live in an area of nearly three million square miles. In theory that gives us a population density of approximately five people to the square mile. However, in practice, the population is not so beautifully even in distribution. Believe it or not Australia has the most urban society on earth.

Because the majority are city dwellers, those wishing to spend their leisure hours in the great outdoors must be prepared to clock up some mileage. So, from Friday afternoon after business hours, it is not surprising to see a trickle of what will become a steady stream of traffic pouring out of the larger cities.

Included among these weekend nomads are some who are going on shooting trips. Unfortunately, an unhealthy proportion hardly measure up to acceptable ideals of sportsmanship. Their little expeditions could, at best, be described as grog-sodden yippie shoots which, naturally, cause no end of problems for bona-fide hunters and landowners alike.

In a country like ours, with so much uninhabited land, it probably seems ridiculous to even suggest that finding suitable hunting grounds is becoming more difficult every day. Yet it is to be expected that the actions of the irresponsible shooters creates the adoption of very negative attitudes towards anyone with guns. Consequently (and with just cause), property owners are becoming increasingly reluctant to allow hunters access to their land.

On Crown land and in National Parks firearms are totally prohibited. So, understandably, when a hunter enjoys a good relationship with farmers, graziers or other landowners he keeps very closed mouthed about it. There's no way he'll risk losing a carefully cultivated working arrangement by advertising its location to all and sundry.

Of course, the use of firearms is subject to restrictions, some of which are quite reasonable and some are not. Even though many Australian hunters have not realised it yet our days of totally uninhibited hunting are numbered. Licensing of firearms has been around for years but licensing requirements and anti-gun legislations are on the increase throughout the country. So too are the penalties for ignoring them. Hunting permits have also been around for years but Rangers and Police are becoming more diligent in checking them. Slowly but surely hunters are beginning to realise that they must pay for what they once got for free, and it hurts.

Australian Game

We are very fortunate in our variety of game in Australia. So fortunate in fact that it would take volumes to give a complete resume of all of it. What is included herein is by necessity excessively brief but hopefully detailed enough to be informative.

This is a vast land full of contrasts in terrain and topography. Almost every climatic condition exists here. We have jungles, open plains, deserts and alpine regions. About the only thing missing are arctic regions but then who needs them.

Such contrasts in habitat in turn bring about many different types of game and considerable variety in styles of hunting. In addition to our own unique fauna there are also many introduced species from other countries, some of which are very welcome, some we'd like to give back.

Like other countries we too have paid the price of indiscriminate over hunting which has sadly led to the irretrievable loss of some species and the near loss of others that almost joined them in extinction. Although game management would be a better approach, endangered species are now totally protected by law. This list is by no means complete and should have provision to include some of the more endangered predators that the 'man on the land' would cheerfully eradicate.

Kangaroo

Beyond a doubt the most hunted animal in Australia is the Kangaroo along with his cousins the Wallaby and the Wallaroo – there are many different species of each. Usually they are docile animals that prefer to run from trouble than fight. More often than not the former option is enough but if cornered and forced to protect themselves they can be ruthlessly formidable. By balancing on their tail and lashing out with those powerful hind feet they can easily annihilate the unwary – man or dog.

Possibly the most popular method of hunting Kangaroo is from the back of fast moving vehicles. This is not very sporting as they don't stand as much chance as a snowball in hell. For this type of hunting (or more correctly, shooting) there is little need for the assistance of a good dog except, perhaps to cut off escape routes inaccessible to vehicles.

A method of Kangaroo hunting being rediscovered is stalking them on foot. This calls for and demands greater skill on the part of the hunter who certainly could use the assistance of a good dog. Many breeds are used including Weimaraners who hold their own and more with the best of them.

Protected Native Fauna

Koala, Platypus, Echinda and Emu are all totally protected throughout Australia. The first two are victims of over-hunting for their pelts. Koalas are ridiculously easy to hunt. They simply sit in trees and wait to be shot at in turn. Incidentally they are not bears but marsupials. Emu (a bird similar to the Ostrich but not quite as big) was also hunted dangerously close to extinction for its feathers.

In the north of Australia there are some species of native water fowl such as the Magpie Geese, and there are Crocodiles both of which are also totally protected. Crocodiles regard dogs as good tucker and since their recent inclusion on the protected list they have become so daring at dog snatching that hunters leave their dogs at home.

Not all of our endangered species are protected, e.g. the magnificent Wedged-tail Eagle, and the Dingo is undisputedly the oldest breed of dog in the world.

Introduced Game

In the eighteenth century each of the separate colonies now collectively known as Australia had its own Acclimatization Society. The purpose of these societies was to assist a predominantly European (mostly British) people to adapt to their new country. They went about it in many ways

Jayteeta Aero owned by Mr & Mrs Wally Finch. By Brydot Orest ex Milajun Baroness.

including the introduction of selected species of Flora and Fauna from their 'old world' as well as Asia and the Americas to a lesser extent. In those days the impact of the consequences of such imports did not warrant a second thought. Some of them were to prove to be disastrous to us their grandchildren, the Australians of today. One of the more notorious imports was the prickly pear which as modern history tells us destroyed untold thousands of acres of prime grazing land before it was brought under control. That was one mistake that was corrected; others never will be.

Rabbits did not take long to reach pest proportions. The hopping invasion even crossed the Nullarbor Plain and into Western Australia. At the time the experts said that rabbits would never survive so much desert but they did. Along Queensland's border with New South Wales is a magical structure called a rabbit-proof fence – complete with rabbits on both sides. One of the more pleasant side effects of this pest is the many pleasant hours which can be spent hunting them. This plays a small part in preventing damage to grazing lands. However, extensive hunting has not done a thing towards controlling rabbit populations, nor has myxomatosis (a mosquito-borne disease introduced to eradicate rabbits) or 'Ten-eighty' (a poison to bait rabbits the success of which is doubtful – it makes rabbits and other animals very sick and renders their meat and pelts useless). Naturally, Weimaraners are very good workers on rabbits.

Deer

Few would argue that the ultimate species to hunt is Deer. Unfortunately, we have no native Deer species in Australia but all is not lost. Through their Acclimatization Societies, our Grandfathers did some things right such as the introduction of Red and Fallow Deer from Europe and Sambar, Hog, Rusa and Chital Deer from Asia. All of these animals have adapted beautifully to the Australian bush without detriment to native fauna or damage to grazing lands.

Hunting regulations for Deer vary from State to State as do the species available. For example, in Victoria, Sambar hunting is legal while in Queensland all Deer are totally protected for no apparent or logical reason.

The Australian Deer Association is successfully working to improve the status of Deer in this country. One of its major breakthroughs in recent years has been to make provision for Queensland hunters to assist the National Parks and Wildlife Department with a limited annual cull. These hunters are taught the fundamentals of taking certain samples and other data which must be forwarded to the Department. A little inconvenience is a small price to pay for the privilege of hunting the noble Red Deer. Especially when this data is making a major contribution to the future of the herd.

Deer hunters fit into two categories – stalkers and hound men. The latter are a minority and are predominantly residents of Victoria. They use their dogs to locate and run the Deer to the hunter. The dogs work in a pack and the most used breed is the Beagle. Some Weimaraners are used but not many even though they perform admirably.

As a rule the stalkers do not use dogs at all. Many of them are either poachers or ex-poachers and consider dogs to be too noisy. There are some who use dogs to assist in locating after the shoot. Weimaraners are better represented in this area and, of course, they perform admirably.

Since the introduction of Deer farming a few years ago some landowners who were once sympathetic to hunters no longer allow them anywhere near their properties. Deer farmers, in some cases, have been known to indulge in illegal trapping on neighbouring properties and there are suspicions that more than the legal limit is being taken. Deer hunters are genuinely concerned that such actions will lead to the end of some well established herds.

With so much activity going on which is associated with our six species of Deer, its ironical that most Australians are completely unaware of their existence.

Buffalo

By far the biggest game animal in Australia is the Water Buffalo which was introduced from Asia as a domestic animal and has since run wild. Dogs do not play a significant role in hunting Buffalo.

Pig

He's mean, vicious, unpredictable, dangerous and downright ugly by anyone's standards. His meat is usually so infested with parasites that it doesn't warrant consideration for consumption by either man or dog. He is the Wild Pig – the domestic Pig gone wild. In spite of all the points against him he is still highly prized as a game animal.

Not all Pig is unfit for human consumption. In a few areas they are reasonably parasite free and hunted commercially for venison. Admittedly venison is universally accepted as Deer meat but, strictly speaking, it is the flesh of any game animal.

Every State has at least some area where Pig can be hunted but the densest populations of pork are found in an area which occupies the northern half of Queensland and is joined by a strip in the west that occupies about a third of the remainder. It begins to narrow at the New South Wales border and continues south to the Victorian border. The further north one goes the meaner they get.

There are a number of methods of Pig hunting. In the west of the area described above hunters favour using the back of fast moving vehicles. Commercial hunters obviously show a definite preference for this method because of its efficiency. Dogs are often used to make sure Pigs don't get away.

Another popular method in areas where the bush is thicker is to hunt them on foot. In one method a variety of rifles are used including shotguns with SG ammunition. The other method, known as 'Pig stickin'', is very similar to the first in locating the quarry but the disposal couldn't be more different. While the dogs hold the Pig at bay or even hold onto it, the hunter moves in with a knife. This method is extremely dangerous and not recommended for the squeamish or the timid. It is very popular with young people in the north of Queensland. In the rest of the country Pig hunters seem to have a bit more common sense.

With the exception of bow hunters, most on-foot Pig hunters use dogs in packs of various sizes. Individual dogs perform in the pack in the following roles: (1) 'Finders' (self-explanatory); (2) 'Bailers' (from the Bushranger expression 'Bail up' – in this case meaning to hold at bay); (3) 'Holders' (the dog physically holds onto the Pig, or at least severely restricts its movement, by latching onto its ear, or wherever, and hanging on for grim death).

Pig hunters are often a rough and ready lot who don't really care in which role, or combination of roles, a dog performs providing it performs well in at least one. Naturally, a dog that performs well in all three roles is preferred.

Breeds used are mostly mongrels of Bull Terrier extraction, which includes, to the disgust of the conscientious, Weimaraner cross Bull Terrier. Enthusiasts of either breed are not impressed with such a callous disregard of untold generations of careful breeding.

In spite of these problems, there are some uncrossed Weimaraners getting their share of the meanest Pigs and proving that the breed is a superb Pig dog in its own right. As a very general rule, as far as the above roles are concerned, Weimaraners tend to be finders or Bailers with some showing talent in all three.

When in confrontation with a Pig, they are usually cool headed, yet courageous and persistent. Those villainous, razor sharp tusks on some of the older Boars command respect and Weimaraners seem to be aware of this. In this situation who needs a foolhardy dog?

The natural increase in Pigs is in the region of 500 per cent per annum. Considering the damage they do to crops it is little wonder they are officially regarded as pests. Helping to control their numbers is another community service provided by those civic-minded Weimaraners and their owners.

Fox

Foxes can be found in most places on the Australian mainland. Tasmania, being an island, is the only State without them. These too are a heritage of our forefathers' mistakes as Foxes are also an official pest. They do some damage to livestock, particularly poultry, but it is minimal in comparison to the irreparable damage to native fauna.

Fox hunting attracts a reasonably large following including some professional hunters. Good quality Fox pelts fetch attractive prices which can make it a very lucrative business. The two main methods of hunting them are spotlighting at night and whistling them in by day. Whistling is an imitation of the cry of a wounded Rabbit – a technique which also works well on Dingo.

Oddly enough Fox hunters in this country don't bother much with using dogs. It's difficult to understand why. Especially when breeds like the Weimaraner do so well at it in other countries. Also Australian Fox hunters don't need to concern themselves about Rabies as this disease does not exist here.

On rare occasions there are attempts to revive the traditional English Fox hunts but they really died a natural death years ago. Besides, this is more the scene for Horses, Beagles and other hounds. On the other hand it would be interesting to try out Weimaraners.

Goat

Every Australian State has some wild Goat herds that were introduced in days gone by. Their quality as game animals is very high and the meat usually quite good. They don't attract all that much attention and dogs aren't much used.

Game Birds

Ducks are the most predominant of our game birds and there are 15 different species throughout the country; some are protected, and the remainder may only be hunted in season which varies from State to State. Fortunately nearly all species which may be hunted are good eating birds. Naturally, the role of the Weimaraner in Duck hunting is that of a Retriever and a passionate one at that.

There are a number of Quail species to choose from including a few that were introduced. Most Australian Quail are small birds without much meat. Some are protected and the remainder may only be hunted in season which also varies from State to State. There are a total of about 30 different species of Quail in the whole country.

155

Quail populations are very transient. A field that is full of them today could be empty tomorrow and for no apparent reason. If that field is hunted one can guarantee they will go away for a long time. Quail hunting does have a definite following but not a large one.

The situation with Snipe is very similar to that with Quail.

Australian Native Swans which, incidentally, are black, do not attract the attention of hunters, nearly all of whom don't give them a second thought as game birds. An ironical attitude when one considers how enthusiastically they are hunted in countries to which they have been exported. Further compounding the irony, in their homeland they are protected and, due to lack of interest, there is very little poaching.

Several species of Australian Native Geese, e.g. the Magpie Goose, are protected but, unlike the Black Swan, they don't escape the attention of poachers. At the beginning of European settlement in Australia these beautiful birds could be found in large numbers in just about every fresh water swamp or lagoon along most of the east coast and all of the north coast. Over hunting at that time wiped them out on the east coast but they are still plentiful in the north from Queensland to Western Australia. As mentioned earlier dogs are not used because of Crocodiles.

Some so-called Australian Native Geese are not true Geese but are actually Ducks, e.g. the various species of Pigmy Geese. A few of these feature prominently in favourite recipes.

A very popular bird in our early history was the Bush Turkey which could be found in large numbers in mountainous areas and rain forest along most of the east coast. Because it was such a good eating bird it was definitely over-hunted but the greatest threat to its existence was the axe not the gun. In other words habitat destruction. Today the Bush Turkey is totally protected but still attracts poachers.

A variety of Pheasant have been (and still are being) released throughout the country but their population could hardly be described as established anywhere. By far the greatest success rate has been in the south east corner of Australia but even there success is limited. Impatient hunters who can't wait for populations to stabilise and predators such as Fox and Feral Cats don't help much.

New Zealand

The first recorded Weimaraners arrived in New Zealand during 1970 from Australia – the dog Scodan Arno (Aust. Ch. Riverdrive v

Caesar/Aust. Ch. Greygraf Eva), and two litter-sisters Spectral Autumn Haze and Spectral Autumn Pixie (Aust. Ch. Riverdrive Silver Blaze/ Aust. Ch. Ghosty Silver Princess), and in 1971 the first litter of puppies was bred from them by their owner Mrs Sandal of the Upton Fells prefix. This first, and subsequent litters were distributed widely to all parts of the country. It is more than probable that there were already odd Weimaraners to be found many years earlier, but unfortunately there does not appear to be any true record of them and in any case they do not apparently figure in pedigrees to be found today in the country.

During the early 1970s there were a number of other imports from Australia and these, together with Mrs Sandal's stock, were the foundation on which kennels were established. The Australian dogs imported were Ch. Riverdrive Penny Tinka CDx who was the foundation bitch for Mr Vic Davy of the Rheinma prefix; Ch. Merrymar Valstorm (born 6.8.71, Aust. Ch. Fritz v Singen/Greygraf Nissa) who was the foundation bitch for Mrs Sylvia Diehl's Waldheim prefix; Ch. Rambai Silver Sahib, a dog imported by Mr Dave Parker and who sired a number of litters under his Gunmettle prefix; born 2.4.73 the bitch Ch. Silberjager Batavi also owned by Mr Parker; Ch. Greylag Fraun (born 1972 by Aust. Ch. Greymar Corey) was the foundation bitch imported by Mr and Mrs Graham Culliford and the start of their Greylag (NZ) prefix; Shadowmar Baron (Aust. Ch. Greymar Noble Monarch/Greyweim Greta) was imported by a keen quail hunter Mr Eric Thompson of Alexandria, and this dog was an excellent worker (unshown) who sired a number of show winners. Ch. Garmisch Waldmeister, a dog, and Ch. Rambai Silver Quail, bitch born 8.10.75, and many others were brought over from Australia, some as pets, others for breeding stock or shooting companions. There are now between 20 and 30 established breeding kennels throughout the country. Nearly all the imports mentioned have UK breeding behind them, which came from the exports from the UK to Australia in the 1950s and 1960s.

The Club's treasurer, Mr Richard Huntington brought in a dog from the USA in 1969, but Rolens Silver Blue Duke was never used at stud. From Germany (after a short spell in the UK) came the dog Arno vom Hohenwald (born 20.2.72, Bird von Reid/Fee von Einkorn) bred by Helmut Scruth, together with a long-haired bitch, Pia aus der Greifenburg (born 11.4.72, Oka aus der Griefenburg/Amber von Schloss Friedrichstanneck) bred by Klaus Hartmann. This pair were brought in by Mr G. Vize and became the foundation stock for all long-haired Weimaraners in New Zealand and Australia; Arno's sire Birk von Ried was also long-haired.

More recent imports from Australia include the dog Silk 'n' Silver Royal Zeus (Ch. Quailmaster Centurion/Ch. Weimas Sudlicher Stern) bred by Mr and Mrs J. Maynard and owned by Mr John Martin. Unshown, but considered to be a most impressive dog, 'Chang' was tragically killed in a road accident in March 1982. His litter-mates retained at home in Australia are both best in show winners: Ch. Silk 'n' Silver Royal Ace and Ch. Silk 'n' Silver Royal Star. 'Chang' had mated three bitches so hopefully his great driving movement and style will not be entirely lost.

As far as direct UK imports are concerned, these began in 1976 with Ragstone Rebhuhn (NZ Ch.) born 22.10.75 by Richtkanonier of Ragstone ex Sh. Ch. Ludmilla of Ragstone; then later on Ragstone Ryulla (NZ Ch.) born 8.2.79 by Ch. Kamsou Moonraker von Bismarck (US import to UK) ex Sh. Ch. Ludmilla of Ragstone, both bred by Mr and Mrs A. Burgoin and imported by Mr and Mrs G. Culliford of the Greylag prefix. The Cullifords also acquired the dog Steniczo Sobe, born 30.12.72 by Ch. Ragstone Remus ex Sh. Ch. Cannylad Olympus Daedalus, bred by Mrs Jones, and who has been imported as a pet and whose owners returned to the UK. Mr and Mrs Rad Drawbridge imported the dog Ambersbury Freischulz born 28.4.77 by Sh. Ch. Gunther of Ragstone ex Sh. Ch. Phayreheidi Chelal of Ambersbury, bred by Mrs M. Wardall, and a bitch, Heronshaw Silver Seagull born 8.2.77 by Sh. Ch. Abbeystag Oceanmist ex Heronshaw Silver Shadow, bred by Mrs D. Chapman. The latest two imports both accompanied their owners; these are the bitch Hiriwa Turehu born 10.8.79 by Merryhell Havoc ex Lindon Enterprize, bred by Mrs L. Horton and owned by Mr and Mrs I. M. Brown; and the dog Ragstone Reckless (HD certified clear) born 6.7.80 by Sh. Ch. Ragstone Ryuhlan ex Ragstone Russelle bred by the Burgoins and owned by Mr and Mrs W. Randall – the Randalls returned to England leaving 'Roo' with his new NZ owners Mr and Mrs D. Stevens.

In 1981 Mr and Mrs John Mayhew of Australia imported from the USA via England the dog Arimar's Rolf von der Reiteralm who gained show titles and was used at stud in each of those three countries. He is by US Dual Ch. Ronamax Rufus von der Reiteralm CD out of US Ch. I've a Dream of Arimar CD (see Show Gallery no. 74, Appendix VIII).

The Weimaraner Club was formed on 20 April 1979 after several

Aus. Ch. Spectral Didgeri Doo owned by Mr & Mrs Wally Finch. By Ghosty Silver Rock ex Spectral Boadicea (Imp. NZ)

informal meetings. Officers and committee members were nominated, rules and aims were discussed and a constitution was drawn up for submission to the New Zealand Kennel Club for official recognition. Club President is Mrs Dianne Webb who, together with Richard Hartington were the prime movers in getting enough people together in order that a club could be formed. In March 1982 the Club membership stood at 110 scattered between Whangarei in the North Island to Invercargill at the tip of the South Island. The Club has its headquarters in Christchurch and is active with social gatherings all year round, obedience and show training, elementary trialling, ribbon parades, etc. The Weimaraner population is estimated to be about 1,250. Registrations during 1973 totalled 52, rising to 289 in 1981.

Championship shows do not attract a very high entry, for example at the prestige show of the year, the 'Fido National' held in Wellington the 1976 entry was 18 in 8 classes; in 1977 the entry was 17 in 7 classes; in 1978 the entry was 24 in 8 classes. The classes are Puppy, Junior, Intermediate and Open, and to become a New Zealand Champion the dog must obtain eight CCs under five different judges and must be over the age of 14 months.

Mr John Tweedie who is the current editor of the Club's quarterly magazine kindly submitted the following information on the types of game and hunting uses for the Weimaraner in New Zealand:

Deer

The dogs are used by the shooter on foot to find deer lying up in heavy cover, or to air scent them off the ridges and indicate the presence of animals in gullies and valleys below. The breed's tracking ability is valuable should an animal be wounded. With the advent of commercial venison recovery of the last decade, and the use of helicopters to shoot remote and inaccessible country, Weimaraners have logged many hours in the cockpit. Believe it or not, the dogs quickly become expert at detecting any movement in the scrub below, enabling the pilot to investigate further. The dogs are used to flush animals hiding in scrub out into the open where they may be captured live, or shot. They are also dropped off to track and recover any wounded animals. In the early days of tranquilliser guns, the dogs were used to track the drugged animals, and trained dogs were sold in excess of $1,000.00. Nowadays the technique is to use nets rather than drugs as fewer animals die of shock. It is the work on deer which, more than any other hunting use, has won a high reputation for the Weimaraner.

160

Chamois

Dogs are used for this game in much the same manner as the work required on deer. I take my own dog out on chamois every time, although many hunters prefer to work without a dog. Unless well-trained, dogs can be a nuisance on a hard climb or a long stalk.

Possums

These animals are hunted for their fur. They are nocturnal in habit, so they are spotlighted at night, the dogs ranging, treeing the possums, then barking to guide the owner to the tree. Possums are also poisoned using a cyanide bait. Dogs are invaluable in recovery of the carcasses, many of which would remain unsighted without the use of a dog.

Wallabies

These are small marsupials related to kangaroos. The dogs point them or flush them from cover as well as retrieve them.

Upland Birds

The main birds are pheasant, quail and Chukkor partridge. Dogs are used in the conventional manner and have earned an excellent reputation for this work.

Water Fowl

Main species are duck and Canada geese. The dogs are used as retrievers from mai-mai (hide) or ponds, and they excel at hunting up creeks and swamplands.

14

The Weimaraner in South Africa

Weimaraners have been present in South Africa since the early 1950s at least, but it was only on 10 January 1981 that the inaugural meeting of the 'Weimaraner Klub' was held. The aim of the Club is to bring together Weimaraner owners with the ultimate goal of maintaining and possibly improving the presently available stock by way of judicious and controlled breeding. For this purpose Breed Wardens have been appointed with a view to evaluating those dogs and bitches intended for use in breeding. Furthermore, a Breed Register has been initiated in order to collect all available information on the breed. The running of the Club is based on the principles of the Weimaraner Club of Germany, being modified to suit local conditions.

Registration figures available from the Kennel Union of South Africa (which includes Zimbabwe) since 1 September 1975 give a total number of 1007 Weimaraners registered during the five year period ending 31 August 1980.

In 1955 East Africa saw the first bitch to be imported from Britain, Strawbridge Enid (Bando von Fohr/Vita von der Haraska) imported by Mr J. Toft. At the same time Strawbridge Franz (Thunderjet/ Cobra von Boberstrand) and Strawbridge Garnet (Bando von Fohr/ Hella aus der Helmeute) were imported into Rhodesia by Mr R. T. Bruford. Shortly afterwards, during 1957 and 1958 Mr D. P. de Villiers Graaff imported into South Africa from Britain Cinders of Strawbridge (Cid von Bolkewehr/Vita von der Haraska), Arco von der Kolfurter Heide and Strawbridge Graf Otto (Ipley Apollo/Cobra von Boberstrand). Arco was a German-bred dog imported into Britain from Germany and after changing hands several times he eventually landed in South Africa where he was unfortunately bitten by a cobra and died leaving no known progeny.

During 1958 a US Naval Attaché, Commander Don Eley, took his Weimaraner dog, Prince Rex of Shimron, and his bitch, Bell von der Bruck, with him to South Africa when he was posted there. Prior to that the dog had been with him on duty in Iran. In the early 1960s Commander Eley was again transferred and this time his Weimaraners were left behind in the care of Mr A. J. Harrison, who subsequently bred four litters from the pair under his Oosterzee prefix which is to be found in many South African pedigrees.

The only other import in the 1950s was Strawbridge Uhlan (Smokey/ Vita von der Haraska) and he too is to be found in many pedigrees with the addition of the Santa Barbara prefix.

Mrs J. Franzsen imported a pair from Britain in the 1960s, Tottens Telstar and Wolfox Clotilda and these two had her 'of Frantoit' suffix added. Also during the 1960s from Britain came Baynard Silver Bomber, Waidman Bonzo and Monroes Otto; from Germany came Harry von Steeg and from the USA von Gaiberg's Flecka of Santa Barbara.

At the 1967 Birmingham Championship Show in England, Mrs G. Troup, who was visiting the Weimaraner benches, said that when she left Rhodesia in 1964 there were no fewer than 63 Weimaraners at the Wanki Game Reserve where they were used for patrol and guard work and also to prevent poaching. The introduction of this stock into Rhodesia was effected by importing nine in-whelp bitches and three unrelated dogs (complete with handlers) from Germany. Prior to deciding on Weimaraners for this type of work, various avenues were explored and it is understood that visits were made to South America, Brazil and sundry other parts of the globe to select a suitable breed and to locate sound representative breeding stock. Mrs Troup was the owner of British bred bitch Strawbridge Penelope (Strawbridge Duke/ Thunderflash).

At the end of 1965 Mr Roy Syddall took his dog Ragnor's Turk to Britain where, after doing his spell of quarantine in Lincolnshire, Turk sired a litter to Schoenfeldt Angelica. This produced two bitches; one was the CC winner Ragstone Renee who had a litter by Ch. Ragstone Ritter in England before going to the USA. Turk eventually returned to Rhodesia and died there. Mr Syddall said that it was he who introduced Lincolnshire Partridges, Pheasants and Bob-white Quail into Rhodesia (imported as eggs) for the benefit of a large shoot owned by Dr Abrey. He also said that at that time Dr Abrey, a veterinary surgeon, was the only breeder in Rhodesia and kept the Weimaraner exclusive to himself and members of his shooting syndicate with the result that no breed other than the Weimaraner was worked there.

163

Unfortunately breed details of the dogs said to be at the Wanki Game Reserve are not available so it is not known if they appear in present-day pedigrees. Dr Abrey's Ragnor prefix is certainly readily apparent and stemmed from the original British imports Strawbridge Franz and Strawbridge Garnet.

During the 1960s, due to a lack of awareness of the potential breeding stock in the country, the possible benefits from the early imports were not fully realised. Islands of good bloodlines were never brought together, mainly due to the vast distances between the main centres. Pioneering of the breed began in the mid-1960s through the promotion in the show ring of some of the progeny of the early imports. Mr Lukas Verch, Mr S. Saffer and Mr D. C. Luke were early campaigners in the show ring, most Weimaraners having been used previously mainly for rough shooting.

The increased interest in the breed in the 1960s received further impetus in the 1970s with new bloodlines being imported into the country. The first was Mr S. Saffer's import from Germany of a long-haired bitch Ona aus der Greifenberg (Alex von Tannenhof/ Krone aus der Greifenberg) bred by Klaus Hartmann, but unfortunately she proved to be sterile. He then imported a long-haired dog, Argus vom Jungholz (Axel vom Schuntertal/Cora von Tannenhof) bred by Manfred Knorp of West Germany and these were the first long-haired Weimaraners to be imported into South Africa. Longhairs do occur through the male import line.

In 1971 Mr L. Verch imported the dog Axel von der Harrasburg (Axel von Gaiersburg/Elken's Fizz von der Reiteralm) from Mrs Helen Schulze of Canada. This dog's Canadian dam had been sent to West Germany to be mated after completing the necessary German field qualifications; he has had a great influence on the breed and appears in most present-day pedigrees. Through Mr Verch, Dr B. Wessels obtained a bitch from Germany in 1973 – Biene vom Annenhof (Marko v Weissen Kreuz/Farah v Fuldatal) bred by Klaus Peter Gay. Mr Verch also imported the bitch Aischa vom Harzblick (Bullerjahn von Gebirgsjaggerhof/Elke von Zenthof) bred by H. Bornmann, West Germany; this bitch arrived in whelp to the German dog Bodo vom Rebhuhnsberg (Akko v Sande/Alfra v Möllenbeck) who was bred by Heinz-Friedrich Strub, but only one puppy survived – this was a long-haired male. More recently Mr Verch has imported the bitch Biene v d Lusshard (Graf v Jungholz/Anka von der Lusshard) bred by E. Ast of West Germany.

SA Ch. Axel v d Harrasburg bred by Helen Schulze and owned by Mr L. Verch. By Alex v Geiersberg (Germany) ex Elkens Fizz v d Reiteralm (Canada)

The top winning Weimaraner in the history of the breed in South Africa is Mr and Mrs C. J. Breyer-Menke's dog Ch. Shepherd's Pride Guenther bred by Mr Verch by Axel von der Harrasburg out of Aischa vom Harzblick. This dog has numerous best of breed awards and 25 Group placings to his credit.

Other imports of note during the 1970s were Mrs A. M. d'Alessandre's American bitch Monomoy Ilse von Eschenfeld (Ch. Monomoy Wheeler Dealer/Centa von Eschenfeld) bred by Phyllis Mason. This bitch whelped a litter in 1973 sired by Axel von der Harrasburg. In 1975 Mr and Mrs Ray Taylor imported Ragstone Rhumbo, a dog, later to be Ch. Ragstone Rhumbo von Stahlberg (Ch. Ragstone Ritter/ Ragstone Rhossignol) from Mr and Mrs A. Burgoin, England. Mated to their bitch Ch. Ansa van Migesta they produced a good litter out of which they retained Ch. Stahlberg's Moondust, who, until her untimely death, was the top winning bitch in the country. More recently the Taylors have imported from the Burgoins the dog Rifleman of Ragstone (Sh. Ch. Ragstone Ryuhlan/Chancel of Castle Garnstone). Mr C. Lee's dog Fatilla Romeo (Sh. Ch. Gunther of Ragstone/Ambersbury Dorabella) bred in Britain by Mr N. Jones was imported into Zimbabwe (which at the present time is still under the jurisdiction of the Kennel Union of South Africa) and has since gained his title. Another English dog Monroes A-Knightsman (Monroes Yarrow/Sh. Ch. Monroes Aequo) bred by Mrs Joan Matuszewska who has visited South Africa and judged the breed, was imported by Mr D. C. Luke. And Knightsman's litter-sister Monroes A-Katya was imported by Mrs F. A. St Clair-Mulley. From West Germany, bred by H. Reuper came Mr and Mrs Breyer-Menke's bitch Perle vom Zenthof (Alan von Forst Horice/ Amsel aus Wald und Feld), and from Britain via Zambia Mr and Mrs Johnson's bitch bred by Mrs A. Farrow, Farthorn Sprite (Sh. Ch. Ragstone Rhion/Senta of Ragstone).

Numerically the breed is limited in the show-ring, but the overall quality has elicited extremely favourable comments from overseas judges from various countries, especially over the past few years. Although the earlier breeders kept the Weimaraner on view in the show-ring it has only been in recent years that the breed has been successful in competition against other breeds. These successes, considering the numbers being shown, are a compliment to the quality of the breed. Prominent dogs that have been major contributors in this success story are the German import Ch. Axel von der Harrasburg; his daughter bred by Mr Verch out of Aida of Shepherd's Pride, Dr C. C. Luke's Ch. Grandbois Calypso of Shepherd's Pride; Mr and Mrs Taylor's bitch Ch. Stahlberg's Moondust, and Mr and Mrs Breyer-Menke's dog Ch. Shepherd's Pride Guenther.

During 1980 the first formal Field Trials for hunt-point-retrieve breeds were held. All the Weimaraners participating were show dogs and it is hoped that through this new venture the dual purpose qualities of the breed will be maintained. During April 1982 the first breed in the hunt-point-retrieve group to gain a Field Qualification in Africa was a Weimaraner – Mr and Mrs Ray Taylor's male Stahlberg Mooncaitiff.

The awarding of Challenge Certificates and Reserve Challenge Certificates is the same as in Britain, except that in South Africa there is also a Restricted Class for dogs which are not competing for the CC or RCC but who can still be considered for best of breed; plus a Champions Class which is restricted to existing champions who also do not wish to compete for the CC or RCC, only for best of breed. This means of course that on many occasions, young stock is competing for the CC without having to be judged against the breed's champions. Naturally, opinions differ about this system! The title of Champion is awarded on a points scheme – five points in total are required, not more than four of these being won in any one centre, and they must be

SA Ch. Shepherd's Pride Guenther bred by Mr L. Verch and owned by Mr & Mrs C. J. Breyer-Menke. By Ch. Axel v d Harrasburg ex Aischa v Harzblik.

won under different judges. A CC wins 1 point if fewer than 10 exhibits of one sex are shown; 2 points if more than 10 exhibits of one sex are shown; one-third of a point for a RCC. Therefore, a dog can be made a Champion with 15 RCCs, not having won a single CC. Apparently the KUSA has recently asked all members to complete a referendum as to whether the RCC should count towards the title of Champion or be cancelled.

15

The Weimaraner in Brazil

The Weimaraner Club of Brazil has a current (1982) membership of around 300 and a Weimaraner population of more than 1,500. It was formed on 17 January 1978, the founder members being Mrs Marisa de Castro Lopes Corrêa and Mr Eduardo Victor Costa to whom grateful acknowledgement is made for the following details of the early days of the breed in Brazil.

Weimaraner history in Brazil started in June 1952 when a ship tied up at the Rio de Janeiro port. On board were two adult Weimaraners from the USA brought in by American sportsman and hunter, Mr Blitz, who later became a naturalised Brazilian. These first two Weimaraners were the litter-sisters Apoll's Silver Lilly and Apoll's Silver Belle (Ch. Apoll Treu Hauentwiete 'V'/Hines Silver Erica) and were followed in October of the same year by an adult male from Germany, Gerd von Bruchholz.

Mr Blitz exhibited 'Lilly' and 'Belle' at several dog shows throughout the country and was successful in finishing both bitches to their championship titles and also successful in winning an all-breed best in show award in the 1950s which was a 'first' for the breed. As well as being show dogs, both these bitches were worked in the field. The first litter to be born in Brazil was out of 'Belle' in 1953 and was the foundation of the first Weimaraner kennel – the Blitz Vymar kennel.

The next kennel to be founded was based on a German imported bitch Diana von der Katzbach (Anko von Kastell Holten/Benigna von der Teufelsposse) brought in by Mr João Moojen de Oliveira in 1953 and was named von Schlossegehege — not to be confused with the old German affix of the same name. Diana's sire was also imported in 1953 from Austria by Mr Euclydes Aranha Neto, but Anko v Kastell Holten (Bodo v Haimberg/Adda v Kleistermoor) was found to be sterile.

From 1952 until the beginning of the 1960s the breeding was virtually controlled by Mr Moojen and Mr Blitz, but then new breeders came along and the number of Weimaraners began to rise. Two of the most notable breeders at that time were Dr Mario de Almeida and Dr Losir Vianna. Dr Almeida acquired an American pair of Weimaraners, Braz. Ch. Schatzi Grafin von Copacabana (Ch. Ann's Wilhelm CD/Gretchen von Kitz) and Braz. Ch. Skipper Graf von Copacabana (Ch. Verdemar's Man O'War/Dymar's Silver Sybil) from whose mating several champions were produced under his kennel name of Itatiaia. Dr Losir Vianna's kennel name was Sumaré and from this came one of the best known Brazilian dogs, Ch. Negão do Sumaré which was a Hunting Dog Speciality Show winner and top best of breed winner. Both Dr Almeida and Dr Vianna helped greatly in fostering the interest shown in the breed.

More importations were made and in the 1970s were founded five important new kennels, among them was Mrs Vincentina Novelli who owned the bitch Ch. Int. and Ch. Song do Sumaré which she mated to her US imported dog Uncle Maxwell von Reiteralm (Ch. Maximilian von der Reiteralm/Elkens Party Gal von Reiteralm) bred by Virginia Alexander. The progeny of these two started the Fonte da Saudade kennel. 'Max' was twice an all-breed best in show winner, Brazilian Champion, International Champion, and top producer.

Mr Alvaro Bastos do Valle's Jaraguá kennel was based on two US imported bitches mated to his dog Ch. Negão do Sumaré; one was bred by Carole Leib and was Scuddahoo's Pepper (Ch. Winage Farm's Maco Scuddahoo/Tannenhof's Diana), and the other by Virginia Alexander, Ruby's Rebel Song Reiteralm (Ch. Brandy's Rebel v Reiteralm/Ch. Rona's Ruby von der Reiteralm). 'Pepper' became a Brazilian Champion and left good offspring from her mating to Negão in the bitch Gr. Ch. and Ch. Flicka do Jaraguá. 'Ruby' had one litter but was later apparently lost after running from her yard. Another American dog influential in the Brazilian breeding was Ch. Green Acres Ode to Reanabuck (Ch. Clark's Buckaru of Green Acres CD NSD NRD/Ch. Reana H. SD RD) acquired from Diane Swanson.

But by the end of the 1970s the main breeders had virtually closed their kennels and there were problems relating to lack of control and lack of goals as the breed had been uncontrolled in its development since the first imports in 1952. Breeding problems arose – close in-breeding and unplanned breeding resulted in many Weimaraners carrying disqualifying faults and therefore very few were taking

170

any major places at dog shows. However, the new generation of Weimaraner owners and future breeders were only too aware of the situation and wished to change this poor state of affairs, and to this end the present-day club was founded.

The Weimaraner Club was founded on 17 January 1978, the brainchild of Mr Edouardo Victor Costa who, with Mrs Marisa de Castro Lopes Corrêa, took over as its first co-ordinators. They were soon joined by several other owners and breeders and so the club was born, the first nucleus in South America whose aims were to improve and control breeding and generally put matters in order. 11 March 1978 saw the first Brazilian Weimaraner Speciality Show in which 33 dogs were entered. The winning male was Ch. Thor of Mar's (Ch. Lord Gray do Itatiaia/Mira do Sumaré) owned by Mr Amaro Mendes de Magalhães, and the winning bitch Gr. Ch. and Ch. Int. and Ch. Alegria da Fonte da Saudade (Ch. Int. and Ch. Uncle Maxwell v Reiteralm/Ch. Int. Song do Sumaré) owned by Mrs Vincentina Novelli.

It might be pertinent at this point to explain the various championship titles which must appear confusing to the British reader. There are three types of champions: (a) Champion; (b) International Champion; and (c) Great (or Grand) Champion. To become a Champion (Ch.) the dog must win five CACs (Championship Aptitude Certificates) from three different judges, plus one best of sex or a group placement. To become an International Champion (Ch. Int.) the dog must win three CACIBs (given to the best of breed winner at an International Dog Show), plus a place in a Field Trial test equalling 'good' or better. To become a Great Champion (Gr. Ch.) the dog must already be a Champion, plus three best of breed wins, plus 60 Great Champion Certificate points. A bitch requires two best of breed wins and 45 points. To date, there have been approximately 120 champions of the three types in Brazil.

Since the formation of the Club, the breed has begun to achieve good placings in groups and also best in show wins at all-breed shows, the latest two of which were taken by the dog Gr. Ch. and Ch. Feitico da Fonte da Saudade (Ch. Int. and Ch. Uncle Maxwell v Reiteralm/ Alvorada da Fonte da Saudade) owned by Mr Renato Inneco Longo; and the bitch Gr. Ch. and Ch. Aloma do Xapaña (Gr. Ch. and Ch. Braco de São Silvestre/Gr. Ch. and Ch. Doçura da Fonte da Saudade) bred and owned by Mrs Sydia Nara M. Vieira. Also in 1980 there were two Speciality Hunting Dogs best in show winners in Am. and Braz.

Ch. Rajah's Mrs Magic v d Reiteralm (Ch. Ronamax Rajah v d Reiteralm/Ch. Brandy's Blizz v d Reiteralm) owned by Mrs Vincentina Novelli, and the Gr. Ch. and Ch. Bianca von der Zara (Biruta D'Aldeia/Brisa do Jaraguá) owned by Mr Sergio Savelli de Menezes.

Among several other achievements, one of the most important was the publication of the first Weimaraner book in Brazil and South America written (in Portuguese) by Eduardo Victor Costa and Marisa de Castro Lopes Corrêa. Several new breeders have emerged, mainly in Rio de Janeiro and São Paulo and a new wave of imports commenced, with some good dogs from Germany but the bulk coming from the USA. For the first time some of the Brazilian bitches have been sent to the USA to be bred to America's top producing sires, such as Ch. Reiteralm's Rio Fonte Saudade and Ch. Colsidex Standing Ovation. Weimaraners have been exported to other South American countries and also to Portugal. Another important factor which is helping to consolidate the breeding aims of the Brazilian Weimaraner fanciers, was the foundation in 1981 of the São Paulo Weimaraner Club which held its own first show in the same year, the winners being: best dog, Am. and Braz. Ch. and Gr. Ch. Nani's Raising Ned at Charmony (Ch. Nani's Silver Slate/Ch. Nani's Soul Sister) bred by Chris and Smokey Medeiros and owned by Mr Jose Bonifacio de Andrada e Silva; best bitch, Gr. Ch. and Ch. Bruna do Canto de Pedra (Biruta D'Aldeia CQN/Gr. Ch. and Ch. Flicka do Jaraguá) bred by Mrs Marisa de Castro Lopes Corrêa and owned by Dr Laercio Gomes Gonçalves.

16

Weimaraners Around the Rest of the World

Argentina

The earliest registration was in 1965, since when 35 Weimaraners have been registered among which would be the solitary British export, Mandy's Cassandra in 1979. As yet there is no separate breed club.

Belgium

Has no separate breed club for Weimaraners which are included in the club for German Pointers. The first litter to be registered was in 1972 and consisted of one dog and two bitches, followed by a litter of two dogs and one bitch in 1973, three litters totalling nine dogs and nine bitches in 1974, two bitches in 1976 and six dogs and two bitches in 1977. Altogether Export Pedigrees have been issued by the Kennel Club for nine Weimaraners from Britain, the earliest being in 1964 – Larry, litter-brother to Ch. Ragstone Remus.

Bermuda

Since the Bermuda Kennel Club set up its own registration records in 1968 only 23 Weimaraners have been registered with them; none was Bermuda-bred and only one was owned by a Bermuda resident – all the others were brought into the Island from the USA or Canada for show purposes only. Since 1956 11 Weimaraners have become Bermuda champions of record, nine have earned the CD title, one the CDx title and one the TD title. The only British export pedigree granted was to Hawsvale Pfennig in 1980.

Hong Kong

Hong Kong has a famous Weimaraner called 'Dewars' who, together with a yellow Labrador, is the pride and joy of the Customs and Excise

Service. In charge of the dog unit is Inspector Poon Yeung-kwong who was sent to the USA on a special course by his Government. He said it took 12 weeks to train 'Dewars' before returning to Hong Kong with him and that his job is to sniff out drugs such as opium, heroin, morphine, marijuana or hashish which he does with great success at various check-points including the post office, container terminals and at Kaitak Airport. The training in America was based on games to ensure the dogs enjoyed their work, and Inspector Poon says that both dogs really look forward to their daily assignments treating the whole affair as a game. He is confident that both dogs will contribute greatly in the effort to stamp out the illicit drug trade.

Six British Weimaraners have gone out to Hong Kong since 1972, two of which, Merryhell Hermes and Hawsvale Kay, bred by Commander and Mrs Val Hawes, both owned by Mr K. P. Ho Chui, have become Hong Kong champions.

Hungary

Magyar Ebtenyēsztōk Orszāgos Egyesülete has none of the breed registered which is perhaps somewhat surprising considering that one of the theories recently put forward is that the Weimaraner is of Hungarian origin, and also bearing in mind the geographical proximity of Austria and other Weimaraner-owning countries.

India

There are no registrations for the breed with the Indian Kennel Club, but since 1955 and up to 1968 three British Weimaraners have been granted export pedigrees. Possibly one of the earliest in India was in 1949 imported from the USA from the Teufelsposse strain by Wing Commander and Mrs Hindley who later had Wolfox Camelot from Mrs Barbara Douglas-Redding, England.

Italy

Ente Nazionale Della Cinofilia Italiana state that the first registration of the breed in their stud book was in 1952 and that from then until 1980 there have been 630 dogs registered. There was a Weimaraner Club but it no longer functions today. From Britain there have been 14 exports, the earliest being in 1958, Strawbridge Quelle. About 300 of the total registration figures were bred by Vito Lattuada of the Allevamento Delle Stoppie affix whose original stock came from Austria, England, Switzerland, Germany and the USA and who currently breeds both long and short-haired Weimaraners.

Malaysia

Three British export pedigrees were granted for Weimaraners sent to the Sultan of Johore in 1968.

Puerto Rico

There have been 31 Weimaraners registered in the 'Book of Origins' of the *Federácion Canofila de Puerto Rico*; the first was in 1968 and named 'Bebo de Puerto Rico' owned by Mrs Maria Gil. Apparently there was a Weimaraner Club at one time but it has ceased to exist.

Republica de Guinea Ecuatorial

Equatorial Guinea, formerly Spanish Guinea, a Republic on the west coast of central Africa, the capital of which is Rey Malabo, has no Weimaraners! But they do have something which so far no other country has, and that is a postage stamp depicting a Weimaraner. It is the highest denomination in a block of eight stamps ranging from a Collie worth one ekuele (100 centimos) to the top-ranking Weimaraner worth 100 ekueles.

Singapore

There are a handful of Weimaraners, the most notable of which until her return to Britain was Mrs Gwen Sowersby's Singapore Champion Hansom Bunny Girl of Westglade. A CC can be awarded to the highest placed specimen of a numerically small breed in a variety class; thus a fourth place behind three different breeds can still win a CC, and a total of three makes a Singapore Champion. Mrs Sowersby was very active in Singapore organising obedience classes for all breeds, where she and her bitch became very well-known for their excellent work. Mr Chee Eng Soon imported the dog Upton Fells von Berhad from New Zealand and has bred several litters with this dog as sire. During 1967 Waidman Jezebel owned by Mr and Mrs Chappell was handled by Corporal Byers to her Malayan Championship title.

Spain

Since 1967 there have been at least 11 exports from Britain to Spain, the first of which Senor F. de Elizabura's Monroes Waidman Gustave gained his championship title. The Dutch-born bandleader Johan Carlquist went to live in Spain for a while after the end of World War II, and whilst there, he imported from Germany the dog Alf von Forsthaus Dieberg and the bitch Nora vom Haimberg from which he bred litters under his von der Weberhof prefix. Unfortunately the Spanish Kennel Club *Real Sociedad Central de Fomento de las Razas Caninas en España* has no record of registrations for the breed and it is therefore impossible to give much in the way of breed details, although there must be quite a number of Weimaraners in the country. The British exports were: Monroes Waidman Gustave, Cannylad Olympus Ceres, Manana Mandygemma, Siegfried Tal, Monroes Solitaire, Ambersbury Baryton, King Silver, Adagio of Monroes, Oneva Thenute, Red Rocks Hidalgo and Hollieseast Angelica.

Switzerland

There are 10 Weimaraners registered with the *Schweizerischer Vorstehhund-Club* – the earliest registration date is not known. Just four British-bred Weimaraners have been granted export pedigrees, the first in 1962 to Derrybeg Ajax, and the last in 1976.

Trinidad and West Indies

Since 1961 seven British-bred Weimaraners have been sent out to the West Indies, one of the first being Mrs D. Shaw's Andelyb's Arwr who was worked in obedience competitions out there before returning to England. Two recent exports sent out by Commander and Mrs Hawes have become Caribbean champions – Hilltop Hawsvale Angostura owned by Ernest Melville, and Merryhell Decoy CDx owned by Maurice de Vertueil.

Zambia

The first listed export to Zambia from Britain was Monroes Otto (Sh. Ch. Monroes Nexus/Sh. Ch. Monroes Idyll). He went to Mr A. C. Fisher who owned the bitch Astrid von Weisses Wasser (Bunduki von

Haraska – not the Austrian prefix/Aura von Weissen Fluss). The pair were mated and the progeny the start of Mr Fisher's Kafue prefix. Ragstone Ritzun (Ch. Ragstone Ritter/Marta of Iken) was the next to leave Britain and he went to Mr and Mrs N. Evans, was made up to Zambia champion and mated to Kundalila Silvermost (Bullitt of Chiredzi/ZsaZsa of Kafue) establishing the Evans' Kundalila prefix; one of the progeny, the dog Kundalila Kinetisch Kosmos being made up to Zambia Champion. Mrs Jenny Miller who owned a dog in England before going out to Zambia soon found herself the owner of several Weimaraners. She bought two pups, one Zambian-bred and one South African-bred, then saw an advertisement in the Kitwe SPCA and bought two bitches which had been left for sale or disposal by the owners who had gone to Germany. To save the bitches from being shot, she bought both, one of which she kept and the other which went to Dar-Es-Salaam. The bitch retained was a two year old skeleton, Kafue Zoe, but nursed back to health she won four CCs in four shows and gained her Zambian championship title. Mrs Miller then imported from Britain Shiana Adamite (Ragstone Rupprecht/ Sidwell Wife of Bath) who also gained his Zambian title; Bredebeck Erica (Sh. Ch. Ragstone Rhion/Bredebeck Sophie); and Farthorn Sprite (Sh. Ch. Ragstone Rhion/Senta of Ragstone) who went on to South Africa with her new owners Mr and Mrs Johnson. Current details of the Weimaraner population in Zambia are not to hand, but there must by now be quite a number.

WEIMARANER CLUBS

The Weimaraner Club of Great Britain
Secretary: Mrs P. LeMon, 6 The Glebe, Cuxton, Rochester, Kent, England.

The Weimaraner Club of America
Box 473, Reynoldsburg, Ohio 43068–0473, USA.

Australia (For up to date addresses of the five clubs, contact the appropriate controlling bodies):

Weimaraner Club of Queensland, Canine Control Council, Exhibition Grounds, Fortitude Valley, Queensland 4006.

Weimaraner Club of New South Wales, RAS Kennel Control, PO Box 74, Paddington, New South Wales 2021.

Weimaraner Club of Victoria, Kennel Control Council, Royal Showgrounds, Epsom Road, Ascotvale, Victoria 3032.

Weimaraner Club of South Australia, South Australian Canine Association, Showgrounds, Wayville, South Australia 5034.

Weimaraner Club of Western Australia, Canine Association of Western Australia (Inc.), PO Box 196, Nedlands, Western Australia 6009.

Austria

Österr. Weimaraner-Verein, Anton Görgl, Jubiläumsstrasse 9, 3701 Grossweikersdorf.

Brazil

Depto. da Raça Weimaraner da SBCCC, Rua Alvaro Alvin 21/7°, CEP: 2003, Rio de Janeiro.

France

Cercle des Amateurs du Braque de Weimar. Secrétaire Général: M. Robert Rudloff, 75c rue de Villevaudé, 77270 – Villeparisis.

Germany

Weimaraner Klub eV, Dr Werner Petri, Konradin-Kreutzer-Strasse 15, 7500 Karlsruhe 21.

Holland

Vereniging 'De Weimarse Staande Hond', Mw C. Jurgen, Toupsbergstraat 103, Kerkrade.

New Zealand

The Weimaraner Club, PO Box 21198, Christchurch.

Scandinavia:

Denmark

Dansk Weimaraner Klub, Niels Jørgen Drost, Friheden 36, 4900 Nakskov.

Norway

Norsk Weimaranerklubb, Miss Eva Eriksen, Ulsrudveien 31, Oslo 6.

Sweden

Svenska Weimaranerklubben, Agneta Kilborn, Ängvaktarvägen 53, 694–00 Hallsberg.

South Africa

Weimaraner Klub of South Africa, Mrs Lilian Taylor, 11 Aster Street, Brackenhurst, 1450 Transvaal.

Appendix I

Federation Cynologique Internationale (FCI)
1976 Standard – Weimaraner – German Breed

Breed Characteristics

1 GENERAL APPEARANCE
A medium to biggish sized dog.
Height at the withers: Dogs 59 to 70 cm.
Bitches 57 to 65 cm.
The dog must show ability to work hard in the field, be graceful in appearance, sinewy and well muscled. The male and female sex must be clearly defined.

2 COLOUR
Silver, deer, or mouse grey as well as shades thereof. Head and ears mostly somewhat lighter. Small white markings are permissible only on the chest and toes. Along the spine often a darker 'eel' streak. Dogs showing a pronounced reddish-yellow tint can only be used for breeding under the condition that the dog shows above average ability and achievement in field trials. In this case permission by the Club is required. However, these dogs cannot obtain a higher mark for conformation other than 'Good'. A brown tint is disqualifying.

3 COAT
        (a) Ideal coat is short, smooth and sleek, sometimes slightly coarser, but short.
More rarely: (b) 'Stockhaarig'.
        (c) Long.
(a) Very short (but longer and denser than in most comparable breeds) and sleek cover without, or with very little, undercoat.
(b) Medium long, dense and straight cover, with dense undercoat. Moderately developed feathers and trousers.
(c) Soft and long cover, with or without undercoat. Smooth or wavy. Sometimes velvety on the ears, long and overhanging the roots of same. Length 3 to 5 cm on the back and flanks. Generally longer on the

180

underside of the neck, chest and belly. Good feathers and trousers, but shorter on the lower parts. Tail well feathered. Covering between the toes. Shorter on the head. (Coat is often only fully developed at the age of two years.)

4 HEAD
Moderately long and in proportion to body size. In dogs broader than in bitches. In both sexes between the ears in proportion to the length of the head. From nose to stop slightly longer than from stop to occipital bone. A median line extending backwards over the forehead, with slightly to medium prominent occiput. Behind the eyes well defined trumpets. Especially in the dog a long and strong jaw. From the profile almost square in appearance. The region between the incisors and the carnassial tooth about equally strong. Strong and complete dentition. Back of the muzzle straight – sometimes slightly arched but never dished. Very moderate stop. Flews moderately deep and pinkish coloured, same as the palate. Small mouth fold – cheeks muscular and well chiselled. 'Dry' head (skin tightly drawn).

5 EARS
Broad and rather long, should reach approximately the angle of the mouth; rounded at the tips; set high and narrow; folded; when attentive slightly turned forward.

6 NOSE
Dark flesh coloured changing into grey. Protruding over the lower jaw.

7 EYES
Amber coloured, from light to dark and of intelligent expression. Round but sometimes slightly almond shaped. Blue in puppies.

8 TEETH
Without fault and with strong, correct scissor-bite.

9 NECK
Clean cut and elegantly carried. Muscular and almost round; not too short. Becoming stronger towards the shoulders and flowing smoothly into the withers and chest. Neck should show no looseness or dewlap at the throat latch.

10 BODY
Well proportioned and muscled. Body length to height at withers approximately in the ratio 12 to 11.

11 CHEST
Strong, not too broad with sufficient depth and length, descending almost to the elbow. Ribs long and arched but not barrel shaped.

12 BACK
A slightly long back is a breed characteristic and NOT faulty provided it is not sagging and not overbuilt at the rear as well as otherwise strong and muscular.

13 TAIL
To be docked at one to two days of age by half in the case of the short-haired variety. In the case of the long-haired type two or three vertebrae should be removed. The root of the tail is set lower than in similar breeds which leads to the assumpton that it was originally carried hanging down.

14 SHOULDERS AND FRONT LEGS
Well angulated, long, set back and snugly fitting, joined with strong muscles. In general 'high' and standing not too far apart, sinewy and strong. From the elbow to the toes approximately equalling the distance from the elbow to the top of the withers. Elbows not turned in or out but lying free and straight. Forelegs to stand well up to the middle of the chest, and parallel.

15 HINDQUARTERS
Long from the hip to the hock. Hip, knee and hock joints well angulated – i.e. thigh shorter than stifle. Hindquarters parallel to each other, neither turned in nor out.

16 FEET AND PADS
Closed and strong. No dew claw on hind foot. Standing straight to the middle of the body. Toes knuckled up; longer middle toe not faulty. Nails light to dark grey. Tough pads touching the ground squarely.

17 MOVEMENT
Forelegs to hindquarters clearly parallel. Back to remain level when trotting. Pacing is to be considered faulty.

18 Testicles of equal size, descended and fully developed in the dog. Bitch to have five pairs of nipples exactly opposite each other.

Faults:

A. DISQUALIFYING FAULTS
Colour other than shades of grey. Brown tint on coat.

Eyes other than amber; eyes too slanted; entropian or ectropian.
Head not typical; stop too pronounced; dished muzzle; pink nose.
Monorchid or cryptorchid dogs; both testicles not visible.
Excessive white chest blaze or white feet.
Undersize; oversize; barrel ribs; weak in bone; straight in stifle; swaybacked.
Hip Dysplasia.
Insufficient hair cover.
Weak character, especially dogs who are shy or show fear.
Serious teeth faults, especially overshot or undershot.
Excessive dewlaps, throat and forechest skin (Bloodhound-type).

B. SERIOUS FAULTS
Lack of more than two premolars.
Poor gait; lack of front or hind driving action; pacing.
Open toes; pad position not squarely on ground; dewclaws on hind feet.
Insufficient angulation – front or rear.
Poor ankle joints or hocks.
Pronounced sagging or roached back; too strongly overbuilt.
Muzzle too short or snipey.
Flews too pronounced; dewlaps.
Ears too short or extremely long.
Doggy bitches or bitchy dogs.
Insufficient depth and length of chest.
Tail too highly placed; broken tail (if not by accident).
Reddish-yellow tint over complete coat.
Bald patches, especially on stomach and ears.
Staring hair and lack of undercoat in 'Stockhaarig' variety.
Testicles too small or unmatched in size.
A little haw showing.

C. FAULTS
Muscles insufficiently developed.
Slight loss of hair on chest or ears.
Nose slightly too short or snipey; nose slightly pink.
Deficient in teeth; level bite instead of scissor bite.
Bowed front legs; cow-hocked.
Back somewhat sagging or roached or overbuilt.
Elbows turned in or out; too straight or loose in shoulders.
Reddish-yellow 'Bloodhound' markings.
Action too short-striding.
Underdeveloped withers; shallow ribcage; back too long.
Eyes a little slanted.
Front legs standing 'east-west'.

183

Tail not raised when excited; too short in the long-haired variety.
Curls in the long-haired variety.
Testicles a little too small.

D. MINOR FAULTS
Tail too short or too long.
Chest and eyebrows slightly yellow.
Spots on nose (loss of pigment).
Neck a little too short.
Back a little too long or swaybacked.
Ribs a little too shallow.
Slight lack of hind angulation.
Feet a little 'east-west', or a little too open.
Slight lack of driving action.
Incorrect number of nipples, or not located in opposite pairs.

Appendix II

Translations of German Documents and Terms

The following is a rough translation of the essential VJP and HZP Trials:

VJP (YOUTH TRIAL)

ORGANISING CLUB:
NAME OF TRIAL:
PLACE OF TRIAL: DATE OF TRIAL:
NAME OF OWNERS:

NAME OF DOG: BREED:
DATE OF BIRTH: REGISTERED No.:

DAM: REGISTERED No.:
SIRE: REGISTERED No.:

Excellent = 12 points   Very Good = 11–9 points   Good = 8–6 points
Sufficient = 5–3 points Poor = 2–1 points   Unsatisfactory = 0 points
FwZ = Multiplication factor

	Working points	× FwZ	Total points
1. Tracking (hare)		2	
2. Nose		2	
3. Search		1	
4. Point		1	
5. Rapport between dog/handler during Trial		1	

Total points:

Method of hunting:	Bark on sight	Bark on trail	No opportunity to give tongue ....
	Silent hunter	Persistent barking or whining during Trial	

Strength on shot:	Steady to shot	Slightly sensitive to shot	Sensitive to shot ....
	Very sensitive to shot	Gun-shy	

Behaviour:	Shyness or nervousness not established	Shy	Easily frightened ....
	Nervous	Hand-shy	Shy of live or wild game ....
	Nervous attitude to strangers (cringing)	Other shortcomings	

185

Teeth:	No faults	Overshot	Undershot ....
	Pincer bite	Crossed teeth	Missing Premolars ....
	Missing Molars	Other missing teeth	
Eyes:	No faults	Entropian	Ectropian ....
Extreme lack of physical body		Testicles missing	

Points:

No marks – completely wrong – such to be eliminated (from breeding, etc.)

The HZP requirements are basically the same as the VJP insofar as method of hunting, gun steadiness, behaviour, teeth and eyes, etc. are concerned, but obviously a higher quality of work is expected of the older, more experienced dogs and scoring is from 11 sections as follows:

	Working points	× FwZ	Total points
1. Tracking (hare)		3	
2. Nose		3	
3. Search		2	
4. Point		2	
5. Rapport between dog/handler during Trial		2	
6. Waterwork			
(a) Hunt in water after duck, using nose, not eyes		3	
(b) Search and retrieve from deep, reedy water		1	
7. Retrieve feathered game		1	
(a) Find shot pheasant, or		1	
(b) Retrieve shot pheasant, or		1	
(c) Trail wounded pheasant		1	
8. Trail hare or rabbit		1	
9. Retrieving style			
(a) Hare or rabbit Points			
(b) Duck Points		1	
(c) Partridge or pheasant Points			
10. Obedience		1	
11. Enthusiasm for work		1	

Total Trial score:

Extra points awarded
if hares are available
on trial

186

Translation of some words to be found on German or Austrian pedigrees

Rude	male	*Leistungbuch*	Field Trial
Hundin	female		Register
Wurf	litter	*Leistungprüfung*	Field Trial
Welpe	whelp – young	*Zur Spur*	Trial
	puppy	*Wasserhundprüfung*	Water Dog Trial
Eltern	parents	*Guter Wasserhund*	Good, very good,
Grosseltern	grandparents	*(W, WW, WWW)*	excellent in water
Urgrosseltern	great-grandparents	*Mannscharf (ms)*	man sharp
Geschlecht	sex	*Raubzeugscharf (rs)*	vermin sharp
gedeckt	date of mating	*Raubzeugschleppe*	Trail of blood-
Wurf Tag (W.T.)	date whelped		thirsty vermin –
Züchter (Z)	breeder		i.e. cat, fox or
Besitzer (B)	owner		polecat
Amme (A)	foster mother	*Schaerfe-nachweis*	Proof of viciousness
Vater (V)	sire (father)	*Schweiss Schleppe*	Blood trail
Mutter (M)	dam (mother)	*Verlorenbringer*	Tracker/retriever
S.Z.	Stud Book	*(Vbr)*	(e.g. on hare
Farbe	colour		at Trials)
sgr – sg	silver-grey	*Bringtreue bewiesen*	natural retriever
mgr – mg	mouse-grey	*(Btr)*	(e.g. retrieve dead
rgr – rg	roe-grey		fox from wood
Angekoert	recommended for		about 150 m
	breeding		from handler)
Haarart	coat (hair)	*Stumm (st)*	silent hunter
Drahthaar	wire-haired	*Sichtlaut*	gives tongue on
Kurzhaar	short-haired	*(sil/slt)*	sight of quarry
Langhaar	long-haired	*Spurlaut (spurl)*	Gives tongue on
Abzeichen	markings		trail
Paar	pair (brace)	*Totverbeller*	Barks at discovery
Zucht Prüfung	Inspected and	*(totverb.)*	of dead game
(Z.Pr.)	passed suitable	*Totverweiser*	Points dead
	for breeding	*(totverw.)*	game
Zuchtwertnachweis	Evaluation of a	*Scharf, Sehr scharf,*	Sharp, Very sharp,
	dog's eligibility	*Rabiat scharf*	Extremely
	for breeding	*(s, ss, sss)*	sharp
Leistung	field training	*Sehr gut, Vorzüglich*	Very good,
Leistungssieger/n	Field Trial	*(auf Ausstellung),*	Excellent in
	Champion of	*(Sg, V)*	Show
	the year	*Zeichenklarung*	Test markings

Jugendbester (J.B.)			Best in Youth Class
J1, J2, J3 = 1st, 2nd, 3rd pr.			1st, 2nd, 3rd prize, Youth Test
Jugendprüfung (VJP)			
H1, H2, H3	=	*1st, 2nd, 3rd pr.*	1st, 2nd, 3rd prize, Autumn
HZ1, HZ2, HZ3	=	*Herbst-Züchtprüfung*	Breeding Test
HZS1, HZS2, HZS3 =		*(HZP)*	
+H1, +H2, +H3 = AZP nach Klubregel			Special trials for dogs too old
			for VJP and HZP Trials

187

G1, G2, G3 = 1st, 2nd, 3rd pr. Gebrauchsprüfung (VGP)	1st, 2nd, 3rd prize, All-round Test
FS1, FS2, FS3 = 1st, 2nd, 3rd pr. Fruhjahrssuche	1st, 2nd, 3rd prize, Spring Test
FZS1, FZS2, FZS3 = 1st, 2nd, 3rd pr. Fruhjahrszuchtsuche	1st, 2nd, 3rd prize, Spring Breeding Test
FJS1, FJS2, FJS3 = 1st, 2nd, 3rd pr. Feldjagdsuche	1st, 2nd, 3rd prize, Field Trial
EFJS1, EFJS2, EFJS3 = 1st, 2nd, 3rd pr. Erweiterte Feldjagdsuche	1st, 2nd, 3rd prize, Advanced Field Trial
VGP1, VGP2, VGP3 = 1st, 2nd, 3rd pr. Vollgebrachsprüfung	1st, 2nd, 3rd prize, Club Utility Dog Trial
S. Pr. Nr. = Scharfeprüfung im OLBJ Vorgemerkt	Kill cat during hunt; not essential for breeding recommendation
4h	Outstanding in hunting test
1a	First quality
V.A.	Select Class
V. Vorzüglich im Formwert	Excellent (conformation)
S.G. = Sehr gut	Very Good
G. = Gut	Good
Gen. = Genügend	Satisfactory
A = Ausreihend	Satisfactory
M. = Mangelhaft	Faulty
O. = Zero	Failed
Sr., Sgrn. = Sieger, Siegerin	Champion dog, bitch
J. Kl. = Jugend Klasse	Youth Class – 12–18 months
JH. Kl. = Junghund Klasse	Young dog Class – 18–24 months
GH. Kl. = Gebrauchshund Klasse	Dogs with SchH I, II, III, training degrees over two years of age
A. Kl. = Alters Klasse	Dogs over two years of age with no training degrees
Schw. Pr. = Schweisspr, nach LJV	Blood trial for Club members
VSwP = Verbandsschweissprüfung	Blood trial for all gundogs
CACIB (FCI) = Schönheitschampionat	International Bench (beauty) Championship
CACIT (FCI) = Arbeitschampionat	Working (F/T) Championship
SchH I, II, III = Schutzhund	Degrees in guard dog tests

Appendix III

The British Affixes

Once the *Strawbridge*, *Ipley* and *Monksway* litters went into circulation, other now well-known affixes began to emerge. Now, some 30 years later, it is not uncommon to have present-day owners ask for information on a particular affix which appeared frequently in the early days, but which may have virtually died out now. Some of those first breeders are still producing stock, but they are few and far between. A run-down on some of the affixes and the foundation bitches may prove interesting. It is not feasible to include *all* the hundreds of affixes used over the years and there is certainly no intention of slighting anybody by omissions! Apology is made for the poor quality of some of the photographs in this section, but obviously they had been packed away in boxes and forgotten for years and we must consider ourselves very fortunate to be able to glean a small idea of what these important bitches were like.

AFFIX	OWNER/S	FOUNDATION BITCH
Strawbridge	Major & Mrs R. Petty	Cobra von Boberstrand, Hella aus der Helmeute, Vita von der Haraska (see Chapter 4).
Monksway	Major Eric Richardson	Anka vom Suntel (see Chapter 4).
Ipley	Mrs Olga Malet	Babette von der Katzbach (see Chapter 4). This prefix was named after Ipley Manor in the Southampton area. Mrs Malet returned to Canada.
Deerswood	Mrs B. M. Davis	Strawbridge Elfrida had five litters by Strawbridge Fury, many of which helped to found the breed in Ireland.
Sandrock	Mr & Mrs L. F. Causeley	Strawbridge Carol had four litters among which was the well-known Sandrock Admiral owned by Dr Alex Mucklow. Carol was shown most successfully; was best of breed at Crufts in 1955 and won one CC in 1962. Some pedigrees name this bitch as Coral which was the original name applied for by the Pettys, but due to a Kennel Club error, she became Carol.

189

Cobra v Boberstrand, by Casar v d Finne ex Alma v Boberstrand.
Sandrock Coral, by Smokey ex Strawbridge Carol.

Lochsloy	Dr W. MacFarlane	Strawbridge Erica will be found mainly in Scottish-originated pedigrees.
Goosefame	Mrs P. M. Wooltorton	Strawbridge Cobra.
Manana	Mrs F. M. Maddocks	Strawbridge Ermegard was no great beauty but from one of her four litters in Devon came that great brood bitch Manana Athene who was the foundation bitch for both the Wolfox and Monroes affixes. Litter-brother to Athene was Manana Adonis whose mating to his daughter Sandrock Blaze produced the Manana B litter, several of which feature in many pedigrees – Bracken, Beguine and Brenda.
Skyrose	Mrs F. Bainbridge	Skyrose Typhoon was the first bitch to have a litter for Mrs Bainbridge who had unsuccessfully tried to breed from two earlier bitches. The Skyrose affix can be found in pedigrees featuring Strawbridge Vespa who had three litters. The best known bitch owned by this lady was Sh. Ch. Strawbridge Czarina who came to her as an adult.
Wolfox	Mrs B. Douglas-Redding	Manana Athene had one litter for this affix and produced two show champions, Wolfox Silverglance and Ace of Acomb. The Wolfox affix was already established in Corgis and German Shepherds and many top winners in Weimaraners came from here, including five UK show champions.
Kingsholt	Mr A. Heyman	Ipley Bodicea.
Kentrish	Major E. K. Rawson-Gardiner	Deerswood Quicksilver.
Whitsands	Mr H. Blake	Gerda of Goosefame.
Monroes	Mrs J. Matuszewska	Manana Athene produced another great dog after coming into this ownership; Sh. Ch. Monroes Dynamic had a very good influence on the breed. The name Monroes came into being from the name of the place in the USA (Monroe) to which Mrs Matuszewska exported her first dog, a German Shepherd. More champions carry the Monroes affix than any other to date; nine in the UK and many more abroad.

Cartford	Mrs A. McNutt	Strawbridge Jane had four litters from which Miss Monkhouse's Sh. Ch. Cabaret Cartford Platinum and Miss Price's Cartford Capricorn CDx both came. This affix was also well-known in Poodles.
Theocsbury	Mr and Mrs G. V. Webb	The Anglo-Saxon name for Tewkesbury was the choice of affix for the Webbs who owned the famous Ch. Strawbridge Oliver. Their first bitch was Sandrock Bella, dam of three litters, including the litter-mates Ch. Theocsbury Abbie and Sh. Ch. Theocsbury Archduke.
Cabaret	Miss R. Monkhouse	One of the first club members, Miss Monkhouse's affix was already well established in Dalmatians. The first bitch to whelp in her ownership was Ivyleaf Storm Witch closely followed by Sh. Ch. Cabaret Cartford Platinum.
Andelyb's	Mr & Mrs J. I. Farquhar	Manana Brenda dam of Ch. Andelyb's Balch.
Barrowdown	Mrs J. Henderson-Hamilton	Tassilo of Whitsands.
Englas	Mr H. Gammon	Strawbridge Madam
Baynard	Mr & Mrs M. G. Simmons	Wolfox Moonsdale Whisper had two litters, was campaigned to her title, was an exceptionally good worker and died at the age of 13 years (see Appendix VII, no. 15).
Derrybeg	Lt Col W. N. S. Donaldson	Inka vom Weissen Kreuz (see Chapter 4).
Hengistholm	Mrs P. M. Wilkinson	Theocsbury Briony.
Halsall	Mrs K. E. Sharman	Sandrock Coral. This affix is also well-known in Old English Sheepdogs. Australian Ch. Halsall Brown Pheasant is to be found in very many Australian pedigrees (see photograph in Australian Chapter).
Sylhill	Mrs S. M. Roberts	Theocsbury Abbie, full champion (see Appendix VII, no. 5).
Waidman	Mrs L. Petrie-Hay	Theocsbury Elsa. This affix is also prominent in German Short-haired Pointers and Hungarian Vizslas. Mrs Petrie-Hay is a field trial judge of the hunt-point-retrieve breeds.
Hepton	Mr J. S. Taylor	Cartford Silver Sand. This affix is also to be found in English Setters.

Gerry Webb with Strawbridge Quiz (Sandrock Ami/Ipley Babette) and Ch. Strawbridge Oliver (Ipley Apollo/Cobra v Boberstrand).

Tottens	Mrs E. R. Kent	Wolfox Andelyb's Awen.
Abingdon	Mr G. C. Hancock	Sylhill Thistle
Arlebroc	Mr E. B. Virgo	Theocsbury Handy Pet. Arlebroc is the Anglo-Saxon name for Aldermarsh which is the area in Worcestershire where the Virgos live.
Ragstone	Mr & Mrs A. Burgoin	The dog, Ch. Ragstone Remus was the cornerstone of this well-known kennel and every pedigree showing Ragstone-affixed Weimaraners will have Remus in it somewhere. As the result of a refused stud enquiry Ragstone Rasheba became the first bitch to own this affix. A pathetically emaciated creature rescued from an unsuitable home, she developed into an extrovert, bread-thief, and unsurpassed lover of puppies.
Greyfilk	Mrs J. Fussell	Requested Greysilk as an affix, but the Kennel Club erroneously granted Greyfilk. Another from the Manana kennels, Manana Donna's Maxine was not a show bitch herself, but produced two super bitches in her first litter. One was Sapphire, the first in a long line of home-bred show champions of excellent colour.
Penates	Mr C. J. H. Takle	Manana Misty Lavinia.
Bilbrook	Mr J. H. Berger	Theocsbury Handy Lass.
Watchant	Mr E. H. Marchant	Lady Minora.
Padneyhill	Mrs M. Goodwin & Mrs V. Webb	Andelyb's Buddugol. Affix also to be found in Whippets and Greyhounds.
Schoenfeldt	Miss B. Schofield	Wolfox Aleeda.
Merse-Side	Mr A. C. Thirlwell	Mist of Merse-Side who produced the famous Sh. Ch. Ballina of Merse-Side for Mrs E. Hackett.
Iken	Mr P. Cutting	Natasha of Abingdon.
Sidwell	Dr M. E. C. Mitchell	Manana Mandy's Quip.
Innisron	Mrs R. Townsend & Miss J. Linz	Bilbrook Brunhilde of Innisron.
Brundholme	Mrs M. Richmond	Minka of Brundholme who was out of Strawbridge Bracken. Brundholme was the name of Mrs Richmond's sister-in-law's house in Keswick and an affix also to be found in Cocker Spaniels.

194

Cannylad	Mr J. G. Lamb	Bimbo of Merse-Side produced two show champions from her first litter: Daedalus and Artemis.
Acombdole	Dr A. W. Mucklow	Dr Mucklow's preference was for dogs and she owned Sandrock Admiral and Sh. Ch. Ace of Acomb before obtaining her first breeding bitch from Mrs Johnson. This was Coninvale Greta of Acombdole, litter-sister to Sh. Ch. Paul. Previously Dr Mucklow had Drake's Bride but did not breed from her.
Dangvord	Mr R. A. F. Ford	Innisron Morgan's Mimic.
Selmore	Mrs B. M. Stephan	Manana Mandy's Yvonne.
Abbeystag	Mr & Mrs A. J. Gray	Waidman Jemima. Affix also in Vizslas.
Gunmetal	Mrs D. Oldershaw	Waidman Giselle won two CCs and a Field Trial Certificate of Merit. Her first litter was docked, but thereafter Mrs Oldershaw refrained from docking puppies and was at the centre of great controversy in the breed. Some puppies were wittily named – Cause Celebre, Laissez Faire, Nonconformist and Ultravires.
Shinglehill	Dr G. E. Nicholls	Watchant Willow.
Heronshaw	Mrs D. Chapman	Monroes Nadine (see Appendix VII, no. 32).
Ambersbury	Mrs M. Wardall	Marta of Iken had three litters. The affix comes from Ambersbury Banks in Epping Forest where Queen Bodicea had her camp, and later (!) whence both Mr & Mrs Wardall originated.
Kympenna's	Mr & Mrs S. Worthing-Davies	Flottheim's Kym (see Chapter 4).
Tarset	Mrs E. Hackett	Astra of Merse-Side, winner of two CCs had one all male litter. Ballina was unable to have puppies; later on Devorgilla was bred from. Tarset is in Northumberland where Mrs Hackett once lived.
Grinshill	Mrs J. Atkinson	Shinglehill Briony had five litters and was one of the first bitches to be cleared through the KC/BVA scheme for Hip Dysplasia.
Boxbury	Mrs J. M. Ralphs	Manana Dorafanta
Willingstone	Mr & Mrs W. Pellant	Gunmetal Gamefinder.

Oneva	Mr & Mrs H. J. T. Bright	Acombdole Athene. One Victoria Avenue was their address – hence the affix which is now to be found in Wire-haired Dachshunds.
Bredebeck	Mrs E. G. Hardman	Manana Dorafila. Bredebeck was the German town where the Hardmans met during the Second World War. Mr Hardman is now a field trial judge for the hunt-point-retrieve breeds.
Hawsvale	Cmdr V. B. Hawes	Monroes Repartee of Hawsvale had five litters. Her offspring are widely scattered throughout the world through Cmdr Hawes' exports.
Merryhell	Mrs B. Hawes	Monroes Quicksilver had five litters, won one CC and lived to a ripe old age, winning nearly all the Club's veteran classes.
Phayreheidi	Mrs P. A. C. Veasey	Manana Donna's Swift had one litter. This affix is derived from Mrs Veasey's maiden name of Phayre plus the bitch's pet name, Heidi.
Hansom	Mr R. M. W. Finch	Originally a Dalmatian breeder, his first Weimaraner came from the Roberts'

Monroes Waidman Jane, by Monroes Invader ex Ch. Andelyb's Balch.

196

Cannylad Lady Hamilton of Fleetapple, by Monroes Nomad ex Bimbo of Merse-Side

		Hansom Sylhill Odette (see Appendix VII, no. 23) and started a line of home-bred show champion bitches.
Hurstlem	Mr & Mrs F. W. LeMon	Hurstlem Selmore Penelope. Hurst was the maiden name of Mrs LeMon, hence the affix.
Athelson's	Mrs J. J. P. Kettle	Queenscoombe Countess.
Rangatira	Mr & Mrs C. M. Brown	Grinshill Phazachalie Jane.
Trafalgar	Dr R. Rogerson	Baynard Silver Cutie.
Aruni	Mrs A. Janson	Monroes Waidman Jane had two litters whilst in Mrs Janson's ownership. Affix is an amalgamation of Ann, Roy and Uni (wife, husband, dog).
Aruni from *Seicer*	Mrs A. Janson	Asta von Gut Blaustauden (see Chapter 4). Seicer is added to all Mrs Janson's long-haired stock.
Castle Garnstone	Mrs O'Keeffe, the former Mrs V. J. Sutton	Grinshill Helga Barnes.
Houblon	Mr & Mrs R. Tranter	Ambersbury Magdelana won one CC.
Helber	Mrs H. M. Carrington-Rice	Athelson's Sophia.
Midwil	Mrs C. M. Haden	Monroes Rosalka.
Fleetapple	Mrs. D. Arrowsmith	Named after a famous show horse, this affix first attached to Cannylad Lady Hamilton who had four litters.

Flimmoric	Mrs C. Alston	Gifford's Lady campaigned to her full title (see Appendix VII, no. 42).
Clackhill	Mr J. R. Holmes	Clackhill Jade.
Ortega	Mr & Mrs G. L. Bain	Opal Solitaire of Ortega.
Hofstetter	Mrs J. Wright	Chawtel of Kenstaff.
Shalina	Mrs C. M. Cutting	Monroes Unity.
Fossana	Mrs S. Fossey	Erika of Trafalgar, dam of Ch. Fossana Bruno and many other good working dogs.
Denmo	Mrs D. Mosey	Aisling Tuathach (see Appendix VII, no. 58). This affix has been very well to the fore in recent years, producing a string of show champions from Hansom Hirondelle.
Kisdon's	Mr & Mrs N. Edminson	Petraqua Wagtail (see Appendix VII, no. 52) campaigned to her full title, bred three show champions in her first litter.

APPENDIX IV

British Breed Registrations and Breed Standard

BREED REGISTRATIONS

Note: Kennel Club records run from 1 April to 31 March annually.

Year	Annual Registrations	Total Registrations
1953	34	34
1954	39	73
1955	20	93
1956	48	141
1957	64	205
1958	42	247
1959	25	272
1960	70	342
1961	110	452
1962	139	591
1963	97	688
1964	127	815
1965	142	957
1966	127	1084
1967	106	1190
1968	177	1367
1969	187	1554
1970	211	1765
1971	213	1978
1972	330	2308
1973	456	2764
1974	327	3091
1975	331	3422
1976	199	3621
1977	113	3734
1978	348	4082
1979	579	4661
1980	705	5366
1981	671	6037
1982	735	6765
1983 *	323	7088

* Six months.

BREED STANDARD – 1971 (with 1976 additions in italics)

CHARACTERISTICS

In the case of the Weimaraner his hunting ability is the paramount concern and any fault of body or mind which detracts from this ability should be penalised. The dog should display a temperament that is fearless, friendly, protective and obedient.

GENERAL APPEARANCE

A medium-sized grey dog with light eyes, he should present a picture of great driving power, stamina, alertness and balance. Above all, the dog should indicate ability to work hard in the field. Movement should be effortless and ground-covering and should indicate smooth co-ordination. When seen from the rear, the hind feet should parallel the front feet. When seen from the side, the top line should remain strong and level.

HEAD AND SKULL

Moderately long and aristocratic, with moderate stop and slight median line extending back over the forehead. Rather prominent occipital bone and ears set well back. Measurement from the top of the nose to stop to equal that from the stop to the occipital prominence. The flews should be moderately deep, enclosing a powerful jaw. Foreface perfectly straight, delicate at the nostrils. Skin tightly drawn. Neck clean cut and moderately long. Expression keen, kind and intelligent.

EARS

Long and lobular, slightly folded and set high. The ear when drawn alongside the jaw should end approximately one inch from the point of the nose.

EYES

Medium-sized in shades of amber or blue-grey, not protruding or too deeply set, placed far enough apart to indicate good disposition and intelligence. When dilated under excitement the eyes may appear almost black.

MOUTH

Well-set, strong and even teeth, well developed and proportionate to jaw with correct scissor bite (the upper teeth protruding slightly over the lower teeth). Complete dentition is greatly desired. Grey nose, lips and gums of pinkish flesh shade.

FOREQUARTERS
Forelegs straight and strong, with measurement from elbow to ground equalling the distance from the elbow to the top of the withers.

BODY
The length of the body from the highest point of the withers to the root of the tail should equal the measurement from the highest point of the withers to the ground. The top line should be level with a slightly sloping croup. The chest should be well developed and deep, shoulders well laid and snug. Ribs well sprung and long. Abdomen firmly held, moderately tucked up flank. The brisket should drop to the elbow.

HINDQUARTERS
Moderately angulated with well turned stifle. The hock joint well let down and turned neither in nor out. Musculation well developed.

FEET
Firm and compact. Toes well arched, pads closed and thick. Nails short and grey or amber in colour. Dewclaws allowable only on imported dogs.

TAIL
Docked, at a point such that the tail remaining shall just cover the scrotum in dogs and the vulva in bitches. The thickness of the tail should be in proportion to the body and it should be carried in a manner expressing confidence and sound temperament. *In the long-haired Weimaraner the tip of the tail should be removed.*

COAT
Short, smooth and sleek. *In the long-haired Weimaraner the coat should be from one to two inches long on the body and somewhat longer on the neck, chest and belly. The tail and the backs of the limbs should be feathered.* should be feathered.

COLOUR
Preferably silver grey, shades of mouse or roe grey are admissible. The colour usually blends to a lighter shade on head and ears. A dark eel

stripe frequently occurs along the back. The whole coat gives an appearance of metallic sheen. Small white mark allowable on the chest but not on any other part of the body. White spots that have resulted from injuries shall not be penalised. *Colour of the long-haired Weimaraner as the short-haired.*

SIZE

Height at withers: Dogs 24–27 inches, *61–69 cm*; Bitches 22–25 inches, *56–64 cm*.

FAULTS

Shyness or viciousness. Any colour or markings other than specified in this Standard.

Male animals should have two apparently normal testicles fully descended into the scrotum.

BREED STANDARD DIFFERENCES

There are basically three breed standards to be found. One is the British which is also accepted in Australia, New Zealand and South Africa; the second is the American which also covers Canada and Latin America; the third is the standard issued by the FCI which covers the Continental countries, Scandinavia, etc. and, of course, the breed's parent country, Germany.

There are a few differences to be found between these three standards which are important to remember, especially when judging abroad, or when exporting stock to, or importing stock from, different countries. Basically, the make and shape of the Weimaraner is universal among the 100,000 in circulation, but more emphasis is put on various points in different countries.

		BRITISH (1976)	AMERICAN (1972)	FCI (1976)
HEIGHT	Dogs:	61–69 cm, 24–27 inches	25–27 inches	59–70 cm
	Bitches:	56–64 cm, 22–25 inches	23–25 inches 1 inch over or under permitted; more than 1 inch over or under to be disqualified.	57–65 cm

The mouth

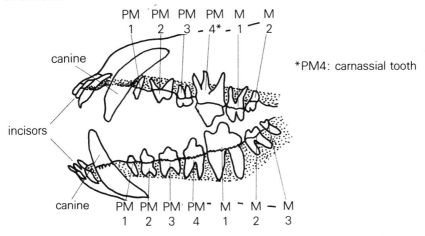

*PM4: carnassial tooth

Complete adult dentition comprises
> 3 Incisors, 1 Canine, 4 Premolars, 2 Molars, top,
> 3 Incisors, 1 Canine, 4 Premolars, 3 Molars, bottom.

> Total 20, top + 22 bottom = 42.

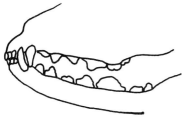

(a) Scissor bite – correct.

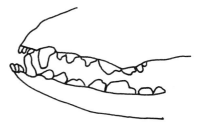

(b) Undershot – incorrect.

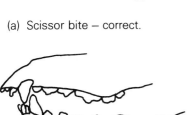

(c) Overshot: extreme case showing position of canine teeth reversed – incorrect.

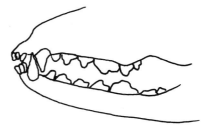

(d) Pincer or level bite – incorrect.

The feet

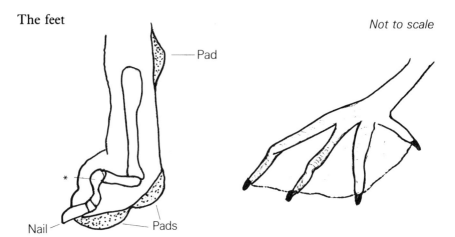

Simplified structure of a single toe showing the well knuckled-up 'cat foot'. In a 'hare foot' the angle * is often non-existent.

This cormorant's foot shows clearly a truly webbed foot.

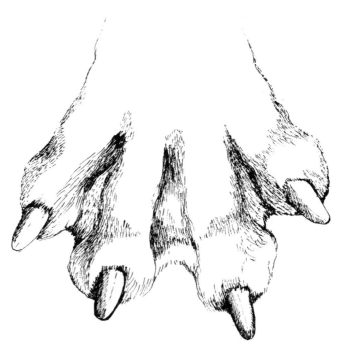

Weimaraner's foot spread out to show the typical slight webbing, common to many breeds.

204

COLOUR	Silver, mouse, roe-grey. White chest spot allowed.	Silver to mouse-grey. White chest spot allowed. Blue or black to be disqualified.	Silver, deer, mouse-grey. White chest spot allowed also white on toes. Brown tint disqualifies as does any shade other than grey, or excessive white on chest or feet.
COAT	Short, smooth and sleek or long-haired.	Short, smooth and sleek. Long coat is to be disqualified.	Short, smooth and sleek, or long-haired, or 'stock-haarig'
EARS	1 inch from end of nose when drawn along jaw.	2 inches from end of nose when drawn along jaw.	Should reach the angle of the mouth.
TEETH	Scissor-bite. Complete dentition greatly desired.	Scissor-bite. Complete dentition desired. It is a major fault to have more than four teeth missing.	Scissor-bite. Faultless. Serious faults especially overshot or undershot to be disqualified.
FEET	Firm, compact, toes well arched, pads closed and thick.	Firm, compact, webbed, toes well arched, pads closed and thick.	Closed and strong, well knuckled, longer middle toe not faulty. Tough pads.
TAIL	Docked at a point to cover scrotum in dog and vulva in bitch when adult; long-hairs docked of the tip.	Docked to be 6 inches in adults. Non-docked tail very serious fault.	Docked at 1 or 2 days by half in short-hairs; by 2 or 3 vertebrae in long-hairs.
TESTICLES	Fully descended in scrotum in male animals.	No mention	To be of even size, descended and fully developed in the dog. Bitches to have 5 pairs of nipples. Monorchid or cryptorchid dogs to be disqualified.
BODY	Length equal height to withers. Level back, sloping from croup.	Back moderate in length, sloping from withers.	Length to height at withers to approximate 12:11. Slightly long back not faulty.

British Field Trial Regulations and Award Winners*

Extracts from Kennel Club Field Trial Regulations, R (1), 10.8.82

9. *The Title of Field Trial Champion*   The following dogs shall be entitled to be described as Field Trial Champions: BREEDS WHICH HUNT, POINT AND RETRIEVE.

A dog which wins two first prizes at two different Field Trials in Open Stakes in which there are no fewer than eight runners. One of the above wins must be in a stake open to all breeds which hunt, point and retrieve.

Show Gundog Working Certificates   A Gundog which has won one or more Challenge Certificates at Shows may be entered for a Show Gundog Working Certificate at a Field Trial Meeting for its breed provided that:

4. For breeds which hunt, point and retrieve, that one of the Judges awarding the Show Gundog Working Certificate is on the official Judges Panel 'A' for these breeds.

5. (b) A dog may not run for a Show Gundog Working Certificate more than three times in all and not more than twice in any one Field Trial season.

   (c) All dogs entered for Show Gundog Working Certificates must be tested during the morning.

   (d) The granting of Show Gundog Working Certificates shall be at the discretion of the Judges at the meeting and all Judges must sign the Certificate.

   (e) Before signing a Certificate the Judges must be satisfied that the dog fulfills the following requirements:

      (1) that the dog has been tested in the line;

      (2) that the dog has shown that it is not gun-shy, and was off the lead during gunfire;

      (4) that it hunts, points and retrieves tenderly and enters water and swims;

      (7) steadiness is not absolutely essential for a Show Gundog Working Certificate.

* Reprinted by kind permission of the Kennel Club.

6. A Gundog which has won one or more first prizes in a Class for its breed at a Show where Challenge Certificates are offered for the breed, may be entered for a Show Gundog Working Certificate at a Specialist Club Show Gundog Field Trial provided that Judge or Judges of the Trial are on Panel 'A' for the breed and subject to Regulations 5(d) and (c) above.

Field Trial Regulations for
Breeds Which Hunt, Point and Retrieve

1. Dogs shall be run singly under two judges.

2. Dogs shall be required to quarter ground in search of game, to point game, to be steady to flush, shot and fall, and to retrieve on command.

3. *Water Retrieve*   Dogs shall be required (i) in Puppy, Novice and Non-Winner stakes to retrieve from or across water a seen bird which has been thrown and shot at whilst in the air; (ii) in all other stakes to make a blind retrieve of a bird from across water, re-entering the water, where practicable, with the bird and with no shot fired.

4. Dogs must not wear any form of collar when under the orders of the judges. All dogs must be kept on a lead when not competing.

5. Any dog which in the opinion of the judges fails to hunt, point, retrieve tenderly, complete the water test, is gun-shy, or is out of control shall not receive any prize. Any dog in any stake must have been tried at least twice in the line, excluding the water retrieve, before receiving a prize.

6. *Eliminations*   Whining or barking, out of control, chasing; failure to hunt, point, retrieve, enter water and swim, face cover; hard mouth; deliberately catching unwounded game.

Kennel Club Guide to Field Trial Judges, R(3)
Breeds Which Hunt, Point and Retrieve

1. Trials should be run as nearly as possible to an ordinary day's shooting. Judges are responsible for the proper conduct of the Trial in accordance with Kennel Club Regulations and with the Schedule for the Stake. They should co-operate with the Host and the Steward of the Beat to achieve the best result in an atmosphere of friendliness and confidence. If conditions force them to depart from usual practice they should explain the reasons to handlers and spectators. Guns and handlers should be briefed at the start.

2. Judges at Open and All Aged stakes should ask the guns to shoot everything, except *directly* over a dog out working. In other stakes judges should ask the guns to shoot only over the 'point' and when the handler is beside his dog, unless otherwise directed.

3. The first round should be taken as drawn. For subsequent rounds judges may call forward dogs at their discretion, so that those showing merit will be thoroughly tested and given every opportunity in roughly comparable conditions of wind, scent and ground. Dogs which are not forward within 15 minutes of being called may be disqualified.

4. Judges should so position themselves that they can see every move of the dogs while in the line. They should regulate the pace of the line to the handler and dog to avoid game being flushed on a part of the beat not yet covered by the dog. Game so flushed should not be counted as missed by the dog.

5. Judges should accede to a request from the handler of a puppy in a Novice or Puppy stake who asks to be excused from retrieving fur.

6. If a dog catches game and the judges are satisfied that the game was unwounded and undamaged, the dog should be eliminated. When it appears that game will not flush for the dog, the handler may ask permission to take up his dog, and should only be marked down for handling if subsequently shown to have been wrong.

7. Judges must confirm the arrangements for the collection of unretrieved and unwanted game.

8. Judges may discuss situations that arise and must agree the categories to be marked, but must not discuss the actual marks they award as these represent their opinions and should be kept strictly to themselves. The marks should represent the work seen on the day, and should not be influenced by past performances.

9. The standard of work in Open and All Aged stakes carrying Field Trial Championship status should be higher than for other stakes. A prize should not be awarded unless the dog has had a productive point, a retrieve in the field and has completed the water retrieve, whatever the conditions of the day. Other stakes may be judged more leniently, but a prize should not be given unless the dog has proved himself a pointer, and a retriever on land or at the water, and has swum. Certificates of Merit are not prizes and may be awarded at the judge's discretion to dogs showing all round qualities and that they swim.

10. Judges should mark the following categories:

(i) *Ground Treatment*   The dog has to hunt the beat allotted thoroughly, making good all ground, missing no game and using the wind correctly. A dog that deliberately runs into game up wind should be discarded, but if he drops to birds rising down wind of him, this is a credit.

(ii) *Pointing*   The dog should point game staunchly, and work out only on word of command. He must be steady to flush, shot and fall. Persistent false pointing should be severely penalised, but an unproductive point, where the dog indicated by nose down and wagging tail where departed game lay should not be marked, but may be credited as a 'point' for the award of Certificate of Merit. It is accepted that hares and rabbits in their forms may not give off scent for the dog to point. Judges should not penalise dogs for failing to point in such conditions.

(iii) *Retrieve*   The retrieve must be on command. If game is shot over the point, and is marked, the dog should go straight to the fall, and any diversion marked down. With blind retrieves, judges should indicate to the handler where the game fell. The dog should go directly as indicated by the handler and any diversion from that line, with consequent waste of time and risk of disturbance of game, should be marked down. On a long blind retrieve, the dog should be taken towards the fall. A handler should be allowed to position himself where he can see to direct the dog according to conditions, but he should be beside the judges for the delivery.

In the case of a strong runner, the judge should give the immediate order for a dog to be sent. Wounded game should be retrieved before dead game. The seen dead game lying in the open does not really test a good dog, should not be highly marked, and should be avoided except in stakes other than Open and All Aged. Not more than two dogs should be tried on the same bird. When a judge goes forward to locate the game, no further dog should be tried on it. If more than one bird is down, and the dog changes birds on the way back, he should be severely marked down.

The pick up should be clean with a quick return and delivery to hand. A dog that puts game down to take a firmer grip should not be severely marked down as he may have had a gruelling stint quartering, but sloppy retrieving and finishing should be penalised.

All game should be examined for hard mouth. A hard mouthed dog seldom gives evidence of hardness. He will simply crush in one or both sides of the bird. Blowing up the feathers will not disclose the damage. Place the bird on the palm of the hand, head forward, and feel the ribs with finger and thumb. They should be round and firm. If they are caved in or flat, this is definite evidence of hard mouth. Be sure the bird reaches your co-judge and the handler for examination. There should be no hesitation or sentiment with 'hard mouth' – the dog should be eliminated. A certain indication of a good mouth is a dog bringing in a live bird whose head is up and eye bright. Superficial damage, if any, in this case can be ignored. At times the rump of a strong runner may be gashed and look ugly. Care should be taken here, as it may be the result of a difficult capture, or lack of experience in mastering a strong runner by a young dog. Judges should always satisfy themselves that any damage done has been caused by the dog, not by the shot or fall, and in cases of doubt the benefit should be given to the dog. Handlers should be given the opportunity of inspecting the damaged game in the presence of the judges, but the decision of the judges is final.

(iv) *Game Finding Ability*   This is of the highest importance. The judges will be looking for it throughout the dog's work by the manner in which he works his beat, finds his game and responds to scent generally, and by the degree of sense of purpose and drive that he displays.

(v) *Steadiness*   The dog must in all cases be steady to flush, shot and fall. He may move to mark the fall, and this may be a credit. A dog that runs in to retrieve and is stopped, and then retrieves on command, should be marked down according to the extent of the break, but the dog that does not stop should be eliminated. Dogs should be steady to fur and feather going away.

(vi) *Facing Cover*   There are occasions, e.g. on a grouse moor when this category cannot be marked. Unless all dogs can be marked, none should be. In general the dog should go boldly into reasonable cover when ordered, either to push out game or to retrieve it. The judges should agree what is reasonable.

(vii) *Style*   This embraces grace of movement, stylishness on point and of the retrieve, and the general appearance of keenness, competence and happiness in what he is doing.

(viii) *Handling*   Noisy, ineffective and over handling should be severely marked down. Usually the best dogs seem to require the least handling, but the dog should be responsive to his handler's signals.

Once a Weimaraner takes to water he works excellently but very many are slow to accept it at first.

(ix) *Water Retrieve*   This should be fully assessed, with special attention to direct, courageous but not suicidal entry, strong swimming, direct emergence and speedy delivery to hand.

In Open and All Aged stakes the water retrieve is blind across water, and should be judged accordingly, including the re-entry into water carrying game.

Eliminations   Whining or barking, out of control, chasing; failure to hunt, point, retrieve, enter water and swim, face cover; hard mouth; deliberately catching unwounded game (myxomatosis rabbits excluded).

Major Faults   Not making ground good, missing birds, unsteadiness, stickiness on point, not acknowledging game going away, failing to find game, disturbing ground, sloppy work, noisy handling, changing birds.

Credits   Game finding ability, style on point, drive, good marking speed and efficiency in gathering game, good waterwork, quiet handling.

211

Winners at Field Trials up to end of 1981/2 Season

1967 *Lotti Go-Lightly* (B) Born 10.5.62. Breeder: Col Murray.
Owner: Lt Col H. D. Tucker.
Sire: Wolfox Sandrock Cha-Cha.
Dam: Kentrish Nickel.
Winner at GSPC Novice Trial.

1972 *Katie Go-Lightly* (B) Born 31.3.69. Breeder/Owner: Lt Col H. D. Tucker.
Sire: Ragstone Radames.
Dam: Lotti Go-Lightly.
Winner at WCGB Novice Trial.

1976 *Waldemar Titus* (D) Born 10.7.70. Breeder: Mrs. J. Mills.
Owner: Mr T. Horsefield.
Sire: Ragstone Rupprecht.
Dam: Silver Siesta.
Winner at GSPC Novice Trial.

1977 *Hillbrow Quest* (B) Born 27.11.75. Breeders: Mr and Mrs J. Andrews.
Owner: Mr T. Horsefield.
Sire: Waldemar Titus.
Dam: Hillbrow Sovereign Suki.
Winner at WCGB Novice Trial.

1980 *Heronshaw Silver* (B) Born 18.2.77. Breeder: Mrs D. Chapman.
Owner: Mr C. Wilkinson.
Sire: Sh. Ch. Greyfilk Knightsman.
Dam: Heronshaw Silver Dawn.
Winner at WCGB Novice Trial and Winner at GSPC Novice Trial.

1981 *Fossana Blue John* (D) Born 11.11.78. Breeder: Mrs S. Fossey.
Owner: Mr R. Jupp.
Sire: Willingstone Brandy.
Dam: Erika of Trafalgar.
Winner at WCGB Novice Trial.

1982 *Czolkins Platinum Cirrus* (D) Born 26.5.79. Breeders: Mr & Mrs L. R. W. Jupp.
Owners: Mr & Mrs M. Turner.
Sire: Sh. Ch. Greyfilk Knightsman.
Dam: Fossana Etta.
Winner at WCGB Novice Trial.

Field Trial Successes*

FT5/56 *Yorkshire Gundog Club.* Trials for Pointers, Setters & Weimaraners on 13/14 April 1955 at Wadworth, near Doncaster, Yorkshire. Judges: Mr J. Forbes and Dr J. B. Maurice.
Novice Stake, 8 runners:
2nd Major R. M. MacGibbon's Strawbridge Baron.

Lotti-Golightly, the breed's first Field Trial winner owned by 'Tommy' Tucker.

FT6/56 *Southern & Western Counties Field Trial Society.* Trials for Pointers, Setters, Weimaraners & GSPs on 25/26 April 1955 at Sutton Manor, Sutton Scotney, Hampshire. Judges: Colonel B. P. Beale, OBE, MC, and Mr J. Delwart.
Puppy Stake, 8 runners:
3rd Mr A. Glucksmann's Ann of Monksway.
Non-Winner Stake, 12 runners:
Res. and Cert. of Merit Mr L. Causeley's Strawbridge Carol.

FT12/56 *Scottish Gundog Assn.* Pointer & Setter Trials on grouse on 29/30 July 1955 at Doune Lodge, Perthshire. Judges: Dr T. Boyd and Mr F. Gillan.
Puppy and Non-Winners Stake, 10 runners:
2nd Mr A. Glucksmann's Ann of Monksway.

FT14/56 *English Setter Club.* Trials on 25/26 July 1955 at Blanchard, County Durham. Judges: Mrs E. L. Buist and Mr J. A. Roberts.
Puppy Stake, 8 runners:
Cert. of Merit Mr J. Banks' Aporto of Monksway.

FT15/56 *Irish Setter Assn (England) and Setter & Pointer Club.* Trials 19/20 July 1955 at Crosby Fell, Shap. Judges: Mr Maurice Morton and Lady Auckland.
Novice Stake, 10 runners:
2nd Mr A. Glucksmann's Ann of Monksway.

FT19/56 *North of Scotland Gundog Assn.* Trials for Pointers and Setters, Weimaraners and GSPs 8/9 August 1955 at Glensaugh, near Fettercairn, Kincardine-

* Unconfirmed: denotes award has not been entered in the Kennel Club Stud Book.

shire and at Fetteesso near Stonehaven, Kincardineshire. Judges: Mrs E. J. Buist and Capt. W. Parlour.
Puppy and Non-Winners Stake, 10 runners:
3rd Major R. M. MacGibbons' Strawbridge Baron.

FT42/62 *German Short-haired Pointer Club.* 6/7 October 1961 at Hailes Castle, East Lothian, Scotland. Judges: Mrs E. J. Buist and Sir John Brooke Bt.
Qual. Cert. to Mr G. V. Webb's Sh. Ch. Strawbridge Oliver.

FT16/65 *German Short-haired Pointer Club.* 21/22 August 1964 at Cerniau, Foel, Welshpool, Mont. Judges: Mr T. R. Bishop and Mr B. Ingham and Mr G. C. Sterne.
Qual. Cert. to Mrs L. Petrie-Hay's Sh. Ch. Andelyb's Balch.
Qual. Cert. to Mr D. G. Roberts' Sh. Ch. Theocsbury Abbie.

FT20/68 *German Short-haired Pointer Club.* 11/12 October 1967 at Wynyard Hall, Wynyard, Stockton on Tees. Judges: Mr G. C. Sterne and Mrs M. Sanderson.
Novice Stake:
1st Lt Col H. D. Tucker's Lotti Go-Lightly.

FT26/69 *German Short-haired Pointer Club.* 19 October 1968 at Eartham, W. Sussex. Judges: Mr G. C. Sterne and Mr T. R. Bishop.
Novice Stake:
2nd Lt Col H. D. Tucker's Lotti Go-Lightly.

German Short-haired Pointer Club. 25 October 1968 at Ford, Northumberland. Judges: Mr G. A. Richmond and Sir M. Leighton.
Novice Stake:
*Cert. of Merit (unconfirmed) to Mr C. L. Church's Border Cleopatra.

FT46/69 *German Short-haired Pointer Club.* 9 November 1968 at Burton-le-Coggles, Grantham, Lincs. Judges: Mr T. R. Bishop and Mrs M. Sanderson.
Qual. Cert. to Mr and Mrs A. Burgoin's Sh. Ch. Ragstone Remus.

German Short-haired Pointer Club. 18 October 1969 at Wootton, Oxford. Judges: Mr J. Gassman and Mrs L. Petrie-Hay.
All-Aged Stake:
*Cert. of Merit (unconfirmed) to Mr C. L. Church's Border Cleopatra.

FT54/71 *Weimaraner Club of Great Britain.* 24 October 1970 at Flixton, Suffolk. Judges: Mr G. C. Sterne and Mrs L. Petrie-Hay.
Novice Stake:
2nd Mr J. Parke's Cloncurry Flash.
Cert. of Merit to Mr J. Parke's Cloncurry Smokey.

FT80/71 *German Short-haired Pointer Club.* 6/7 November 1970 at Ford Northumberland. Judges: Mr G. A. Richmond and Mrs. M. Sanderson.
All-Aged Stake, 12 runners:
3rd Lt Col H. D. Tucker's Lotti Go-Lightly.

FT50/72 *Weimaraner Club of Great Britain.* 16 October 1971 at Gorhambury, Herts. Judges: Mr J. Gassman and Mrs L. Petrie-Hay.
Novice Stake: All awards to GSPs.

FT34/73 *Weimaraner Club of Great Britain.* 7 October 1972 at Flixton, Suffolk. Judges: Mrs M. Sanderson and Mr G. Sherring.
Novice Stake:
1st Lt. Col. H. D. Tucker's Katie Go-Lightly.

FT64/74 *Weimaraner Club of Great Britain*. 20 October 1973 at Moreton-in-Marsh, Glos. Judges: Mr J. Gassman and Mr C. L. Church.
Novice Stake, 13 runners:
3rd Mr J. R. Holmes' Tottens Cinzano.
Cert. of Merit to Mr and Mrs J. M. Jeffrey's Ambersbury Melot.
Cert. of Merit to Mrs V. J. Sutton's Grinshill Malplaquet of Castle Garnstone.

FT33/75 *Weimaraner Club of Great Britain*. 4 October 1974 at Flixton, Suffolk. Judges: Mrs L. Petrie-Hay and Mr G. Sherring.
Novice Stake, 13 runners:
Cert. of Merit to Mr and Mrs J. M. Jeffrey's Ambersbury Melot.
Cert. of Merit to Mr T. Horsefield's Waldemar Titus.

FT123/75 *Hungarian Vizsla Club*. 23 October 1974 at Bishopsbourne, Kent. Judges: Mrs P. Maurice and Mr I. E. T. Sladden.
Novice Stake, 12 runners:
Res. and Cert. of Merit to Mrs V. J. Sutton's Grinshill Malplaquet of Castle Garnstone.
Cert. of Merit to Mr T. Horsefield's Waldemar Titus.

FT32/75 *German Short-haired Pointer Club*. 5 October 1974 at Flixton, Suffolk. Judges: Mrs L. Petrie-Hay and Mr I. E. T. Sladden.
Open Stake, 12 runners:
Cert. of Merit to Mrs D. Oldershaw's Gunmetal Emma.

FT70/75 *Lothians & Border Gundog Assn*. 12 October 1974 at Cardross, Stirling-shire. Judges: Mrs M. Sanderson and Lord Joicey.
Open (Qualifying) Stake, 11 runners:
Cert. of Merit to Lt Col H. D. Tucker's Katie Go-Lightly.

FT74/75 *German Short-haired Pointer Club*. 26 October 1974 at Burton-le-Coggles, Lincs. Judges: Mrs M. Sanderson and Mr C. L. Church.
Qual. Cert. to Mr and Mrs A. Burgoin's Sh. Ch. Ragstone Ritter.

FT35/76 *German Short-haired Pointer Club*. 11 October 1975 at Laughton, Lincs. Judges: Mr I. E. T. Sladden and Mr G. Farrand.
Novice Stake, 12 runners:
Cert. of Merit to Mr T. Horsefield's Waldemar Titus.

FT54/76 *Weimaraner Club of Great Britain*. 10 October 1975 at Harwich, Essex. Judges: Lord Joicey and Mr G. Sherring.
Novice Stake, 12 runners:
Reserve Mrs S. Weatherill's Waldemar Tara.
Cert. of Merit to Mr T. Horsefield's Waldemar Titus.

FT70/76 *German Short-haired Pointer Assn*. 1 November 1975 at Dalemain Estate, Penrith. Judges: Mrs M. Sanderson and Mr R. Flett.
Novice Stake, 11 runners:
Reserve Mr T. Horsefield's Waldemar Titus.

FT55/76 *Weimaraner Club of Great Britain*. 18 October 1975 at Somerleyton, Suffolk. Judges: Mrs L. Petrie-Hay and Mr C. L. Church.
Open Stake, 12 runners: All awards to GSPs.

FT21/77 *German Short-haired Pointer Assn.* 2 October 1976 at Laughton, Lincs.
Judges: Mr I. E. T. Sladden and Mr G. Roberts.
Open Stake (Non-Qualifying), 11 runners:
2nd Mr T. Horsefield's Waldemar Titus.

FT132/77 *German Short-haired Pointer Club.* 27 November 1976 at Eyke, Hollesley.
Judges: Mrs L. Petrie-Hay and Major G. Wilkinson MBE.
Novice Stake, 12 runners:
1st Mr T. Horsefield's Waldemar Titus.

FT16/77 *German Short-haired Pointer Assn.* 30 August 1976 at Leck Fell, Cumbria.
Judges: Sir M. Leighton and Mr D. Layton.
Qual. Cert. to Mrs S. Weatherill's Dapifers Huxel Mandelhang.

FT80/77 *Weimaraner Club of Great Britain.* 29 October 1976 at Boxted, Essex.
Judges: Mr M. Brander and Mr C. L. Church.
Novice Stake, 12 runners: No Weimaraners awarded prizes.

FT49/78 *German Short-haired Pointer Assn.* 8 October 1977 at Laughton, Lincs.
Judges: Mr I. E. T. Sladden and Mr R. Miles.
Open (Non-Qualifying) Stake, 12 runners:
2nd Mr T. Horsefield's Waldemar Titus.

FT85/78 *Weimaraner Club of Great Britain.* 21 October 1977 at Dullingham, and 22
October 1977 at Debenham, Suffolk. Novice Stake Judges: Mrs L. Petrie-Hay and Mr
C. L. Church. Open Stake Judges: Mrs L. Petrie-Hay and Mr G. Sterne.
Novice Stake, 12 runners:
1st Mr T. Horsefield's Hillbrow Quest.
Res. and Cert. of Merit to Mr. L. Horsefield's Clackhill Bambi.

FT56/78 *German Short-haired Pointer Club.* 8 October 1977 at Braintree, Essex.
Judges: Mrs M. Davison and Mr C. L. Church.
Qual. Cert. to Mrs C. Alston's Sh. Ch. Gifford's Lady.

FT46/79 *German Short-haired Pointer Club.* 7 October 1978 at Braintree, Essex.
Judges: Mr C. L. Church and Mr J. Kew.
Novice Stake, 12 runners:
3rd Mr and Mrs L. R. W. Jupp's Fossana Algenon.

FT212/79 *German Short-haired Pointer Club.* 17 January 1979 at Ringwood, Hants.
Judges: Mrs L. Petrie-Hay and Mr R. Kuban.
Open (Qualifying) Stake, 12 runners:
Cert. of Merit to Mr and Mrs L. R. W. Jupp's Fossana Algenon.

FT77/79 *Weimaraner Club of Great Britain.* 18 October 1978 at Wishanger, Surrey.
Judges: Major G. Wilkinson, MBE, and Mr G. Sherring.
Novice Stake, 10 runners (all Weimaraners). No first prize awarded.
2nd Mrs E. D. Knight's Fossana Heidi.
Cert. of Merit to Mrs E. G. Hardman's Bredebeck Sophie.
Cert. of Merit to Mr M. Phillips' Fay of Rujanta.
Qual. Cert. to Mrs V. J. O'Keeffe's Fossana Bruno.

FT192/79 *Weimaraner Club of Great Britain.* 30 December 1978 at Wiston, Essex.
Judges: Mr C. L. Church and Mr G. Sherring.
Open Stake, 12 runners:
Cert. of Merit to Mr T. Horsefield's Hillbrow Quest.

FT57/79 *German Short-haired Pointer Assn.* 13 October 1978 at Loton Park, Salop. Judges: Sir M. Leighton and Mr G. Dixon.
Qual. Cert. to Mrs D. Arrowsmith's Sh. Ch. Wotan of Ragstone.
Qual. Cert. to Mrs P. Edminson's Sh. Ch. Petraqua Pagtail.

FT58/80 *German Short-haired Pointer Club.* 13 October 1979 at Burton-le-Coggles, Lincs. Judges: Mr C. L. Church and Mr B. Botterman.
Novice Stake, 12 runners:
2nd Mr E. Hardman's Bredebeck Sophie.

FT39/80 *German Short-haired Pointer Assn.* 6 October 1979 at Osberton, Notts. Judges: Mr I. E. T. Sladden and Mr G. Nixon.
Novice Stake, 12 runners:
Res. and Cert. of Merit to Mrs M. Booker's Hofstetter Beau (Handler: Mr T. Chivers).

FT100/80 *German Short-haired Pointer Club.* 27 October 1979 at Blackmore End. Judges: Mr G. Wilkinson and Mr. B. Botterman.
All-Aged Stake, 12 runners:
Cert. of Merit to Mr E. Hardman's Bredebeck Sophie.

FT97/80 *German Short-haired Pointer Assn.* 26 October 1979 at Lichfield, Staffs. Judges: Mrs M. Davidson and Mr T. Horsefield.
Novice Stake, 12 runners:
Cert. of Merit to Mrs M. Booker's Hofstetter Beau (Handler: Mr T. Chivers).

FT187/80 *Hungarian Vizsla Club.* 7 December 1979 at Woodbridge, Suffolk. Judges: Mr D. Layton and Mr G. Nixon.
Novice Stake, 12 runners:
Reserve Mr and Mrs L. R. W. Jupp's Fossana Algenon.

FT119/80 *German Short-haired Pointer Club.* 3 November 1979 at Bicester. Judges: Mrs L. Petrie-Hay and Mr A. G. Williams.
Novice Stake, 10 runners:
2nd Mr and Mrs L. R. W. Jupp's Fossana Algenon.

FT139/80 *German Short-haired Pointer Assn.* 8 November 1979 at East Markham, Notts. Judges: Mrs L. Petrie-Hay and Mr H. Fisher.
All-Aged Stake, 12 runners:
Res. and Cert. of Merit to Mr and Mrs Edminson's Ch. Petraqua Wagtail.

FT204/80 *Weimaraner Club of Great Britain.* 29 December 1979 at Wiston, Essex. Judges: Mr C. L. Church and Mr G. Nixon.
All-Aged Stake, 12 runners:
Reserve Mrs M. Booker's Hofstetter Beau.

FT32/80 *Weimaraner Club of Great Britain.* 18 January 1980 at Tisted, Hants. Judges: Mr D. Layton and Mr T. Horsefield.
Novice Stake for Weimaraners only, 9 runners:
1st Mr C. Wilkinson's Heronshaw Silver.
2nd Mrs M. Booker's Hofstetter Beau.
3rd Mr E. Hardman's Bredebeck Sophie.
*4th and Cert. of Merit (unconfirmed) Mrs J. Matuszewska's Monroes Fieldfare (Long-haired) handled by Mr T. Griggs.
Cert. of Merit to Mr and Mrs L. R. W. Jupp's Fossana Algenon.
Qual. Cert. to Mr and Mrs R. George's Sh. Ch. Kamsou Moonraker v Bismarck.
Qual. Cert. to Mr M. Mitchener's Sh. Ch. Helber Camillo.

FT241/80 *Weimaraner Club of Great Britain*. 1 February 1980 at Hoar Cross, Staffs. Judges: Mrs L. Petrie-Hay and Mr C. L. Church.
Open Stake, 12 runners:
*Cert. of Merit (unconfirmed) Mrs M. Booker's Hofstetter Beau.

FT72/81 *German Short-haired Pointer Club*. 11 October 1980 at Burton-le-Coggles, Lincs. Judges: Mrs M. Davidson and Mr E. Wheeler.
Novice Stake, 12 runners:
1st Mr C. Wilkinson's Heronshaw Silver.

FT154/81 *German Short-haired Pointer Club*. 5 November 1980 at Sevenoaks. Judges: Mr C. L. Church and Mr C. Hales.
Open Stake:
Cert. of Merit to Mr C. Wilkinson's Heronshaw Silver.

FT64/81 *Large Munsterlander Club*. 8 October 1980 at Beaconsfield. Judges: Major G. Wilkinson and Mrs S. Kuban.
Novice Stake, 12 runners:
2nd Mr and Mrs L. R. W. Jupp's Fossana Algenon.

FT154/81 *German Short-haired Pointer Club*. 6 November 1980 at Swanley. Judges: Major G. Wilkinson and Mr Jim Field.
All-Aged Stake:
Cert. of Merit to Mr C. Wilkinson's Heronshaw Silver.

FT176/81 *German Short-haired Pointer Club*. 15 November 1980 at Bicester. Judges: Major G. Wilkinson and Mr G. Nixon.
Novice Stake:
Show Gundog Working Cert. to Mrs S. Bradley's Shalina Sky Diver.

FT190/81 *German Short-haired Pointer Club*. 28 November 1980 at Westerham, Kent. Judges: Mr R. Kuban and Mr A. Jackson.
Novice Stake, 12 runners:
Reserve Mr and Mrs L. R. W. Jupp's Fossana Blue John.

FT205/81 *Large Munsterlander Club*. 16 December 1980 at Preesall, Lancs. Judges: Mr M. Davidson and Mr G. Nixon.
Novice Stake:
Cert. of Merit to Mrs J. Turner's Czolkins Platinum Cirrus.

FT216/81 *Weimaraner Club of Great Britain*. 2 January 1981 at Colchester, Essex. Judges: Mr C. L. Church and Mr G. Kew.
All-Aged Open (Non-Qualifying) Stake. No first prize awarded.
2nd Mr C. Wilkinson's Heronshaw Silver.
Reserve Mrs S. Bradley's Shalina Sky Diver.

FT214/81 *German Short-haired Pointer Assn*. 3 January 1981 at Hints, Staffs. Judges: Mr G. Farrand and Mrs M. Layton.
Cert. of Merit to Mrs V. J. O'Keeffe's Loren of Fleetapple.
Cert. of Merit to Mr and Mrs R. George's Ch. Kamsou Moonraker v Bismarck handled by Mrs. V. J. O'Keeffe.

FT241/81 *Weimaraner Club of Great Britain*. 14 January 1981 at Tisted, Hants. Judges: Major G. Wilkinson and Mr G. Sherring.
Novice Stake, 10 runners, confined to Weimaraners.
1st Mr and Mrs L. R. W. Jupp's Fossana Blue John.

2nd Mr and Mrs R. George's Ch. Kamsou Moonraker v Bismarck handled by Mrs V. J. O'Keeffe.
3rd Mr and Mrs Knight's Czolkins Fioletta.
Cert. of Merit to Mr V. Clarke's Verrami Abbaca.
Cert. of Merit to Mr K. Absalom's Sh. Ch. Lodgewater Amber.
Show Gundog Working Cert. to Mrs D. Arrowsmith's Sh. Ch. Ragstone Rune.
Show Gundog Working Cert. to Mr and Mrs R. George's Sh. Ch. Denmo Blueberry Muffin.

FT251/81 *German Short-haired Pointer Club*. 20 January 1981 at Somerley, Hants.
Judges: Mrs L. Petrie-Hay and Mr R. Kuban.
Open Stake:
Reserve Mr and Mrs L. R. W. Jupp's Fossana Blue John.

FT258/81 *Weimaraner Club of Great Britain*. 31 January 1981 at Hoar Cross, Staffs.
Judges: Lord Joicey and Mr T. Horsefield.
Open Championship Stake, 12 runners. No Weimaraners were drawn to run.

FT51/82 *Weimaraner Club of Great Britain*. 3 October 1981 at High Wycombe, Bucks. Judges: Mr R. Kuban and Mr T. Horsefield.
Novice Stake, 12 runners:
Cert. of Merit to Mr and Mrs L. R. W. Jupp's Fossana Blue John.

FT57/82 *Large Munsterlander Club*. 7 October 1981 at Beaconsfield. Judges: Mr D. Layton and Mr G. Nixon.
Novice Stake, 12 runners:
Cert. of Merit to Mrs. J. George's Ch. Denmo Blueberry Muffiin.

FT57/82 *Large Munsterlander Club*. 6 October 1981 at Shoreham, Kent. Judges: Major G. Wilkinson and Mr T. Horsefield.
All-Aged (Non-Qualifying) Stake, 12 runners:
Cert. of Merit to Mr C. Wilkinson's Heronshaw Silver.

FT69/82 *Weimaraner Club of Great Britain*. 10 October 1981 at Fordham, Essex.
Judges: Mr C. L. Church and Mr E. Hales.
Open Qualifying Stake, Championship Status, 12 runners:
3rd Mrs S. Bradley's Ch. Shalina Sky Diver.
Cert. of Merit to Mr and Mrs L. R. W. Jupp's Fossana Algenon.

FT95/82 *German Short-haired Pointer Assn*. 21 October 1981 at Belvoir, Grantham, Lincs. Judges: Sir M. Leighton Bt., and Mr B. Miles.
Novice Stake, 12 runners:
3rd Mrs J. Turner's Czolkins Platinum Cirrus.

FT159/82 *German Short-haired Pointer Club*. 7 November 1981 at Thornham, Suffolk. Judges: Mr C. L. Church and Mr M. J. Field.
Novice Stake, 12 runners:
2nd Mr and Mrs L. R. W. Jupp's Fossana Blue John.
Cert. of Merit to Mr and Mrs M. Turner's Fossana Quartz.

FT170/82 *German Short-haired Pointer Club*. 11 November 1981 at Sevenoaks, Kent. Judges: Mrs L. Petrie-Hay and Mr E. Hales.
Open Qualifying Stake, 12 runners:
3rd Mr C. Wilkinson's Heronshaw Silver.

FT173/82 *Weimaraner Club of Great Britain.* 12 November 1981 at Swanley, Kent. Judges: Mr C. L. Church and Mr A. Greville-Williams.
Open Qualifying Stake, 12 runners: No Weimaraners awarded prizes.

FT185/82 *Weimaraner Club of Great Britain.* 18 November 1981 at Wishanger, Surrey. Judges: Mrs L. Petrie-Hay and Mr G. Sherring.
All-Aged Stake (Non-Qualifying), 12 runners:
Cert. of Merit to Mr and Mrs L. R. W. Jupp's Fossana Blue John.
Cert. of Merit to Mr J. Holmes' Clackhill Christian.

FT243/82 *Weimaraner Club of Great Britain.* 13 January 1982 at Tisted, Hants. Judges: Mr G. Kew and Mr J. Field.
Novice Stake for Weimaraners only:
1st Mrs J. Turner's Czolkins Platinum Cirrus.
2nd Mr T. Griggs' Aruni of Index.
3rd Mr E. Hardman's Bredebeck Sophie.
Cert. of Merit to Mr R. Quiddington's Fineshade Quality Fair.
Cert. of Merit to Mr T. Horsefield's Fineshade Quail Run.
Cert. of Merit to Mr M. Phillips' Vanwilkie Naughty Nancy.
Show Gundog Working Cert. to Mrs G. Sowersby's Monroes Ambition of Westglade CDx UDx.

FT57/83 *German Short-haired Pointer Club.* 2 October 1982 at Wheldrake. Judges: Mr G. Kew and Mr J. Beckon.
Novice Stake, 12 runners:
Cert. of Merit to Mr and Mrs N. Elder's Aucassin of Llangynog.

FT53/83 *Weimaraner Club of Great Britain.* 2 October 1982 at High Wycombe. Judges: Mr B. Botterman and Mr J. Field.
Novice Stake, 12 runners:
2nd Mrs J. Turner's Czolkins Platinum Cirrus.
3rd Mr L. R. W. Jupp's Fossana Blue John.

FT77/83 *Weimaraner Club of Great Britain.* 9 October 1982 at Fordham. Judges: Mr C. L. Church and Mr F. Musselwhite.
Open (Qualifying) Stake: No Weimaraners awarded prizes.

FT80/83 *Large Munsterlander Club.* 9 October 1982 at Hall Barn. Judges: Mr R. Kuban and Mr P. Howard.
Novice Stake, 12 runners:
1st Mrs J. Turner's Czolkins Platinum Cirrus.

FT90/83 *Weimaraner Club of Great Britain.* 14 October 1982 at Rotherfield Park. Judges: Mrs L. Petrie-Hay and Mr E. J. Hardman.
Novice Stake, 12 runners: No Weimaraners awarded prizes.

FT137/83 *German Short-haired Pointer Assn.* 30 October 1982 at Belvoir. Judges: Mr G. Kew and Mr H. Fisher.
Novice Stake, 12 runners:
Cert. of Merit to Mr and Mrs E. Hardman's Bredebeck Jutta.

FT186/83 *Weimaraner Club of Great Britain.* 10 November 1982 at Cliffe, Kent. Judges: Mr J. Kew and Mr T. Horsefield.
No Weimaraners awarded prizes.

FT209/83 *Weimaraner Club of Great Britain.* 17 November 1982 at Radbourne. Judges: Mr D. Layton and Mr G. Sherring.
All-Aged Stake: No Weimaraners awarded prizes.

FT210/83 *German Short-haired Pointer Club.* 17 November 1982, Kent. Judges: Mr C. Church and Mr M. Casserley.
Novice Stake, 12 runners:
Cert. of Merit to Mr and Mrs E. Hardman's Bredebeck Jutta.

FT288/83 *Weimaraner Club of Great Britain.* 13 January 1983 at Tisted. Judges: Mr P. Godby and Mrs V. J. O'Keeffe.
Novice Stake for Weimaraners only.
No 1st or 2nd prizes awarded.
3rd Mr and Mrs S. Johnson's Castle Garnstone Caisson.
Cert. of Merit to Mr R. Quiddington's Fineshade Quality Fair.
Cert. of Merit to Mr and Mrs A. H. Simons' Greyfilk Lexion.
Cert. of Merit to Mrs L. J. Shea's Ragstone Renegade.

FT296/83 *German Short-haired Pointer Club.* 18 January 1983 at Somerley. Judges: Mr R. Kuban and Mr G. Nixon.
Open (Qualifying) Stake:
Cert. of Merit to Mr C. Wilkinson's Heronshaw Silver.

Note: NOVICE STAKE is for dogs and bitches which have not won two first prizes in Novice, one first prize in Open, or a win and two places in any Field Trial up to the closing date of entry.
ALL-AGED STAKE is an Open stake but restricted by the regulations of the promoting society.
OPEN STAKE CHAMPIONSHIP STATUS is for open dogs and bitches where the award of first prize counts towards the title of Field Trial Champion.

APPENDIX VI

British Working Trial and Obedience Regulations and Award Winners

EXTRACTS FROM KENNEL CLUB RULES FOR WORKING TRIALS
AND OBEDIENCE CLASSES, S,
AND WORKING TRIAL REGULATIONS, S (1), 10.8.82*

The Title of Working Trial Champion   A Kennel Club Working Trial Certificate will be awarded to any dog winning a TD or PD Stake at a Championship Working Trial provided that it has obtained 70 per cent or more marks as indicated in the Schedule of Points in the appropriate columns for each group of exercises separately shown in that Schedule and has also been awarded the qualification 'Excellent' by obtaining at least 80 per cent of the possible total of marks for the stake.

Two Kennel Club Working Trial Certificates awarded by different judges at Championship Working Trials duly licensed by the General Committee as Championship fixtures shall qualify a dog for the title of Working Trial Champion.

Certificates   The Judge or Judges shall give certificates at a Championship Working Trial PD (Police Dog), TD (Tracking Dog), WD (Working Dog), UD (Utility Dog), and CD (Companion Dog) Stake to those dogs which have obtained 70 per cent or more marks in each group of exercises in the Stake entered (provided that the dog has complied with any additional requirements for that Stake). The added qualification 'Excellent' shall be awarded should the dog also obtain 80 per cent or more marks of the total for the Stake.

SCHEDULE OF EXERCISES AND POINTS
COMPANION DOG (CD) STAKE

	Marks	Group Total	Minimum Group Qualifying Mark
GROUP I. *Control*			
1. Heel on Leash	5		
2. Heel Free	10		
3. Recall to Handler	5		
4. Sending the dog away	10	30	21

* Reprinted by kind permission of the Kennel Club.

	Marks	Group Total	Minimum Group Qualifying Mark
GROUP II. *Stays*			
5. Sit (2 minutes)	10		
6. Down (10 minutes)	10	20	14
GROUP III. *Agility*			
7. Scale (3) Stay (2) Recall (5)	10		
8. Clear Jump	5		
9. Long Jump	5	20	14
GROUP IV. *Retrieving and Nosework*			
10. Retrieve a dumb-bell	10		
11. Elementary Search	20	30	21
Totals	100	100	70

UTILITY DOG (UD) STAKE

	Marks	Group Total	Minimum Group Qualifying Mark
GROUP I. *Control*			
1. Heel Free	5		
2. Sending the dog away	10		
3. Retrieve a dumb-bell	5		
4. Down (10 minutes)	10		
5. Steadiness to Gunshot	5	35	25
GROUP II. *Agility*			
6. Scale (3) Stay (2) Recall (5)	10		
7. Clear Jump	5		
8. Long Jump	5	20	14
GROUP III. *Nosework*			
9. Search	35		
10. Track (95) Article (15)	110	145	102
Totals	200	200	141

WORKING DOG (WD) STAKE

	Marks	Group Total	Minimum Group Qualifying Mark
GROUP I. *Control*			
1. Heel Free	5		
2. Sending the dog away	10		
3. Retrieve a dumb-bell	5		
4. Down (10 minutes)	10		
5. Steadiness to Gunshot	5	35	25

	Marks	Group Total	Minimum Group Qualifying Mark
GROUP II. *Agility*			
6. Scale (3) Stay (2) Recall (5)	10		
7. Clear Jump	5		
8. Long Jump	5	20	14
GROUP III. *Nosework*			
9. Search	35		
10. Track (90) Articles (10 + 10 = 20)	110	145	102
Totals	200	200	141

TRACKING DOG (TD) STAKE

	Marks	Group Total	Minimum Group Qualifying Mark
GROUP I. *Control*			
1. Heel Free	5		
2. Sendaway and Directional Control	10		
3. Speak on Command	5		
4. Down (10 minutes)	10		
5. Steadiness to Gunshot	5	35	25
GROUP II. *Agility*			
6. Scale (3) Stay (2) Recall (5)	10		
7. Clear Jump	5		
8. Long Jump	5	20	14
GROUP III. *Nosework*			
9. Search	35		
10. Track (100) Articles (10 + 10 + 10 = 30)	130	165	116
Totals	220	220	155

POLICE DOG (PD) STAKE

	Marks	Group Total	Minimum Group Qualifying Mark
GROUP I. *Control*			
1. Heel Free	5		
2. Sendaway and Directional Control	10		
3. Speak on Command	5		
4. Down (10 minutes)	10		
5. Steadiness to Gunshot	5	35	25
GROUP II. *Agility*			
6. Scale (3) Stay (2) Recall (5)	10		
7. Clear Jump	5		
8. Long Jump	5	20	14

	Marks	Group Total	Minimum Group Qualifying Mark
GROUP III. *Nosework*			
9. Search	35		
10. Track (60) Articles (10 + 10 = 20)	80	115	80
GROUP IV. *Patrol*			
11. Quartering the Ground	45		
12. Test of Courage	20		
13. Search and Escort	25		
14a. Recall from Criminal	30		
14b. Pursuit and Detention of Criminal	30	150	105
Totals	320	320	224

Working Trial and Obedience Title Holders

Strawbridge Irene (B)
  CDx, Obed. CC

17.4.56. Breeder: Mrs E. M. Petty.
Owner: Mrs. S. M. Milward.
Sire: Casar von Bolkewehr.
Dam: Vita von der Haraska.

Cartford Capricorn (D)
  CDx, 2 CCs

25.7.60. Breeder: Mrs A. McNutt.
Owner: Miss K. Price.
Sire: Sandrock Admiral.
Dam: Strawbridge Jane.

Gunmetal Guy (D)
  CDx, UDx

6.4.64. Breeder: Mrs Callaghan.
Owner: Mrs D. Oldershaw.
Sire: Wolfox Magnus.
Dam: Moonsville Starlight.

Grinshill Malplaquet of Castle Garnstone (D)   CDx, UDx

19.8.71. Breeder: Mrs J. Atkinson.
Owner: Mrs V. Sutton.
Sire: Sh. Ch. Cannylad Olympus Daedalus.
Dam: Shinglehill Briony.

Waidman Giselle (B)
  CDx, 2 CCs

2.6.66. Breeder: Mrs L. Petrie-Hay.
Owner: Mrs D. Oldershaw.
Sire: Monroes Invader.
Dam: Ch. Andelyb's Balch.

Sidwell Gentil Knight (D)
  CDx

7.3.70. Breeder: Dr M. Mitchell.
Owner: Mrs T. Cass.
Sire: Tottens Thengel.
Dam: Sidwell Olivia.

'Metpol' Monroes Thor (D)
  UDx, WDx, PDx

31.7.70. Breeder: Mrs J. Matuszewska.
Owners: The Commissioners of Police.
Handler: PC Paul Dodd.
Sire: Monroes Orest.
Dam: Monroes Pandora.

Heatherdam Phantom (B)
CDx

17.11.70. Breeder: Mrs E. Linge.
Owner: Mrs Thompson.
Sire: Belazieths Silver Ace.
Dam: Innisron Aphrodite.

Gunmetal Emma (B)
CDx, F.T. C.o.M.

21.6.69. Breeder/Owner: Mrs D. Oldershaw.
Sire: Sh. Ch. Monroes Nexus.
Dam: Waidman Giselle, CDx.

Cristal of Bulow (B)
CDx, UDx, WDx, 1 CC

24.1.72. Breeder: Mrs P. Way.
Owner: Mrs D. Shaw.
Sire: Ch. Ragstone Ritter.
Dam: Ragstone Fantasma.

Ragstone Rhodora (B)
CDx

3.3.72. Breeders: Mr and Mrs A. Burgoin.
Owner: Mrs Fenn.
Sire: Ragstone Radames.
Dam: Ragstone Rakete.

Fossana Bruno, Ch. (D)
CDx, UDx WDx, TD

28.2.75. Breeder: Mrs S. Fossey.
Owner: Mrs V. O'Keeffe.
Sire: Willingstone Brandy.
Dam: Erika of Trafalgar.

Sachs of Castle Garnstone (D)
CDx

1.8.75. Breeder: Mrs J. Matuszewska.
Owner: Mrs V. O'Keeffe.
Sire: Sh. Ch. Gunther of Ragstone.
Dam: Uhlan Fantasia.

Ragstone Raufbold (D)
CDx

14.9.75. Breeders: Mr and Mrs A. Burgoin.
Owner: Mr L. Chapman.
Sire: Ch. Wotan of Ragstone.
Dam: Ragstone Rhossignol.

Grinshill Rana Vanessa (B)
CDx, UDx, WDx, TDx

13.6.76. Breeder: Mrs J. M. Atkinson.
Owner: Miss A. Cooke.
Sire: Waidman Hank.
Dam: Shinglehill Briony.

Ziggy of Bwthyn (D)
CDx

8.2.76. Breeder: Mrs A. Farrow.
Owner: Mrs H. Greening.
Sire: Sh. Ch. Ragstone Rhion.
Dam: Senta of Ragstone.

Grinshill Sweet Solario, Sh. Ch. (B)
CDx, UDx, WD

9.1.77. Breeder: Mrs J. M. Atkinson.
Owner: Mrs S. Walkden.
Sire: Grinshill Maxamillian.
Dam: Monroes Xpatriate.

Toby of Sanceriph (D)
CDx, UDx, WDx

21.4.78. Breeder: Miss A. King.
Owner: Mrs A. L. Williams.
Sire: Sh. Ch. Greyfilk Equerry.
Dam: Miefag Beda.

Monroes Ambition of Westglade, Ch. (D) CDx, UDx, WDx

18.2.79. Breeder: Mrs J. Matuszewska.
Owner: Mrs G. Sowersby.
Sire: Sh. Ch. Kympenna's Tristan.
Dam: Sh. Ch. Monroes Aequo.

Shalina Melody Man (D) CDx, UDx, WDx

31.5.78. Breeder: Mrs C. M. Cutting.
Owner: Mr C. Sagoe-Staff.
Sire: Sh. Ch. Midwil Zak.
Dam: Monroes Unity.

Gentil Thundercloud (D) CDx, UDx, WD

26.8.77. Breeder: Miss S. M. Insley.
Owner: Mrs T. Cass.
Sire: Sidwell Gentil Knight, CDx.
Dam: Phayreheidi Fogle Flush.

Kapitada Lysander (D) CDx, UDx, WDx

28.3.79. Breeder: Mrs M. Bettesworth.
Owner: Mr T. Castle.
Sire: Sh. Ch. Gunther of Ragstone.
Dam: Valhalla Harlequin.

Fleetapple Wargo (D) CDx, UDx

29.2.80. Breeder: Mrs D. Arrowsmith.
Owners: Mr and Mrs Johnson.
Sire: Ch. Wotan of Ragstone.
Dam: Ch. Ragstone Rune.

'Metpol' Monroes Prangen (D) CDx, UDx, WDx

23.8.79. Breeder: Mrs J. Matuszewska.
Owners: The Commissioners of Police.
Handler: PC Paul Dodd.
Sire: Waidman Hank.
Dam: Matilda of Monroes (NAF).

Shampers Sooty Forluck (D) CDx

3.12.79. Breeder: Mrs W. H. Foskett.
Owner: Miss C. Summers.
Sire: Ch. Fossana Bruno, CDx, UDx, WDx,
TD.
Dam: Bonville Helen.

Maulbeere Abba (B) CD

7.1.79. Breeders: Mr and Mrs M. Mulberry.
Owner: Mrs J. Lawrence.
Sire: Imposter of Monroes.
Dam: Aruni Domira from Seicer (L/H).

Hillmist Abacus (D) CDx, UDx

7.4.81. Breeders: Mr and Mrs P. C.
Gledhill.
Owner: Mr D. Marsh.
Sire: Fleetapple Overture.
Dam: Phayreheidi Harmony of Hillmist.

Brancaster Maximillian (D) CDx, UDx, WDx, TDx

5.5.79. Breeder: Mrs A. Marriott.
Owner: Ms E. Myers.
Sire: Sh. Ch. Midwil Zak.
Dam: Florimell of Artegall.

Miroko Argus (D)
    CDx, UDx, WDx

4.2.82. Breeder: Mr S. R. Sharpe.
Owner: Mr E. Rowley.
Sire: Ch. Wotan of Ragstone.
Dam: Valestock Contessa.

Reeman Aruac (D)
    CDx, UDx, WDx

15.1.81. Breeder: Miss D. L. Reid.
Owner: Mr R. Lynch.
Sire: Sh. Ch. Arimars Rolf von der
    Reiteralm.
Dam: Hawsvale Merganser.

Brigkeena Boy (D)
    CDx, UDx, WDx

7.11.81. Breeders: Mr and Mrs D.
    Chambers.
Owner: Mr D. C. Guiver.
Sire: Ch. Kamsou Moonraker von
    Bismarck.
Dam: Kregnell Carrinka.

Legend of Hawsvale (D)
    UDx

31.8.77. Breeder: Mr P. F. Goss.
Owner: Miss J. Jones.
Sire: Phyl's Flight.
Dam: Hawsvale Illusion.

Appendix VII

British Championships

Kennel Club Rules Relating to Championships, Lists of Champions, Sires and Dams, Breeders, Junior Warrant Holders and H.D. – Free Stock

Extract from Kennel Club Rules 'A' Relating to Championships, etc. 26.4.82.*

The title of Show Champion (abbreviation Sh. Ch.) shall attach to any Gundog awarded three Challenge Certificates under three different judges provided that at least one of the Challenge Certificates was awarded when the dog was more than 12 months of age. If it has obtained a prize, Award of Honour, Diploma of Merit or Certificate of Merit at a Field Trial under the Rules of the Kennel Club and of the Field Trials Committee or under rules of the Irish Kennel Club or a Show Gundog Working Certificate which conforms to the conditions set out in Kennel Club Field Trial Regulation no. 21 or the Rules of the Irish Kennel Club, then it shall be recorded as a Champion.

The title of Obedience Champion (abbreviation Ob. Ch.) shall attach to any dog (i) awarded three Obedience Certificates under three different judges in accordance with the Kennel Club Regulations for Tests for Obedience classes, or (ii) which has won a Kennel Club Obedience Championship.

List of Champions to 30 September 1983:

(Abbreviations: JW: Junior Warrant; GS: Irish Green Star; FQ: Field Qualified.)

NO.	YEAR	NAME	CCs WON	
1	1960	Wolfox Silverglance, Sh. Ch.	7	
2		Strawbridge Oliver, Ch.	13	FQ
3	1961	Strawbridge Czarina, Sh. Ch.	7	
4	1962	Wolfox Lycidas, Sh. Ch.	4	
5	1963	Theocsbury Abbie, Ch.	5	FQ
6		Ace of Acomb, Sh. Ch.	7	
7		Monroes Dynamic, Sh. Ch.	9	
8	1964	Andelyb's Balch, Ch.	5	FQ

* Reprinted by kind permission of the Kennel Club.

NO.	YEAR	NAME	CCs WON	
9		Strawbridge Yuri, Sh. Ch.	5	
10		Wolfox Bittersweet, Sh. Ch.	6	
11		Ragstone Remus, Ch.	16	FQ JW 3GS
12	1964	Cabaret Cartford Platinum, Sh. Ch.	6	
13	1966	Wolfox Nyria, Sh. Ch.	4	
14		Theocsbury Archduke, Sh. Ch.	4	
15	1967	Wolfox Moonsdale Whisper, Sh. Ch.	3	
16		Monroes Idyll, Sh. Ch.	3	
17		Coninvale Paul of Acombdole, Sh. Ch.	7	JW
18		Knowdale Annabella, Sh. Ch.	4	JW
19	1968	Ballina of Merse-Side, Sh. Ch.	31	JW
20		Waidman Gunnar, Sh. Ch.	3	
21		Monroes Nexus, Sh. Ch.	9	
22	1969	Greyfilk Sapphire, Sh. Ch.	3	
23		Hansom Sylhill Odette, Sh. Ch.	6	
24	1970	Ragstone Ritter, Ch.	22	FQ
25		Arlebroc Brigand, Sh. Ch.	3	
26		Monroes O'Netti, Sh. Ch.	6	
27	1971	Cannylad Olympus Daedalus, Sh. Ch.	4	
28	1972	Hansom Hobby Hawk, Sh. Ch.	13	
29		Greyfilk Equerry, Sh. Ch.	10	
30		Abbeystag Oceanmist, Sh. Ch.	6	
31	1973	Kympenna's Tristan, Sh. Ch.	6	
32		Monroes Nadine, Sh. Ch.	4	
33		Monroes Serena, Sh. Ch.	6	
34		Cannylad Olympus Artemis, Sh. Ch.	6	
35	1974	Gunther of Ragstone, Sh. Ch.	31	JW
36		Greyfilk Granella, Sh. Ch.	3	
37	1975	Ludmilla of Ragstone, Sh. Ch.	11	
38		Monroes Ubiquitous, Sh. Ch.	3	
39		Ragstone Rhion, Sh. Ch.	3	
40		Cannylad Balenciaga le Dix, Sh. Ch.	3	
41	1976	Aruni Calidore, Sh. Ch.	3	JW
42		Gifford's Lady, Ch.	4	FQ
43		Brundholme Bronella, Sh. Ch.	6	JW
44		Reymar's Aurora, Sh. Ch.	4	
45	1976	Wotan of Ragstone, Ch.	10	FQ
46	1977	Helber Camillo, Ch.	11	FQ
47		Tarset Catriona, Sh. Ch.	4	
48		Heronshaw Silver Fortune, Sh. Ch.	3	
49		Midwil Zak, Sh. Ch.	3	
50		Monroes Aequo, Sh. Ch.	8	
51		Oneva Trenodia, Sh. Ch.	3	
52		Petraqua Wagtail, Ch.	11	FQ
53		Flimmoric Fieldday, Sh. Ch.	16	JW
54		Phayreheidi Chelal of Ambersbury, Sh. Ch.	4	
55	1978	Fleetapple Wilmar, Sh. Ch.	3	
56		Greyfilk Kirsty, Sh. Ch.	3	
57		Kamsou Moonraker von Bismarck, Ch.	8	FQ

NO.	YEAR	NAME	CCs WON	
58		Aisling Tuathach, Sh. Ch.	3	
59		Greyfilk Knightsman, Sh. Ch.	12	
60	1979	Grinshill Sweet Solario, Sh. Ch.	4	JW CDx UDx WD
61		Hansom Cordon Bleu, Sh. Ch.	4	
62		Kisdon's Artist, Sh. Ch.	4	
63		Hansom Hirondelle, Sh. Ch.	4	
64		Wivelees Wicked Charmer, Sh. Ch.	8	
65		Fossana Bruno, Ch.	4	FQ CDx UDx WDx TD
66		Kisdon's Arabella, Sh. Ch.	6	JW
67	1980	Kisdon's Asti of Nevedith, Sh. Ch.	27	JW
68		Denmo Roadrunner, Sh. Ch.	3	JW
69		Lodgewater Amber, Ch.	8	FQ
70		Rangatira Deerstalker, Sh. Ch.	3	JW
71		Silvilee Lyra, Sh. Ch.	5	
72		Ragstone Rune, Ch.	3	FQ JW
73		Denmo Blueberry Muffin, Ch.	3	FQ JW
74		Arimar's Rolf v d Reiteralm, Sh. Ch.	3	
75		Ragstone Ryuhlan, Sh. Ch.	15	JW
76	1981	Jehnvar of Greyfilk, Sh. Ch.	4	
77	1981	Shalina Sky Diver, Ch.	3	FQ
78		Verrami Aphrodite, Sh. Ch.	4	JW
79		Bredebeck Ilka, Sh. Ch.	7	JW
80	1982	Fossana Quartz, Ch.	9	FQ
81		Denmo Debutante, Sh. Ch.	3	
82		Denmo Side-Car, Sh. Ch.	10	JW
83		Monroes Ambition of Westglade, Ch.	4	FQ CDx UDx WDx
84		Cleimar Country Cobbler of Flimmoric, Sh. Ch.	6	
85		Denmo Raspberry Highball, Sh. Ch.	6	
86		Hansom Brandyman of Gunalt, Sh. Ch.	11	JW
87		Hansom Hospitality, Sh. Ch.	3	
88	1983	Flashman of Flimmoric, Sh. Ch.	9	JW
89		Denmo Prairie Oyster, Sh. Ch.	3	
90		Silvron Sonnet, Sh. Ch.	3	JW
91		Denmo Broadway Melody, Sh. Ch.	3	
92		Czolkins Platinum Cirrus, Ch.	3	JW FT

Champion Producing Sires to 30 September 1983

NO. OF CH.	NAME	SIRE OF:
9	*Ch. Kamsou Moonraker von Bismarck* (US Import)	Denmo Roadrunner, Denmo Side-Car, Denmo Broadway Melody, Denmo Blueberry Muffin, Ragstone Ryuhlan, Denmo Raspberry Highball, Denmo Prairie Oyster, Hansom Brandyman of Gunalt, Hansom Hospitality
7	*Ch. Ragstone Remus*	Knowdale Annabella, Ragstone Ritter, Hansom Sylhill Odette, Oneva Trenodia, Gunther of Ragstone, Wotan of Ragstone, Ludmilla of Ragstone
7	*Sh. Ch. Greyfilk Knightsman*	Kisdon's Artist, Kisdon's Arabella, Kisdon's Asti of Nevedith, Bredebeck Ilka, Czolkins Platinum Cirrus, Cleimar Country Cobbler of Flimmoric, Silvron Sonnet
4	*Sandrock Admiral*	Wolfox Silverglance, Ace of Acomb, Monroes Dynamic, Cabaret Cartford Platinum
4	*Sh. Ch. Cannylad Olympus Daedalus*	Hansom Hobby Hawk, Monroes Ubiquitous, Brundholme Bronella, Cannylad Balenciaga le Dix
4	*Sh. Ch. Jehnvar of Greyfilk*	Flimmoric Fieldday, Greyfilk Knightsman, Greyfilk Kirsty, Lodgewater Amber
3	*Abbot of Monksway*	Theocsbury Abbie, Strawbridge Yuri, Theocsbury Archduke
3	*Wolfox Monroes Hengist*	Monroes Nexus, Monroes Nadine, Monroes O'Netti
3	*Ch. Ragstone Ritter*	Abbeystag Oceanmist, Cannylad Olympus Daedalus, Cannylad Olympus Artemis
3	*Sh. Ch. Flimmoric Fieldday*	Silvilee Lyra, Denmo Debutante, Flashman of Flimmoric
2	*Sh. Ch. Monroes Dynamic*	Wolfox Bittersweet, Monroes Idyll
2	*Wolfox Kentrish Kanonier*	Wolfox Moonsdale Whisper, Wolfox Lycidas
2	*Greyfilk Critic*	Greyfilk Equerry, Greyfilk Granella
2	*Sh. Ch. Monroes Nexus*	Kympenna's Tristan, Monroes Aequo
2	*Greyfilk Gallant*	Reymar's Aurora, Helber Camillo
2	*Ortega Opal Mint*	Tarset Catriona, Aisling Tuathach
2	*Sh. Ch. Abbeystag Oceanmist*	Rangatira Deerstalker, Heronshaw Silver Fortune
2	*Richtkanonier of Ragstone*	Hansom Cordon Bleu, Ragstone Rune
2	*Willingstone Brandy*	Fossana Bruno, Fossana Quartz
2	*Sh. Ch. Kympenna's Tristan*	Aruni Calidore, Monroes Ambition of Westglade
1	*Ipley Apollo*	Strawbridge Oliver
1	*Wolfox Andelyb's Arwydd*	Wolfox Nyria

NO. OF CH.	NAME	SIRE OF:
1	*Cid von Bolkewehr*	Strawbridge Czarina
1	*Derrybeg Argus*	Ragstone Remus
1	*Strawbridge Oberon*	Andelyb's Balch
1	*Sh. Ch. Ace of Acomb*	Coninvale Paul of Acombdole
1	*Arlebroc Abbot*	Ballina of Merse-Side
1	*Monroes Invader*	Waidman Gunnar
1	*Monroes Horsa*	Greyfilk Sapphire
1	*Sh. Ch. Theocsbury Archduke*	Arlebroc Brigand
1	*Monroes Orest*	Monroes Serena
1	*Ragstone Radames*	Ragstone Rhion
1	*Sh. Ch. Ragstone Rhion*	Hansom Hirondelle
1	*Amfrid of Jacarini*	Gifford's Lady
1	*Monroes Upholder*	Midwil Zak
1	*Monroes Uhlan*	Petraqua Wagtail
1	*Sh. Ch. Greyfilk Equerry*	Phayreheidi Chelal of Ambersbury
1	*Ch. Wotan of Ragstone*	Fleetapple Wilmar
1	*Grinshill Maxamillian*	Grinshill Sweet Solario
1	*Bewohner of Hawsvale*	Wivelees Wicked Charmer
1	*Sh. Ch. Gunther of Ragstone*	Jehnvar of Greyfilk
1	*Sh. Ch. Midwil Zak*	Shalina Sky Diver
1	*Clackhill Christian*	Verrami Aphrodite

Champion Producing Dams to 30 September 1983

NO. OF CH.	NAME	DAM OF:
6	*Sh. Ch. Hansom Hirondelle*	Denmo Roadrunner, Denmo Side-Car, Denmo Broadway Melody, Denmo Blueberry Muffin, Denmo Raspberry Highball, Denmo Prairie Oyster
4	*Sh. Ch. Hansom Hobby Hawk*	Hansom Hirondelle, Hansom Cordon Bleu, Hansom Brandyman of Gunalt, Hansom Hospitality
3	*Manana Athene*	Wolfox Silverglance, Monroes Dynamic, Ace of Acomb
3	*Ch. Andelyb's Balch*	Waidman Gunnar, Monroes O'Netti, Monroes Nadine
3	*Dinna vom Morebach* (Austrian Import)	Gunther of Ragstone, Ludmilla of Ragstone, Wotan of Ragstone
3	*Ch. Petraqua Wagtail*	Kisdon's Artist, Kisdon's Arabella, Kisdon's Asti of Nevedith
3	*Monroes Waidman Jane*	Monroes Ubiquitous, Aruni Calidore, Cannylad Balenciaga le Dix

NO. OF CH.	NAME	DAM OF:
2	Sandrock Bella	Theocsbury Abbie, Theocsbury Archduke
2	Cannylad's Bimbo of Merse-Side	Cannylad Olympus Daedalus, Cannylad Olympus Artemis
2	Monroes Xpatriate	Petraqua Wagtail, Grinshill Sweet Solario
2	Greyfilk Haldana	Greyfilk Knightsman, Greyfilk Kirsty
2	Sh. Ch. Ludmilla of Ragstone	Ragstone Rune, Ragstone Ryuhlan
2	Erika of Trafalgar	Fossana Bruno, Fossana Quartz
1	Cobra v Boberstrand (German Import)	Strawbridge Oliver
1	Vita v d Haraska (Austrian Import)	Strawbridge Czarina
1	Sh. Ch. Wolfox Silverglance	Wolfox Lycidas
1	Strawbridge Query	Strawbridge Yuri
1	Wolfox Andelyb's Awen	Wolfox Bittersweet
1	Strawbridge Vanessa	Ragstone Remus
1	Strawbridge Jane	Cabaret Cartford Platinum
1	Wolfox Waidman Bena	Wolfox Nyria
1	Wolfox Silvania	Wolfox Moonsdale Whisper
1	Monroes Helline	Monroes Idyll
1	Theocsbury Bodicea	Coninvale Paul of Acombdole
1	Mist of Merse-Side	Ballina of Merse-Side
1	Monroes Classic	Monroes Nexus
1	Manana Donna's Maxine	Greyfilk Sapphire
1	Ch. Theocsbury Abbie	Hansom Sylhill Odette
1	Cleo Wildmoss	Ragstone Ritter
1	Theocsbury Handy Pet	Arlebroc Brigand
1	Sh. Ch. Hansom Sylhill Odette	Hansom Hobby Hawk
1	Sh. Ch. Greyfilk Sapphire	Greyfilk Equerry
1	Waidman Jemima	Abbeystag Oceanmist
1	Flottheim's Kym (U.S. Import)	Kympenna's Tristan
1	Sh. Ch. Wolfox Nyria	Monroes Serena
1	Greyfilk Emmaclan Angelique	Greyfilk Granella
1	Ragstone Rakete	Ragstone Rhion
1	Greyfilk Caprice	Gifford's Lady
1	Brundholme Brunhilde	Brundholme Bronella
1	Sh. Ch. Monroes Serena	Reymar's Aurora
1	Athelson's Sophia	Helber Camillo
1	Tarset Devorgilla of Merse-Side	Tarset Catriona
1	Sh. Ch. Monroes Nadine	Heronshaw Silver Fortune

NO. OF CH.	NAME	DAM OF:
1	*Monroes Rosalka*	Midwil Zak
1	*Sh. Ch. Monroes Ubiquitous*	Monroes Aequo
1	*Acombdole Athene*	Oneva Trenodia
1	*Ch. Gifford's Lady*	Flimmoric Fieldday
1	*Heidicopse Lisa*	Phayreheidi Chelal of Ambersbury
1	*Cannylad's Lady Hamilton of Fleetapple*	Fleetapple Wilmar
1	*Heronshaw Silver Chimes*	Aisling Tuathach
1	*Hawsvale Furstin*	Wivelees Wicked Charmer
1	*Gretchen of Sandstone*	Lodgewater Amber
1	*Grinshill Phazachalie Jane*	Rangatira Deerstalker
1	*Greymorn Cloud*	Silvilee Lyra
1	*Greyfilk Ginza*	Jehnvar of Greyfilk
1	*Monroes Unity*	Shalina Sky Diver
1	*Gerda of High Garrett*	Verrami Aphrodite
1	*Bredebeck Minna*	Bredebeck Ilka
1	*Sh. Ch. Aisling Tuathach*	Denmo Debutante
1	*Sh. Ch. Monroes Aequo*	Monroes Ambition of Westglade
1	*Flimmoric Fairdinkum*	Cleimar Country Cobbler of Flimmoric
1	*Sh. Ch. Wivelees Wicked Charmer*	Flashman of Flimmoric
1	*Sh. Ch. Silvilee Lyra*	Silvron Sonnet
1	*Fossana Etta*	Czolkins Platinum Cirrus

Breeders of more than One Champion at 30 September 1983

(* and † denote litter-mates)

NO. OF CH.	BREEDER AND AFFIX	CHAMPIONS OR SHOW CHAMPIONS
10	Mrs J. Matuszewska, *Monroes*	Monroes Dynamic, Monroes Idyll, Monroes Nexus, Monroes Serena, Monroes Nadine.* Monroes O'Netti,* Monroes Ambition of Westglade, Monroes Ubiquitous,† Cannylad Balenciaga le Dix,† Monroes Aequo
7	Mrs D. Mosey, *Denmo*	Denmo Roadrunner,* Denmo Broadway Melody,* Denmo Blueberry Muffin,* Denmo Debutante, Denmo Side-Car,† Denmo Prairie Oyster,† Denmo Raspberry Highball†
5	Mrs B. Douglas-Redding, *Wolfox*	Ace of Acomb,* Wolfox Silverglance,* Wolfox Lycidas, Wolfox Nyria, Wolfox Bittersweet

NO. OF CH.	BREEDER AND AFFIX	CHAMPIONS OR SHOW CHAMPIONS
5	Mrs J. Fussell, *Greyfilk*	Greyfilk Sapphire, Greyfilk Equerry, Greyfilk Knightsman,★ Greyfilk Kirsty,★ Greyfilk Granella
5	Mr R. M. W. Finch, *Hansom*	Hansom Hobby Hawk, Hansom Cordon Bleu, Hansom Hirondelle, Hansom Hospitality,★ Hansom Brandyman of Gunalt★
3	Mrs E. M. Petty, *Strawbridge*	Strawbridge Czarina, Strawbridge Oliver, Strawbridge Yuri
3	Mrs E. L. Fearn, *Ragstone* (registered)	Gunther of Ragstone,★ Ludmilla of Ragstone,★ Wotan of Ragstone★
3	Mr and Mrs A. Burgoin, *Ragstone*	Ragstone Rhion, Ragstone Rune, Ragstone Ryuhlan
3	Mrs P. Edminson and Mr J. N. Newton, *Kisdon's*	Kisdon's Artist,★ Kisdon's Asti of Nevedith,★ Kisdon's Arabella★
2	Mr and Mrs G. Webb, *Theocsbury*	Theocsbury Abbie,★ Theocsbury Archduke★
2	Mr J. Lamb, *Cannylad*	Cannylad Olympus Daedalus,★ Cannylad Olympus Artemis★

Junior Warrant

To obtain the title of Junior Warrant, the dog must obtain 25 points whilst under the age of 18 months. The scale of points is as follows: (i) 3 points for each first prize in breed classes at Championship Shows where CCs are on offer; (ii) 1 point for each first prize in breed classes at Championship Shows where no CCs are on offer, or at Open Shows.

JNR WARRANT WINNERS	OWNER	SIRE AND DAM
Ragstone Remus, Ch. (the first in 1964)	Mr and Mrs A. Burgoin	Derrybeg Argus Strawbridge Vanessa
Coninvale Paul of Acombdole, Sh. Ch.	Dr A. Mucklow	Sh. Ch. Ace of Acomb Theocsbury Bodicea
Knowdale Annabella, Sh. Ch.	Mr G. Taylor	Ch. Ragstone Remus Hepton Queen
Ballina of Merse-Side, Sh. Ch.	Mrs E. Hackett	Arlebroc Abbot Mist of Merse-Side
Keppel Kurt	Mr A. F. Wallace	Kympenna's Samson Monroes Quip
Gunther of Ragstone, Sh. Ch.	Mr and Mrs P. H. Wardall	Ch. Ragstone Remus Dinna vom Morebach
Heronshaw Silver Dawn	Mrs D. Chapman	Sh. Ch. Abbeystag Oceanmist Sh. Ch. Monroes Nadine
Brundholme Bronella, Sh. Ch.	Mrs J. Hensey	Ch. Ragstone Remus Minka of Brundholme

236

APPENDIX VII

JNR WARRANT WINNERS	OWNER	SIRE AND DAM
Aruni Calidore, Sh. Ch.	Mr and Mrs B. Mulberry	Sh. Ch. Kympenna's Tristan Monroes Waidman Jane
Brundholme Banachek	Mrs M. Richmond	Sh. Ch. Ragstone Rhion Minka of Brundholme
Bredebeck Fritz	Mrs M. Cox	Sh. Ch. Gunther of Ragstone Bredebeck Sophie
Flimmoric Fieldday, Sh. Ch.	Mrs C. Alston	Sh. Ch. Jehnvar of Greyfilk Ch. Gifford's Lady
Fleetapple Overture	Mr J. Loch	Sh. Ch. Abbeystag Oceanmist Cannylad's Lady Hamilton of Fleetapple
Abbisline Greta	Mr and Mrs R. Quiddington	Sh. Ch. Gunther of Ragstone Webbdant's Arabesque
Ragstone Rune, Ch.	Mrs D. Arrowsmith	Richtkanonier of Ragstone Sh. Ch. Ludmilla of Ragstone
Rangatira Deerstalker, Sh. Ch.	Mr J. Loch	Sh. Ch. Abbeystag Oceanmist Grinshill Phazachalie Jane
Grinshill Sweet Solario, *Sh. Ch.* CDx, UDx	Mrs S. Walkden	Grinshill Maxamillian Monroes Xpatriate
Gentil Thundercloud, CDx	Mrs T. Cass	Sidwell Gentil Knight Phayreheidi Fogleflush
Merryhell Havoc	Mr D. Hawes	Sh. Ch. Kympenna's Tristan Monroes Quicksilver
Perdita of Fleetapple	Mrs S. Marshall	Ch. Wotan of Ragstone Grafin Silbern
Denmo Blueberry Muffin, Ch.	Mrs J. George	Ch. Kamsou Moonraker v Bismarck Sh. Ch. Hansom Hirondelle
Ragstone Ringtaube	Mr and Mrs A. Burgoin	Richtkanonier of Ragstone Ragstone Rhydriad
Denmo Roadrunner, Sh. Ch.	Mrs D. Mosey	Ch. Kamsou Moonraker v Bismarck Sh. Ch. Hansom Hirondelle
Kisdon's Arabell, Sh. Ch.	Lt Cdr J. Bond	Sh. Ch. Greyfilk Knightsman Ch. Petraqua Wagtail
Kisdon's Asti of Nevedith, *Sh. Ch.*	Mr and Mrs N. Edminson	Sh. Ch. Greyfilk Knightsman Ch. Petraqua Wagtail
Verrami Aphrodite, Sh. Ch.	Mrs D. Bushby	Clackhill Christian Gerda of High Garrett
Ragstone Ryuhlan, Sh. Ch.	Mr and Mrs A. Burgoin	Ch. Kamsou Moonraker v Bismarck Sh. Ch. Ludmilla of Ragstone
Bredebeck Ilka, Sh. Ch.	Mr and Mrs W. Fairlie	Sh. Ch. Greyfilk Knightsman Bredebeck Minna

Hansom Brandyman of
  Gunalt, Sh. Ch.
	Mr and Mrs S. Hollings	Ch. Kamsou Moonraker v
		  Bismarck
		Sh. Ch. Hansom Hobby Hawk

237

JNR WARRANT WINNERS	OWNER	SIRE AND DAM
Sterling Tumbling Dice	Mrs S. Topley	Merryhell Havoc Lindon Enterprize
Czolkins Captivatin' Cushat	Mr and Mrs L. R. W. Jupp	Sh. Ch. Greyfilk Knightsman Fossana Etta
Czolkins Platinum Cirrus, Ch.	Mr and Mrs P. A. Turner	Sh. Ch. Greyfilk Knightsman Fossana Etta
Denmo Side-Car, Sh. Ch.	Mrs J. Barry	Ch. Kamsou Moonraker v Bismarck Sh. Ch. Hansom Hirondelle
Ragstone Reedwren	Mr and Mrs C. Helm	Sh. Ch. Ragstone Ryuhlan Ragstone Russelle
Domaset Grey Sovereign	Mrs M. Bennett	Son of Seth Malbremer Jane
Cleimar Dainty Dove of Rangatira	Messrs J. Loch and C. Brown	Sh. Ch. Flimmoric Fieldday Sh. Ch. Wivelees Wicked Charmer
Flashman of Flimmoric, Sh. Ch.	Mrs C. Alston	Sh. Ch. Flimmoric Fieldday Sh. Ch. Wivelees Wicked Charmer
Vanwilkie Nearly Napoleon	Mr and Mrs C. R. Wilkinson	Sh. Ch. Arimars Rolf v d Reiteralm Aruni Gemma
Pipwell Pipedreamer	Mr R. E. Wroe	Sh. Ch. Jehnvar of Greyfilk Hofstetter Hannah
Silvron Sonnet, Sh. Ch.	Mr and Mrs R. Bates	Sh. Ch. Greyfilk Knightsman Sh. Ch. Silvilee Lyra
Hollieseast Engelchen	Mr A. Rochford	Sh. Ch. Greyfilk Knightsman Terrag Heloise of Hollieseast
Datrix Minto Renown	Mrs J. Barry	Sh. Ch. Denmo Roadrunner Carnoustie Silver Liebchen
Shalina Fieldsman of Cannylad	Mr J. Lamb	Ch. Shalina Sky Diver Rujanta Blackthorn
Czersieger Clever Clown	Mr and Mrs C. Hill	Fossana Algenon Heronshaw Silver Solveig
Sireva Skylark	Miss G. Averis	Sh. Ch. Ragstone Ryuhlan Sh. Ch. Denmo Raspberry Highball
My Girl Quest of Mikanda	Mr and Mrs C. Bullock	Monroes A-Joker Mikanda's Junoesque
Aylmarch Aldous of Tasairgid	Mr and Mrs W. Fairlie	Sh. Ch. Greyfilk Knightsman Bredebeck Mercedes
Glinstre Saracen	Mrs A. Williams	Kisdon's Blakeney Silberprior la Rocca
Gunalt Anais-Anais	Mr and Mrs S. Hollings	Sh. Ch. Hansom Brandyman of Gunalt Vimana Viveca of Gunalt
Kisdon's Derring-Do	Mr and Mrs N. Edminson	Sh. Ch. Ragstone Ryuhlan Sh. Ch. Kisdon's Asti of Nevedith

238

JNR WARRANT WINNERS	OWNER	SIRE AND DAM
Ambersbury Jazzman	Mrs M. Wardall	Hawsvale Hermod Ambersbury Impromptu
Ryanstock Ashkanazy	Mr and Mrs K. J. Grewcock	Sh. Ch. Flimmoric Fieldday Monroes Ash Lady of Ryanstock
Rujanta Game Plucker	Mrs P. C. Thompson	Ch. Fossana Quartz Vanwilkie Naughty Nancie
Lucky Lady	Mr R. Allen	Fleetapple Ramsey Silberprior Blithe
Hansom Misty Blue	Mr R. M. W. Finch	Sh. Ch. Jehnvar of Greyfilk Sh. Ch. Hanson Cordon Bleu

Weimaraners Certified Clear of Hip Dysplasia by the BVA/KC Official Scheme

(Note: only dogs issued with a BVA/KC Certificate are listed; other dogs have been unofficially cleared but have no certificate of proof.)

SEX	NAME	SIRE AND DAM
D	*Ragstone Radamès*	Ragstone Remus/Andelyb's Buddugol
B	*Arlebroc Celeste*	Coninvale Paul of Acombdole/Arlebroc Amber
B	*Bilbrook Brunhilde of Innisron*	Derrybeg Andy/Theocsbury Handy Lass
B	*Shinglehill Briony*	Greyfilk Ambassador/Watchant Willow
D	*Ragstone Rhion, Sh. Ch.*	Ragstone Radamès/Ragstone Rakete
B	*Ragstone Fantasia*	Englas Odin/Phantom Star
D	*Waidman Hank*	Kympenna's Tristan/Abbeystag Gytha
B	*Flimmoric Solitaire*	Ragstone Ritter/Gifford's Lady
B	*Willingstone Chartreuse*	Sidwell Prospero/Gunmetal Gameflusher
B	*Dreenhill Cyran Sara of Gunmetal*	Gunmetal Growth Stock/Midwil Zsa Zsa
D	*Gunmetal Giles*	Helber Camillo/Gunmetal Emma
B	*Ambersbury Engelstimme*	Gunther of Ragstone/Phayreheidi Chelal of Ambersbury
B	*Abbisline Greta*	Gunther of Ragstone/Webbdant's Arabesque
D	*Grinshill Tudor Minstrel*	Ragstone Radamès/Shinglehill Briony
B	*Grinshill Athene Wildmoss*	Waidman Hank/Shinglehill Briony
D	*Hofstetter Beau*	Greyfilk Equerry/Chantel of Kenstaff
D	*Kiltimach Spike*	Shadow of Stavrovouni/Miss Jackie
B	*Nettle of Nevedith*	Monroes Uhlan/Monroes Zena
B	*Hofstetter Hannah*	Greyfilk Equerry/Chantel of Kenstaff
D	*Bredebeck Fritz*	Gunther of Ragstone/Bredebeck Sophie
B	*Reymar's Zana*	Greyfilk Equerry/Monroes Serena
B	*Groundsel Girl*	Rhions Gray Apollo/Juniper Jane
B	*Amarna Lubeck Lisa*	Helber Camillo/Groundsel Girl
B	*Firebrau of Fleetapple*	Wotan of Ragstone/Grafin Silbern
D	*Denmo Roadrunner, Sh. Ch.*	Kamsou Moonraker v Bismarck/Hansom Hirondelle
B	*Cillyn Samantha*	Helber Camillo/Ranmore Sombra
B	*Alcyde Amy*	Helber Camillo/Merryhell Glorious
D	*Clackhill Christian*	Fossana Algenon/Clackhill Jade
D	*Houblon Euryalus*	Jehnvar of Greyfilk/Houblon Clytie

SEX	NAME	SIRE AND DAM
B	*Galgo Gooseberry*	Rangatira Deerstalker/Amarna Marie Helle at Galgo
B	*Grinshill Sweet Solario, Sh. Ch.*	Grinshill Maxamillian/Monroes Xpatriate
D	*Frojan Napley Wildefrost of Plusila*	Gunther of Ragstone/Helber Dorcas
D	*Denmo Side-Car, Sh. Ch.*	Kamsou Moonraker v Bismarck/Hansom Hirondelle
B	*Pondridge Asta Melody* (L/H)	Walberg Astor Claudius/Aruni Darienne From Seicer
D	*Benjamin Beau*	Wotan of Ragstone/Hansom Mystere
D	*Ragstone Ryuhlan, Sh. Ch.*	Kamsou Moonraker v Bismarck/Ludmilla of Ragstone
B	*Gunmetal Acceptor*	Gunmetal Giles/Dreenhill Cyran Sara of Gunmetal
B	*Bredebeck Mercedes*	Greyfilk Equerry/Bredebeck Else
D	*Ragstone Reckless*	Ragstone Ryuhlan/Ragstone Russelle
B	*Kapitada Timandra*	Gunther of Ragstone/Valhalla Harlequin
B	*Claranjay Araphnataph*	Gunther of Ragstone/Firebrau of Fleetapple
B	*Ambersbury Impromptu*	Ambersbury Maestersinger/Ambersbury Engelstimme
D	*Vanwilkie Nearly Napoleon*	Arimar's Rolf v d Reiteralm/Aruni Gemma
D	*Frojan Molyvos Crisp*	Gunther of Ragstone/Helber Dorcas
B	*Gunmetal Debtor*	Gunmetal Giles/Dreenhill Cyran Sara of Gunmetal
B	*Sterling Tumbling Dice*	Merryhell Havoc/Lindon Enterprize
B	*Vanwilkie Velvet Valentine*	Clackhill Christian/Heronshaw Silver
D	*Ragstone Rasputin*	Ragstone Ryotsquad/Ragstone Ringtaube
B	*Houblon Erato*	Jehnvar of Greyfilk/Houblon Clytie
D	*Aylmarch Aldous of Tasairgid*	Greyfilk Knightsman/Bredebeck Mercedes
B	*Gunmetal Joanna*	Gunmetal Giles/Gunmetal Peach Blush
B	*Sireva Skylark*	Ragstone Ryuhlan/Denmo Raspberry Highball
D	*Sireva Saker Falcon*	Ragstone Ryuhlan/Denmo Raspberry Highball
B	*Cassandra Darlin'*	Richtkanonier of Ragstone/Angelica of High Garrett
B	*Denmo Prairie Oyster, Sh. Ch.*	Kamsou Moonraker v Bismarck/Hansom Hirondelle
B	*Aylmarch Adella*	Greyfilk Knightsman/Bredebeck Mercedes
B	*Aylmarch Astrid*	Greyfilk Knightsman/Bredebeck Mercedes
B	*Philhalle Carillon*	Grinshill Maxamillian/Lotte of Philhalle
B	*Bisque of Fleetapple*	Wotan of Ragstone/Hansom Mystere

The Show Gallery

THE 92 BRITISH CHAMPIONS TO DATE

Show Champion *Wolfox Silverglance* (B) 157 AT.
Born: 1.1.58. Died: 1969.
Breeder/Owner: Mrs B. Douglas-Redding.
Winner of 7 CCs.

	Strawbridge Duke	*Ipley Apollo*
		Hella aus der Helmeute
Sandrock Admiral		
	Strawbridge Carol	*Cid von Bolkewehr*
		Vita von der Haraska
	Ipley Apollo	*Erich vom Haimberg*
		Babette von der Katzbach
Manana Athene		
	Strawbridge Ermegard	*Bando von Fohr*
		Vita von der Haraska

Champion *Strawbridge Oliver* (D) 160 AT.
Born: 17.7.57. Died: 1968.
Breeder: Mrs E. M. Petty. Owner: Mr G. Webb.
Winner of 7 CCs; Field Qualified.
Oliver was the first Weimaraner to gain full championship status when he qualified at the GSP Trial at Hailes Castle in October 1962.

	Erich v Haimberg	*Bobo v Schwanebusch*
		Asta v Haimberg
Ipley Apollo		
	Babette v d Katzbach	*Bobo v Reiningen*
		Benigna v d Teufelsposse
	Casar v d Finne*	*Arco v Bruchholz*
		Alix v d Finne
Cobra von Boberstrand		
	Alma v Boberstrand	*Arras v Zauchebruch*
		Ank v Hohenleite

* Later exported ex-Germany to USA; gained title.

244

Show Champion *Strawbridge Czarina* (B) 281 AT.
Born: 6.7.53. Died: 1965.
Breeder: Mrs E. M. Petty. Owner: Mrs F. Bainbridge.
Winner of 7 CCs.

Cid v Bolkewehr	Asso v Uplengen	Bodo v Hohenleite
		Antje v Bruchholz
	Centa v d Burg	Bodo v Hohenleite
		Asta v Schloss Weitmar
Vita v d Haraska	Sidi v Brunneckerhof	Fels v Diendorf
		Quella v d Sonnseite
	Ata v Thayaschloss	Alf v Schlossanger
		Diana v Waldenfels

Show Champion *Wolfox Lycidas* (D) 1249 AU.
Born: 13.10.59.
Breeder/Owner: Mrs B. Douglas-Redding.
Winner of 4 CCs.

Wolfox Kentrish Kanonier	Alex of Monksway	Casar v Bolkewehr
		Anka v Suntel
	Deerswood Quicksilver	Strawbridge Fury
		Strawbridge Elfrida
Sh. Ch. Wolfox Silverglance	Sandrock Admiral	Strawbridge Duke
		Strawbridge Carol
	Manana Athene	Ipley Apollo
		Strawbridge Ermegard

Champion *Theocsbury Abbie* (B) 1413 AV.
Born: 29.10.59. Died: 1973.
Breeder: Mr G. Webb. Owner: Mr D. G. Roberts.
Winner of 5 CCs; Field Qualified 1964.

Abbot of Monksway	Strawbridge Duke	Ipley Apollo
		Hella aus der Helmeute
	Amber of Monksway	Casar von Bolkewehr
		Anka vom Suntel
Sandrock Bella	Manana Adonis	Ipley Apollo
		Strawbridge Ermegard
	Strawbridge Carol	Cid von Bolkewehr
		Vita von der Haraska

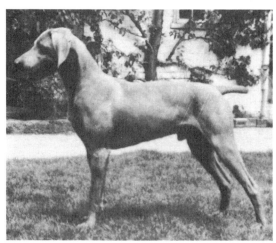

Show Champion *Ace of Acomb* (D) 1134 AT.
Born: 1.1.58. Died: 1966.
Breeder: Mrs B. Douglas-Redding. Owner: Dr A. W. Mucklow.
Winner of 7 CCs.

Sandrock Admiral	*Strawbridge Duke*	*Ipley Apollo* *Hella aus der Helmeute*
	Strawbridge Carol	*Cid von Bolkewehr* *Vita von der Haraska*
Manana Athene	*Ipley Apollo*	*Erich von Haimberg* *Babette von der Katzbach*
	Strawbridge Ermegard	*Bando von Fohr* *Vita von der Haraska*

Show Champion *Monroes Dynamic* (D) 2537 AU.
Born: 15.7.59. Died: 1965.
Breeder/Owner: Mrs J. Matuszewska.
Winner of 9 CCs.
Dynamic was the first Weimaraner to gain a Best in Show award which was at the 1964 Hampshire Gundog Club show.

Sandrock Admiral	*Strawbridge Duke*	*Ipley Apollo* *Hella a d Helmeute*
	Strawbridge Carol	*Cid v Bolkewehr* *Vita v d Haraska*
Manana Athene	*Ipley Apollo*	*Erich v Haimberg* *Babette v d Katzbach*
	Strawbridge Ermegard	*Bando v Fohr* *Vita v d Haraska*

Champion *Andelyb's Balch* (B) 144 AW.
Born: 24.10.61. Died: 1973.
Breeder: Mrs Farquhar.
Owner: Mrs L. Petrie-Hay and Mrs J. Matuszewska.
Winner of 5 CCs; Field Qualified 1964.

Strawbridge Oberon	*Ipley Apollo*	*Erich v Haimberg* *Babette v d Katzbach*
	Cobra v Boberstrand	*Casar v d Finne* *Alma v Boberstrand*
Manana Brenda	*Manana Adonis*	*Ipley Apollo* *Strawbridge Ermegard*
	Sandrock Blaze	*Manana Adonis* *Strawbridge Carol*

Show Champion *Strawbridge Yuri* (B) 459 AV.
Born: 26.1.61. Died: 1971.
Breeder: Mrs E. M. Petty. Owner: Mrs S. M. Roberts.
Winner of 5 CCs.

Abbot of Monksway	*Strawbridge Duke*	*Ipley Apollo* *Hella a d Helmeute*
	Amber of Monksway	*Casar v Bolkewehr* *Anka v Suntel*
Strawbridge Query	*Sandrock Ami*	*Strawbridge Duke* *Strawbridge Carol*
	Ipley Babette	*Woodcock's Argus* *Ipley Athene*

Show Champion *Wolfox Bittersweet* (B) 2844 AW.
Born: 14.5.62.
Breeder/Owner: Mrs B. Douglas-Redding.
Winner of 6 CCs.

	Sandrock Admiral	*Strawbridge Duke*
		Strawbridge Carol
Sh. Ch. Monroes Dynamic		
	Manana Athene	*Ipley Apollo*
		Strawbridge Ermegard
	Valhalla's Helmsman Arrow	*US Ch. Casar v Haussermann*
		Marward's Brenda
Wolfox Andelyb's Awen		
	Manana Brenda	*Manana Adonis*
		Sandrock Blaze

Champion *Ragstone Remus* (D) 365 AX.
Born: 4.6.63. Died: 1974.
Breeders: Mr and Mrs J. H. Milward. Owners: Mr and Mrs A. Burgoin.
Winner of 16 CCs and 3 Green Stars; Field Qualified.
First Weimaraner to attain Junior Warrant. Weimaraner of the Year 1967.

	Sandrock Admiral	*Strawbridge Duke*
		Strawbridge Carol
Derrybeg Argus		
	Inka v Weissen Kreuz	*Kuno aus der Helmeute*
		Fanny von Reiningen
	Ipley Apollo	*Erich vom Haimberg*
		Babette von der Katzbach
Strawbridge Vanessa		
	Sh. Ch. Strawbridge Czarina	*Cid von Bolkewehr*
		Vita von der Haraska

Photo: Cooke.

Show Champion *Cabaret Cartford Platinum* (B) 1252 AU.
Born: 25.7.60.
Breeder: Mrs McNutt. Owner: Miss R. C. Monkhouse.
Winner of 6 CCs.

	Strawbridge Duke	*Ipley Apollo*
		Hella a d Helmeute
Sandrock Admiral		
	Strawbridge Carol	*Cid v Bolkewehr*
		Vita v d Haraska
	Alex of Monkway	*Casar v Bolkewehr*
		Anka v Suntel
Strawbridge Jane		
	Cobra v Boberstrand	*Casar v d Finne*
		Alma v Boberstrand

Drawing by Anne Johnson.

251

252

Show Champion *Wolfox Nyria* (B) 248 AY.
Born: 17.4.64. Died: 1974.
Breeder/Owner: Mrs B. Douglas-Redding.
Winner of 4 CCs.

Wolfox Andelyb's Arwydd	*Valhalla's Helmsman Arrow*	*US Ch. Casar v Haussermann* / *Marward's Brenda*
	Manana Brenda	*Manana Adonis* / *Sandrock Blaze*
Wolfox's Waidman Bena	*Theocsbury Deerstalker*	*Ch. Strawbridge Oliver* / *Strawbridge Madam*
	Theocsbury Elsa	*Ch. Strawbridge Oliver* / *Cartford Silver Cloud*

Photo: Cooke.

Show Champion *Theocsbury Archduke* (D) 514 AV.
Born: 29.10.59. Died: 1967.
Breeder: Mr G. Webb. Owner: Mr B. Virgo.
Winner of 3 CCs.

Abbot of Monksway	*Strawbridge Duke*	*Ipley Apollo* / *Hella aus der Helmeute*
	Amber of Monksway	*Casar von Bolkewehr* / *Anka vom Suntel*
Sandrock Bella	*Manana Adonis*	*Ipley Apollo* / *Strawbridge Ermegard*
	Strawbridge Carol	*Cid von Bolkewehr* / *Vita von der Haraska*

Show Champion *Wolfox Moonsdale Whisper* (B) 1251 AU.
Born: 28.6.60. Died: 1973.
Breeder: Mrs J. Hodgson. Owner: Mr M. G. Simmons.
Winner of 3 CCs.

Wolfox Kentrish Kanonier	*Alex of Monksway*	*Casar v Bolkewehr* / *Anka v Suntel*
	Deerswood Quicksilver	*Strawbridge Fury* / *Strawbridge Elfrida*
Wolfox Silvania	*Sandrock Admiral*	*Strawbridge Duke* / *Strawbridge Carol*
	Manana Athene	*Ipley Apollo* / *Strawbridge Ermegard*

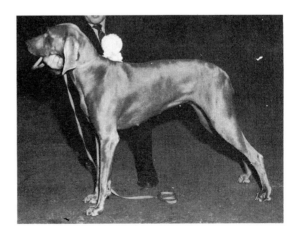

Show Champion *Monroes Idyll* (B) 748 AY.
Born: 15.4.63.
Breeder/Owner: Mrs J. Matuszewska.
Winner of 3 CCs.

	Sandrock Admiral	Strawbridge Duke
		Strawbridge Carol
Sh. Ch. Monroes Dynamic		
	Manana Athene	Ipley Apollo
		Strawbridge Ermegard
	Wolfox's Sandrock Cha Cha	Smokey
		Strawbridge Carol
Monroes Helline		
	Manana Athene	Ipley Apollo
		Strawbridge Ermegard

Show Champion *Coninvale Paul of Acombdole* (D) 2146 AY.
Born: 15.7.64. Died: 1974.
Breeder: Mr B. E. Johnson. Owner: Dr A. W. Mucklow.
Winner of 7 CCs; Junior Warrant.
Weimaraner of the Year Award 1966.

	Sandrock Admiral	Strawbridge Duke
		Strawbridge Carol
Sh. Ch. Ace of Acomb		
	Manana Athene	Ipley Apollo
		Strawbridge Ermegard
	Ch. Strawbridge Oliver	Ipley Apollo
		Cobra v Boberstrand
Theocsbury Boadacea		
	Sandrock Bella	Manana Adonis
		Strawbridge Carol

Show Champion *Knowdale Annabella* (B) 309 BA.
Born: 5.4.66.
Breeder/Owner: Mr G. Taylor.
Winner of 4 CCs; Junior Warrant.

	Derrybeg Argus	Sandrock Admiral
		Inka v Weissen Kreuz
Ch. Ragstone Remus		
	Strawbridge Vanessa	Ipley Apollo
		Sh. Ch. Strawbridge Czarina
	Sh. Ch. Theocsbury Archduke	Abbot of Monksway
		Sandrock Bella
Hepton Queen		
	Cartford Silver Sand	Valhalla's Helmsman Arrow
		Strawbridge Jane

256

Show Champion *Ballina of Merse-Side* (B) 1082 BA.
Born: 31.12.66. Died: 1980.
Breeder: Mr A. C. Thirlwell. Owner: Mrs E. Hackett.
Winner of 31 CCs; Junior Warrant. Record holder for CCs in bitches.
Weimaraner of the Year Award 1968 and 1973.

	Sh. Ch. Theocsbury Archduke	*Abbot of Monksway*
		Sandrock Bella
Arlebroc Abbot		
	Theocsbury Handy Pet	*Ch. Strawbridge Oliver*
		Strawbridge Quiz
	Strawbridge Bando	*Bando von Fohr*
		Cobra von Boberstrand
Mist of Merse-Side		
	Rana of Tulliebole	*Ranter of Lochsloy*
		Anka of Monksway

Photo: Pearce.

Show Champion *Waidman Gunnar* (D) 95 BA.
Born: 2.6.66.
Breeder: Mrs L. Petrie-Hay. Owner: Mr J. N. Newton.
Winner of 3 CCs.
Exported to Japan.

	Sh. Ch. Monroes Dynamic	*Sandrock Admiral*
		Manana Athene
Monroes Invader		
	Monroes Helline	*Wolfox's Sandrock Cha Cha*
		Manana Athene
	Strawbridge Oberon	*Ipley Apollo*
		Cobra v Boberstrand
Ch. Andelyb's Balch		
	Manana Brenda	*Manana Adonis*
		Sandrock Blaze

Show Champion *Monroes Nexus* (D) 612 AZ.
Born: 10.5.65. Died: 1974.
Breeder/Owner: Mrs J. Matuszewska.
Winner of 9 CCs.

	Wolfox's Sandrock Cha Cha	*Smokey*
		Strawbridge Carol
Wolfox Monroes Hengist		
	Manana Athene	*Ipley Apollo*
		Strawbridge Ermegard
	Sandrock Admiral	*Strawbridge Duke*
		Strawbridge Carol
Monroes Classic		
	Manana Athene	*Ipley Apollo*
		Strawbridge Ermegard

Show Champion *Greyfilk Sapphire* (B) 145 AZ.
Born: 21.8.64. Died: 1971.
Breeder/Owner: Mrs J. Fussell.
Winner of 3 CCs.

	Wolfox's Sandrock Cha Cha	*Smokey*
Monroes Horsa		*Strawbridge Carol*
	Manana Athene	*Ipley Apollo*
		Strawbridge Ermegard
	Manana Halsall Sea Count	*Ch. Strawbridge Oliver*
Manana Donna's Maxine		*Sandrock Coral*
	Manana Beguine	*Manana Adonis*
		Sandrock Blaze

Show Champion *Hansom Sylhill Odette* (B) 574 BC.
Born: 14.11.65. Died: 1974.
Breeder: Mrs S. M. Roberts. Owner: Mr R. M. W. Finch.
Winner of 6 CCs.

	Derrybeg Argus	*Sandrock Admiral*
Ch. Ragstone Remus		*Inka v Weissen Kreuz*
	Strawbridge Vanessa	*Ipley Apollo*
		Sh. Ch. Strawbridge Czarina
	Abbot of Monksway	*Strawbridge Duke*
Ch. Theocsbury Abbie		*Amber of Monksway*
	Sandrock Bella	*Manana Adonis*
		Strawbridge Carol

Champion *Ragstone Ritter* (D) 1748 BC.
Born: 29.3.67. Died: 1975.
Breeder: Mr D. Modi. Owners: Mr and Mrs A. Burgoin.
Winner of 22 CCs; Field Qualified.
Won 11 Best in Show awards, 7 of them at ALL-BREED shows.
Won the Weimaraner of the Year award for three consecutive years 1969/70/71.
Won the Dog CC at Crufts five years in succession from 1970 onwards.

	Derrybeg Argus	*Sandrock Admiral*
Ch. Ragstone Remus		*Inka v Weissen Kreuz*
	Strawbridge Vanessa	*Ipley Apollo*
		Sh. Ch. Strawbridge Czarina
	Sh. Ch. Monroes Dynamic	*Sandrock Admiral*
Cleo Wildmoss		*Manana Athene*
	Lotti Go-Lightly	*Wolfox's Sandrock Cha-Cha*
		Kentrish Nickel

Photo: Pearce.

Show Champion *Arlebroc Brigand* (D) 2045 BA.
Born: 11.7.66.
Breeder: Mr E. B. Virgo. Owner: Mrs J. Putsman.
Winner of 3 CCs.

Sh. Ch. Theocsbury Archduke	*Abbot of Monksway*	*Strawbridge Duke* *Amber of Monksway*
	Sandrock Bella	*Manana Adonis* *Strawbridge Carol*
Theocsbury Handy Pet	*Ch. Strawbridge Oliver*	*Ipley Apollo* *Cobra v Boberstrand*
	Strawbridge Quiz	*Sandrock Ami* *Ipley Babette*

Show Champion *Monroes O'Netti* (B) 442 BD.
Born: 14.1.68. Died: 1972.
Breeder: Mrs J. Matuszewska. Owner: Mr J. N. Newton.
Winner of 6 CCs.

Wolfox Monroes Hengist	*Wolfox's Sandrock Cha-Cha*	*Smokey* *Strawbridge Carol*
	Manana Athene	*Ipley Apollo* *Strawbridge Ermegard*
Ch. Andelyb's Balch	*Strawbridge Oberon*	*Ipley Apollo* *Cobra von Boberstrand*
	Manana Brenda	*Manana Adonis* *Sandrock Blaze*

Show Champion *Cannylad Olympus Daedalus* (D) 714 BE.
Born: 10.10.68. Died 1979.
Breeder/Owner: Mr J. Lamb.
Winner of 4 CCs.

Ch. Ragstone Ritter	*Ch. Ragstone Remus*	*Derrybeg Argus* *Strawbridge Vanessa*
	Cleo Wildmoss	*Sh. Ch. Monroes Dynamic* *Lotti Go-Lightly*
Cannylad's Bimbo of Merse-Side	*Arlebroc Abbot*	*Sh. Ch. Theocsbury Archduke* *Theocsbury Handy Pet*
	Mist of Merse-Side	*Strawbridge Bando* *Rana of Tulliebole*

Photo: Pearce.

Show Champion *Hansom Hobby Hawk* (B) 2007 BF.
Born: 26.1.70. Died: 1983.
Breeder/Owner: Mr R. M. W. Finch.
Winner of 13 CCs.
First championship show group winner, 1974 Birmingham.

Sh. Ch. Cannylad Olympus Daedalus	*Ch. Ragstone Ritter*	*Ch. Ragstone Remus* *Cleo Wildmoss*
	Cannylad's Bimbo of Merse-Side	*Arlebroc Abbot* *Mist of Merse-Side*
Sh. Ch. Hansom Sylhill Odette	*Ch. Ragstone Remus*	*Derrybeg Argus* *Strawbridge Vanessa*
	Ch. Theocsbury Abbie	*Abbot of Monksway* *Sandrock Bella*

Show Champion *Greyfilk Equerry* (D) 2510 BF.
Born: 1.5.70. Died: 1980.
Breeder/Owner: Mrs J. Fussell.
Winner of 10 CCs.
Weimaraner of the Year Award 1972.

Greyfilk Critic	*Greyfilk Ambassador*	*Wolfox's Monroes Hengist* *Manana Donna's Maxine*
	Kilfenora Heidi	*Monroes Horsa* *Sylhill Nettle*
Sh. Ch. Greyfilk Sapphire	*Monroes Horsa*	*Wolfox's Sandrock Cha Cha* *Manana Athene*
	Manana Donna's Maxine	*Manana Halsall Sea Count* *Manana Beguine*

Show Champion *Abbeystag Oceanmist* (D) 3201 BE.
Born: 18.4.69.
Breeder: Mr A. J. Gray. Owner: Mr C. Dunk.
Winner of 6 CCs.

Ch. Ragstone Ritter	*Ch. Ragstone Remus*	*Derrybeg Argus* *Strawbridge Vanessa*
	Cleo Wildmoss	*Sh. Ch. Monroes Dynamic* *Lotti Go-Lightly*
Waidman Jemima	*Monroes Invader*	*Sh. Ch. Monroes Dynamic* *Monroes Helline*
	Ch. Andelyb's Balch	*Strawbridge Oberon* *Manana Brenda*

Photo: Pearce.

264

Show Champion *Kympenna's Tristan* (D) 2248 BF.
Born: 2.8.70.
Breeder: Mrs S. Worthing-Davies. Owner: Mrs J. Matuszewska.
Winner of 6 CCs.

	Wolfox Monroes Hengist	*Wolfox's Sandrock Cha Cha*
		Manana Athene
Sh. Ch. Monroes Nexus		
	Monroes Classic	*Sandrock Admiral*
		Manana Athene
	US Ch. Flottheim's Goldey	*Nurmie v Haimberg*
		Flottheim's Wilhamina
Flottheim's Kym*		
	Pat v d Heide	*US Ch. Prent's Grey Roamer*
		Lee's Honeycomb Miss of Keeler

* US import.

Show Champion *Monroes Nadine* (B) 713 BE.
Born: 14.1.68. Died: 1980.
Breeder: Mrs J. Matuszewska. Owner: Mrs D. Chapman.
Winner of 4 CCs.

	Wolfox's Sandrock Cha-Cha	*Smokey*
		Strawbridge Carol
Wolfox Monroes Hengist		
	Manana Athene	*Ipley Apollo*
		Strawbridge Ermegard
	Strawbridge Oberon	*Ipley Apollo*
		Cobra von Boberstrand
Ch. Andelyb's Balch		
	Manana Brenda	*Manana Adonis*
		Sandrock Blaze

Show Champion *Monroes Serena* (B) 448 BG.
Born: 10.6.70.
Breeders: Mrs J. Matuszewska and Mrs B. Douglas-Redding.
Owner: Mr W. Reypert.
Winner of 6 CCs.

	Sh. Ch. Monroes Nexus	*Wolfox Monroes Hengist*
		Monroes Classic
Monroes Orest		
	Sh. Ch. Monroes Idyll	*Sh. Ch. Monroes Dynamic*
		Monroes Helline
	Wolfox Andelyb's Arwydd	*Valhalla's Helmsman Arrow*
		Manana Brenda
Sh. Ch. Wolfox Nyria		
	Wolfox's Waidman Bena	*Theocsbury Deerstalker*
		Theocsbury Elsa

266

Show Champion *Cannylad Olympus Artemis* (B) 2485 BE.
Born: 10.10.68. Died: 1980.
Breeder: Mr J. Lamb. Owner: Mr A. E. Jones.
Winner of 6 CCs.

Ch. Ragstone Ritter	*Ch. Ragstone Remus*	*Derrybeg Argus* *Strawbridge Vanessa*
	Cleo Wildmoss	*Sh. Ch. Monroes Dynamic* *Lotti Go-Lightly*
Cannylad's Bimbo of Merse-Side	*Arlebroc Abbot*	*Sh. Ch. Theocsbury Archduke* *Theocsbury Handy Pet*
	Mist of Merse-Side	*Strawbridge Bando* *Rana of Tulliebole*

Photo: Cooke.

Show Champion *Gunther of Ragstone* (D) 2796 BH.
Born: 3.12.72. Died: 1981.
Breeder: Mrs E. L. Fearn. Owner: Mr and Mrs W. H. Wardall
Winner of 31 CCs. Record holder in dogs. Junior Warrant.
Championship show group winner at Leicester 1979.
Weimaraner of the Year Award 1977.

Ch. Ragstone Remus	*Derrybeg Argus*	*Sandrock Admiral* *Inka vom Weissen Kreuz*
	Strawbridge Vanessa	*Ipley Apollo* *Sh. Ch. Strawbridge Czarina*
Dinna vom Morebach★	*Axel vom Wehrturm*	*Beau von der Haraska* *Romy vom Mitterberg*
	Cilli von Tattendorf	*Arko von der Krahenhutte* *Ussi von der Murwitz*

★ Austrian import.

Photo: Pearce.

Show Champion *Greyfilk Granella* (B) 1524 BI.
Born: 8.2.72.
Breeder: Mrs J. Fussell. Owners: Mrs J. Fussell and Mrs. M. E. Holmes.
Winner of 3 CCs.

Sh. Ch. Greyfilk Equerry	*Greyfilk Critic*	*Greyfilk Ambassador* *Kilfenora Heidi*
	Sh. Ch. Greyfilk Sapphire	*Monroes Horsa* *Manana Donna's Maxine*
Greyfilk Emmaclan Angelique	*Sh. Ch. Monroes Nexus*	*Wolfox Monroes Hengist* *Monroes Classic*
	Wildmoss Hestia	*Ch. Ragstone Remus* *Cleo Wildmoss*

Show Champion *Ludmilla of Ragstone* (B) 581 BI.
Born: 3.12.72.
Breeder: Mrs E. L. Fearn. Owner: Mr and Mrs A. Burgoin.
Winner of 11 CCs.

	Derrybeg Argus	*Sandrock Admiral*
		Inka vom Weissen Kreuz
Ch. Ragstone Remus		
	Strawbridge Vanessa	*Ipley Apollo*
		Sh. Ch. Strawbridge Czarina
	Axel vom Wehrturm	*Beau von der Haraska*
		Romy vom Mitterberg
Dinna vom Morebach★		
	Cilli von Tattendorf	*Arko von der Krahenhutte*
		Ussi von der Murwitz

★ Austrian import.

Show Champion *Monroes Ubiquitous* (B) 786 BG.
Born: 18.7.71. Died: 1975.
Breeder/Owner: Mrs J. Matuszewska.
Winner of 3 CCs.

	Ch. Ragstone Ritter	*Ch. Ragstone Remus*
		Cleo Wildmoss
Sh. Ch. Cannylad Olympus Daedalus		
	Cannylad's Bimbo of Merse-Side	*Arlebroc Abbot*
		Mist of Merse-Side
	Monroes Invader	*Sh. Ch. Monroes Dynamic*
		Monroes Helline
Monroes Waidman Jane		
	Ch. Andelyb's Balch	*Strawbridge Oberon*
		Manana Brenda

Show Champion *Ragstone Rhion* (D) 1132 BH.
Born: 31.7.71. Died: 1977.
Breeder/Owner: Mr and Mrs A. Burgoin.
Winner of 3 CCs.

	Ch. Ragstone Remus	*Derrybeg Argus*
		Strawbridge Vanessa
Ragstone Radames		
	Andelyb's Buddugol	*Strawbridge Oberon*
		Manana Brenda
	Ch. Ragstone Remus	*Derrybeg Argus*
		Strawbridge Vanessa
Ragstone Rakete		
	Ragstone Rasheba	*Silver Eric*
		Hillandale Dina

Photo: Burgoin.

270

Show Champion *Cannylad Balenciaga le Dix* (B) 1568 BH.
Born: 18.7.71. Died: 1976.
Breeder: Mrs J. Matuszewska. Owner: Mr J. Lamb.
Winner of 3 CCs.

	Ch. Ragstone Ritter	*Ch. Ragstone Remus*
		Cleo Wildmoss
Sh. Ch. Cannylad Olympus Daedalus		
	Cannylad's Bimbo of Merse-Side	*Arlebroc Abbot*
		Mist of Merse-Side
	Monroes Invader	*Sh. Ch. Monroes Dynamic*
		Monroes Helline
Monroes Waidman Jane		
	Ch. Andelyb's Balch	*Strawbridge Oberon*
		Manana Brenda

Photo: Burgoin.

Show Champion *Aruni Calidore* (D) 1257 BJ.
Born: 30.5.74.
Breeder: Mrs A. Janson. Owners: Mr and Mrs M. Mulberry.
Winner of 3 CCs; Junior Warrant.

	Sh. Ch. Monroes Nexus	*Wolfox Monroes Hengist*
		Monroes Classic
Sh. Ch. Kympenna's Tristan		
	Flottheim's Kym	*US Ch. Flottheim's Goldey*
		Pat von der Heide
	Monroes Invader	*Sh. Ch. Monroes Dynamic*
		Monroes Helline
Monroes Waidman Jane		
	Ch. Andelyb's Balch	*Strawbridge Oberon*
		Manana Brenda

Champion *Gifford's Lady* (B) 2797 BH.
Born: 14.2.72.
Breeder: Mr P. Gifford Nash. Owner: Mrs C. Alston.
Winner of 4 CCs; Field Qualified.

	Greyfilk Ambassador	*Wolfox Monroes Hengist*
		Manana Donna's Maxine
Amfrid of Jacarini		
	Kilfenora Heidi	*Monroes Horsa*
		Sylhill Nettle
	Baynard Silver Bomber	*Sh. Ch. Monroes Dynamic*
		Sh. Ch. Wolfox Moonsdale Whisper
Greyfilk Caprice		
	Manana Donna's Maxine	*Manana Halsall Sea Count*
		Manana Beguine

Show Champion *Brundholme Bronella* (B) 1465 BJ.
Born: 17.2.74.
Breeder: Mrs M. Richmond. Owner: Mrs J. Whitehead.
Winner of 6 CCs; Junior Warrant.

	Ch. Ragstone Ritter	*Ch. Ragstone Remus*
		Cleo Wildmoss
Sh. Ch. Cannylad Olympus Daedalus		
	Cannylad's Bimbo of Merse-Side	*Arlebroc Abbot*
		Mist of Merse-Side
	Ch. Ragstone Remus	*Derrybeg Argus*
		Strawbridge Vanessa
Brundholme Brunhilde		
	Minka of Brundholme	*Wolfox Monroes Hengist*
		Strawbridge Bracken

Photo: Pearce.

Show Champion *Reymar's Aurora* (B) 2258 BJ.
Born: 27.11.73.
Breeder/Owner: Mr W. Reypert.
Winner of 4 CCs.

	Sh. Ch. Greyfilk Equerry	*Greyfilk Critic*
		Sh. Ch. Greyfilk Sapphire
Greyfilk Gallant		
	Greyfilk Emmaclan Angelique	*Sh. Ch. Monroes Nexus*
		Wildmoss Hestia
	Monroes Orest	*Sh. Ch. Monroes Nexus*
		Sh. Ch. Monroes Idyll
Sh. Ch. Monroes Serena		
	Sh. Ch. Wolfox Nyria	*Wolfox Andelyb's Arwydd*
		Wolfox's Waidman Bena

Champion *Wotan of Ragstone* (D) 879 BJ.
Born: 3.12.72.
Breeder: Mrs E. L. Fearn. Owner: Mrs D. Arrowsmith.
Winner of 10 CCs; Field Qualified.
Championship Show group winner at East of England 1978.

	Derrybeg Argus	*Sandrock Admiral*
		Inka vom Weissen Kreuz
Ch. Ragstone Remus		
	Strawbridge Vanessa	*Ipley Apollo*
		Sh. Ch. Strawbridge Czarina
	Axel vom Wehrturm	*Beau von der Haraska*
		Romy vom Mitterberg
Dinna vom Morebach*		
	Cilli von Tattendorf	*Arko von der Krahenhutte*
		Ussi von der Murwitz

* Austrian import.

273

Champion *Helber Camillo* (D) 646 BK.
Born: 30.5.74.
Breeder: Mrs H. M. Carrington Rice. Owner: Mr A. Mitchener.
Winner of 11 CCs; Field Qualified.

	Sh. Ch. Greyfilk Equerry	Greyfilk Critic Sh. Ch. Greyfilk Sapphire
Greyfilk Gallant		
	Greyfilk Emmaclan Angelique	Sh. Ch. Monroes Nexus Wildmoss Hestia
	Sh. Ch. Kympenna's Tristan	Sh. Ch. Monroes Nexus Flottheim's Kym
Athelson's Sophia		
	Queenscoombe Countess	Manana Mandy's Racer Queenscoombe Ziggi

Photo: Garwood.

Show Champion *Tarset Catriona* (B) 1401 BJ.
Born: 12.3.74.
Breeder/Owner: Mrs E. Hackett.
Winner of 4 CCs.
Weimaraner of the Year Award 1975.

	Fritz of Dunbriar	Halsall Sea Pirate Tessa of Carlsdorf
Ortega Opal Mint		
	Silverburn Shuna	Arlebroc Abbot Greyfilk Alana
	Arlebroc Abbot	Sh. Ch. Theocsbury Archduke Theocsbury Handy Pet
Tarset Devorgilla of Merse-Side		
	Mist of Merse-Side	Strawbridge Bando Rana of Tulliebole

Show Champion *Heronshaw Silver Fortune* (D) 1046 BK.
Born: 10.10.73.
Breeder: Mrs D. Chapman. Owner: Mrs F. Dow.
Winner of 3 CCs.

	Ch. Ragstone Ritter	Ch. Ragstone Remus Cleo Wildmoss
Sh. Ch. Abbeystag Oceanmist		
	Waidman Jemima	Monroes Invader Ch. Andelyb's Balch
	Wolfox Monroes Hengist	Wolfox's Sandrock Cha-Cha Manana Athene
Sh. Ch. Monroes Nadine		
	Ch. Andelyb's Balch	Strawbridge Oberon Manana Brenda

Show Champion *Midwil Zak* (D) 431 BK.
Born: 14.3.74.
Breeder: Mrs C. Haden. Owner: Mrs T. Cutting.
Winner of 3 CCs.

	Sh. Ch. Cannylad Olympus Daedalus	*Ch. Ragstone Ritter* *Cannylad's Bimbo of Merse-Side*
Monroes Upholder		
	Monroes Waidman Jane	*Monroes Invader* *Ch. Andelyb's Balch*
	Sh. Ch. Monroes Nexus	*Wolfox's Monroes Hengist* *Monroes Classic*
Monroes Rosalka		
	Sh. Ch. Wolfox Nyria	*Wolfox Andelyb's Arwydd* *Wolfox's Waidman Bena*

Show Champion *Monroes Aequo* (B) 1258 BJ.
Born: 19.1.74.
Breeder/Owner: Mrs J. Matuszewska.
Winner of 8 CCs.

	Wolfox Monroes Hengist	*Wolfox's Sandrock Cha Cha* *Manana Athene*
Sh. Ch. Monroes Nexus		
	Monroes Classic	*Sandrock Admiral* *Manana Athene*
	Sh. Ch. Cannylad Olympus Daedalus	*Ch. Ragstone Ritter* *Cannylad's Bimbo of Merse-Side*
Sh. Ch. Monroes Ubiquitous		
	Monroes Waidman Jane	*Monroes Invader* *Ch. Andelyb's Balch*

Photo: A. Burgoin.

Show Champion *Oneva Trenodia* (B) 3686 BI.
Born: 27.7.72.
Breeder: Mr and Mrs H. Bright. Owner: Mrs V. G. Burdge.
Winner of 3 CCs.

	Derrybeg Argus	*Sandrock Admiral* *Inka v Weissen Kreuz*
Ch. Ragstone Remus		
	Strawbridge Vanessa	*Ipley Apollo* *Sh. Ch. Strawbridge Czarina*
	Sh. Ch. Arlebroc Brigand	*Sh. Ch. Theocsbury Archduke* *Theocsbury Handy Pet*
Acombdole Athene		
	Coninvale Greta of Acombdole	*Sh. Ch. Ace of Acomb* *Theocsbury Bodicea*

Champion *Petraqua Wagtail* (B) 1322 BL.
Born: 9.5.75.
Breeder: Mrs Davies. Owners: Mr and Mrs N. Edminson.
Winner of 11 CCs; Field Qualified.

Monroes Uhlan	*Sh. Ch. Cannylad Olympus Daedalus*	*Ch. Ragstone Ritter*
		Cannylad's Bimbo of Merse-Side
	Monroes Waidman Jane	*Monroes Invader*
		Ch. Andelyb's Balch
Monroes Xpatriate	*Sh. Ch. Kympenna's Tristan*	*Sh. Ch. Monroes Nexus*
		Flottheim's Kym
	Padneyhill Monroes Quill	*Sh. Ch. Monroes Nexus*
		Monroes Waidman Jane

Show Champion *Flimmoric Fieldday* (D) 1574 BL.
Born: 1.2.76.
Breeder/Owner: Mrs C. Alston.
Winner of 16 CCs; Junior Warrant.

Sh. Ch. Jehnvar of Greyfilk	*Sh. Ch. Gunther of Ragstone*	*Ch. Ragstone Remus*
		Dinna vom Morebach
	Greyfilk Ginza	*Sh. Ch. Greyfilk Equerry*
		Greyfilk Emmaclan Angelique
Ch. Gifford's Lady	*Amfrid of Jacarini*	*Greyfilk Ambassador*
		Kilfenora Heidi
	Greyfilk Caprice	*Baynard Silver Bomber*
		Manana Donna's Maxine

Photo: Pearce.

Show Champion *Phayreheidi Chelal of Ambersbury* (B) 3488 BH.
Born: 8.2.72. Died: 1979.
Breeder: Mrs P. A. C. Veasey. Owner: Mrs M. Wardall.
Winner of 4 CCs.

Sh. Ch. Greyfilk Equerry	*Greyfilk Critic*	*Greyfilk Ambassador*
		Kilfenora Heidi
	Sh. Ch. Greyfilk Sapphire	*Monroes Horsa*
		Manana Donna's Maxine
Heidicopse Lisa	*Sh. Ch. Monroes Nexus*	*Wolfox Monroes Hengist*
		Monroes Classic
	Manana Donna's Swift	*Manana Halsall Sea Count*
		Manana Beguine

Photo: Foyle.

Show Champion *Fleetapple Wilmar* (D) 3079 BK.
Born: 5.9.74.
Breeder: Mrs D. Arrowsmith. Owner: Mrs S. Marshall.
Winner of 3 CCs.

	Ch. Ragstone Remus	*Derrybeg Argus*
		Strawbridge Vanessa
Ch. Wotan of Ragstone		
	Dinna v Morebach	*Axel vom Wehrturm*
		Cilli von Tattendorf
	Monroes Nomad	*Wolfox Monroes Hengist*
		Monroes Classic
Cannylad's Lady Hamilton of Fleetapple		
	Cannylad's Bimbo of Merse-Side	*Arlebroc Abbot*
		Mist of Merse-Side

Photo: Pearce.

Show Champion *Greyfilk Kirsty* (B) 2027 BL.
Born: 26.2.76.
Breeder: Mrs J. Fussell. Owner: Mr and Mrs M. Mulberry.
Winner of 3 CCs.

	Sh. Ch. Gunther of Ragstone	*Ch. Ragstone Remus*
		Dinna vom Morebach
Jehnvar of Greyfilk		
	Greyfilk Ginza	*Sh. Ch. Greyfilk Equerry*
		Greyfilk Emmaclan Angelique
	Greyfilk Gallant	*Sh. Ch. Greyfilk Equerry*
		Greyfilk Emmaclan Angelique
Greyfilk Haldana		
	Greyfilk Elphine	*Greyfilk Critic*
		Sh. Ch. Greyfilk Sapphire

Champion *Kamsou Moonraker von Bismarck* (D) 3202 BL.
Born: 14.10.75.
Breeders: Kamsou Kennels and Edith Huntley.
Imported from the USA by owners Richard and Jane George.
Winner of 8 CCs; Field Qualified.

	US/Can. Ch. Gwinner's Arco Wheel	*US Ch. Gwinner's Pinwheel*
		Lake Acres Silver Lady
US Ch. Kam's Tempest		
	Kam's Redhill Reverie	*US Ch. Warhorse Billy of Redhill*, CD
		US Ch. Kris-Miss Shadow, CD
	US/Mex. Ch. Gretchenhof Silver Thor	*US Ch. Hans v d Gretchenhof*, CD
		US Ch. Silver Dust XVI, CD
US Ch. Kam's Dusty Moonshine		
	US Ch. Kris-Miss Shadow, CD	*Monarch of Long Beach*
		Duchess Amber

282

Show Champion *Aisling Tuathach* (B) 3081 BK.
Born: 18.3.75. Died: 1979.
Breeder: Mr P. D. Causer. Owner: Mrs D. Mosey.
Winner of 3 CCs.

	Fritz of Dunbriar	*Halsall Sea Pirate*
		Tessa of Carlsdorf
Ortega Opal Mint		
	Silverburn Shuna	*Arlebroc Abbot*
		Greyfilk Alana
	Ch. Ragstone Remus	*Derrybeg Argus*
		Strawbridge Vanessa
Heronshaw Silver Chimes		
	Sh. Ch. Monroes Nadine	*Wolfox Monroes Hengist*
		Ch. Andelyb's Balch

Show Champion *Greyfilk Knightsman* (D) 3013 BL.
Born: 26.2.76.
Breeder/Owner: Mrs J. Fussell.
Winner of 12 CCs.

	Sh. Ch. Gunther of Ragstone	*Ch. Ragstone Remus*
		Dinna vom Morebach
Sh. Ch. Jehnvar of Greyfilk		
	Greyfilk Ginza	*Sh. Ch. Greyfilk Equerry*
		Greyfilk Emmaclan Angelique
	Greyfilk Gallant	*Sh. Ch. Greyfilk Equerry*
		Greyfilk Emmaclan Angelique
Greyfilk Haldana		
	Greyfilk Elphine	*Greyfilk Critic*
		Sh. Ch. Greyfilk Sapphire

Show Champion *Grinshill Sweet Solario* (B), CDex, UDex, WD, 793 BM.
Born: 9.1.77.
Breeder: Mrs J. M. Atkinson. Owner: Mrs S. Walkden.
Winner of 4 CCs; Junior Warrant Winner.

	Ragstone Radames	*Ch. Ragstone Remus*
		Andelyb's Buddugol
Grinshill Maxamillian		
	Shinglehill Briony	*Greyfilk Ambassador*
		Watchant Willow
	Sh. Ch. Kympenna's Tristan	*Sh. Ch. Monroes Nexus*
		Flottheim's Kym
Monroes Xpatriate		
	Padneyhill Monroes Quill	*Sh. Ch. Monroes Nexus*
		Monroes Waidman Jane

Photo: Garwood.

Show Champion *Hansom Cordon Bleu* (B) 1462 BL.
Born: 12.4.76.
Breeder/Owner: Mr R. M. W. Finch.
Winner of 4 CCs.

	Ch. Ragstone Ritter	*Ch. Ragstone Remus*
Richtkanonier of Ragstone		*Cleo Wildmoss*
	Waldemar Tara	*Ragstone Rupprecht*
		Silver Siesta
	Sh. Ch. Cannylad Olympus Daedalus	*Ch. Ragstone Ritter*
Sh. Ch. Hansom Hobby Hawk		*Cannylad's Bimbo of Merse-Side*
	Sh. Ch. Hansom Sylhill Odette	*Ch. Ragstone Remus*
		Ch. Andelyb's Balch

Photo: McFarlane.

Show Champion *Kisdon's Artist* (D) 370 BN.
Born: 21.5.78. Exported to New Zealand 1982.
Breeder: Mrs P. Edminson and Mr J. N. Newton. Owner: Mrs P. Edminson.
Winner of 4 CCs.

	Jehnvar of Greyfilk	*Sh. Ch. Gunther of Ragstone*
Sh. Ch. Greyfilk Knightsman		*Greyfilk Ginza*
	Greyfilk Haldana	*Greyfilk Gallant*
		Greyfilk Elphine
	Monroes Uhlan	*Sh. Ch. Cannylad Olympus Daedalus*
Ch. Petraqua Wagtail		*Monroes Waidman Jane*
	Monroes Xpatriate	*Sh. Ch. Kympenna's Tristan*
		Padneyhill Monroes Quill

Show Champion *Hansom Hirondelle* (B) 1323 BL.
Born: 14.9.75.
Breeder: Mr R. M. W. Finch. Owner: Mrs D. Mosey.
Winner of 4 CCs.

	Ragstone Radames	*Ch. Ragstone Remus*
Sh. Ch. Ragstone Rhion		*Andelyb's Buddugol*
	Ragstone Rakete	*Ch. Ragstone Remus*
		Ragstone Rasheba
	Sh. Ch. Cannylad Olympus Daedalus	*Ch. Ragstone Ritter*
Sh. Ch. Hansom Hobby Hawk		*Cannylad's Bimbo of Merse-Side*
	Sh. Ch. Hansom Sylhill Odette	*Ch. Ragstone Remus*
		Ch. Theocsbury Abbie

285

Show Champion *Wivelees Wicked Charmer* (B) 743 BM.
Born: 4.8.76.
Breeder: Mrs B. Brown. Owner: Mrs M. Tipney.
Winner of 8 CCs.

	Monroes Supremo	*Monroes Orest*
		Sh. Ch. Wolfox Nyria
Bewohner of Hawsvale		
	Cannylad Olympus Hadria	*Ch. Ragstone Ritter*
		Cannylad's Bimbo of Merse-Side
	Sh. Ch. Gunther of Ragstone	*Ch. Ragstone Remus*
		Dinna v Morebach
Hawsvale Furstin		
	Uhlan Champelle of Hawsvale	*Ortega Opal Mint*
		Gray Moonshadow of Duenna

Champion *Fossana Bruno* (D), CDex, UDex, WDex, TD, 1321 BL.
Born: 28.2.75.
Breeder: Mr S. Fossey. Owner: Mrs V. O'Keeffe.
Winner of 4 CCs; Field Qualified.
Weimaraner of the Year Award 1978 and 1979.

	Sidwell Prospero	*Cartford Capricorn*, CDx
		Manana Mandy's Quip
Willingstone Brandy		
	Gunmetal Gameflusher	*Gunmetal Guy*, CDx, UDx
		Teige of Whitsands
	Ortega Opal Mint	*Fritz of Dunbriar*
		Silverburn Shuna
Erika of Trafalgar		
	Baynard Silver Cutie	*Ch. Ragstone Ritter*
		Baynard Silver Belle

Show Champion *Kisdon's Arabella* (B) 2019 BN.
Born: 21.5.78.
Breeders: Mrs P. Edminson and Mr J. N. Newton. Owner: Lt Cdr J. Bond, RN.
Winner of 6 CCs; Junior Warrant.

	Jehnvar of Greyfilk	*Sh. Ch. Gunther of Ragstone*
		Greyfilk Ginza
Sh. Ch. Greyfilk Knightsman		
	Greyfilk Haldana	*Greyfilk Gallant*
		Greyfilk Elphine
	Monroes Uhlan	*Sh. Ch. Cannylad Olympus Daedalus*
		Monroes Waidman Jane
Ch. Petraqua Wagtail		
	Monroes Xpatriate	*Sh. Ch. Kympenna's Tristan*
		Padneyhill Monroes Quill

Photo: Garwood.

288

Show Champion *Kisdon's Asti of Nevedith* (B) 2109 BN.
Born: 21.5.78.
Breeders: Mrs P. Edminson and Mr J. N. Newton. Owner: Mrs P. Edminson.
Winner of 27 CCs; Junior Warrant.

	Jehnvar of Greyfilk	*Sh. Ch. Gunther of Ragstone*
		Greyfilk Ginza
Sh. Ch. Greyfilk Knightsman		
	Greyfilk Haldana	*Greyfilk Gallant*
		Greyfilk Elphine
	Monroes Uhlan	*Sh. Ch. Cannylad Olympus Daedalus*
		Monroes Waidman Jane
Ch. Petraqua Wagtail		
	Monroes Xpatriate	*Sh. Ch. Kympenna's Tristan*
		Padneyhill Monroes Quill

Photo: Garwood.

Show Champion *Denmo Roadrunner* (D) 573 BP.
Born: 5.8.78.
Breeder/Owner: Mrs D. Mosey.
Winner of 3 CCs; Junior Warrant.

	US Ch. Kam's Tempest	*US/Can. Ch. Gwinner's Arco Wheel*
		Kam's Redhill Reverie
Ch. Kamsou Moonraker v Bismarck*		
	US Ch. Kam's Dusty Moonshine	*US/Mex. Ch. Gretchenhof Silver Thor*
		US Ch. Kris-Miss Shadow, CD
	Sh. Ch. Ragstone Rhion	*Ragstone Radames*
		Ragstone Rakete
Sh. Ch. Hansom Hirondelle		
	Sh. Ch. Hansom Hobby Hawk	*Sh. Ch. Cannylad Olympus Daedalus*
		Sh. Ch. Hansom Sylhill Odette

* US import.

Champion *Lodgewater Amber* (B) 105 BN.
Born: 15.3.77.
Breeder: Mr G. Blowfield. Owner: Mr K. Absalom.
Winner of 8 CCs; Field Qualified.

	Sh. Ch. Gunther of Ragstone	*Ch. Ragstone Remus*
		Dinna vom Morebach
Jehnvar of Greyfilk		
	Greyfilk Ginza	*Sh. Ch. Greyfilk Equerry*
		Greyfilk Emmalclan Angelique
	Sh. Ch. Greyfilk Equerry	*Greyfilk Critic*
		Sh. Ch. Greyfilk Sapphire
Gretchen of Sandstone		
	Gretchen of Janau	*Ghost of Gunsmoke*
		Arlebroc Della

Photo: Garwood.

290

Show Champion *Rangatira Deerstalker* (D) 1938 BM.
Born: 21.1.77.
Breeders: Mr and Mrs C. Brown. Owner: Mr J. Loch.
Winner of 3 CCs; Junior Warrant.

	Ch. Ragstone Ritter	*Ch. Ragstone Remus* *Cleo Wildmoss*
Sh. Ch. Abbeystag Oceanmist		
	Waidman Jemina	*Monroes Invader* *Ch. Andelyb's Balch*
	Cabaret Catapult	*Valhalla's Helmsman Arrow* *Sh. Ch. Cabaret Cartford Platinum*
Grinshill Phazachalie Jane		
	Grinshill Gretchen	*Cabaret Crumbcrusher* *Theocsbury Briony*

Show Champion *Silvilee Lyra* (B) 830 BN.
Born: 6.7.77.
Breeder: Mrs. E. M. Waite. Owner: Mrs Bates.
Winner of 5 CCs.

	Sh. Ch. Jehnvar of Greyfilk	*Sh. Ch. Gunther of Ragstone* *Greyfilk Ginza*
Sh. Ch. Flimmoric Fieldday		
	Ch. Gifford's Lady	*Amfrid of Jacarini* *Greyfilk Caprice*
	Sh. Ch. Gunther of Ragstone	*Ch. Ragstone Remus* *Dinna vom Morebach*
Greymorn Cloud		
	Tallyham Silver Dream	*Duenna Gray Ghost* *Simonslane Sheba*

Champion *Ragstone Rune* (B) 517 BM.
Born: 20.6.76.
Breeder: Mr and Mrs A. Burgoin. Owner: Mrs D. Arrowsmith.
Winner of 3 CCs; Field Qualified.

	Ch. Ragstone Ritter	*Ch. Ragstone Remus* *Cleo Wildmoss*
Richtkanonier of Ragstone		
	Waldemar Tara	*Ragstone Rupprecht* *Silver Siesta*
	Ch. Ragstone Remus	*Derrybeg Argus* *Strawbridge Vanessa*
Sh. Ch. Ludmilla of Ragstone		
	Dinna vom Morebach	*Axel vom Wehrturm* *Cilli von Tattendorf*

Champion *Denmo Blueberry Muffin* (B) 829 BN.
Born: 5.8.78.
Breeder: Mrs D. Mosey. Owners: Mr and Mrs R. George.
Winner of 3 CCs; Junior Warrant; Field Qualified.

US Ch. Kam's Tempest	*US/Can. Ch. Gwinner's Arco Wheel*
*Ch. Kamsou Moonraker v Bismarck**	*Kam's Redhill Reverie*
US Ch. Kam's Dusty Moonshine	*US/Mex. Ch. Gretchenhof Silver Thor*
	US Ch. Kris-Miss Shadow, CD
Sh. Ch. Ragstone Rhion	*Ragstone Radames*
Sh. Ch. Hansom Hirondelle	*Ragstone Rakete*
Sh. Ch. Hansom Hobby Hawk	*Sh. Ch. Cannylad Olympus Daedalus*
	Sh. Ch. Hansom Sylhill Odette

* US import.

Photo: R. George.

Show Champion *Arimar's Rolf v d Reiteralm* (D) 3468 BP.
Born: 15.1.79.
Breeder: Mrs J. Isabell. Owners: Mr and Mrs J. Mayhew (Australia).
Winner of 3 CCs. Imported from USA 1979, handled by Mrs Jane George for Mr and Mrs Mayhew. Exported to Australia in November 1980.

Am. Ch. Val Knight Ranck, BROM
Am. Ch. Maxamilian von der Reiteralm, NSD, BROM
Bella von der Reiteralm, BROM

Am. & Can. Dual Ch. Ronamax Rufus v d Reiteralm, CD, SDx, RDx

Am. Ch. Graves Rogue
Am. Ch. Norman's Rona von der Reiteralm, NRD, SD, BROM
Shadowmar Valentress, BROM

Am. Ch. Eichenhof's Ginger Man, BROM
Am. Dual Ch. Arimar's Ivan, CD, NSD
Am. Ch. Arimar's Desert Diana, NSD, BROM

Am. Ch. I've A Dream of Arimar, CD, NSD

Am. Ch. Doug's Dauntless von Dor, BROM
Am. Ch. Arimar's Desert Dream, SD, NRD, V
Am. Ch. Halanns Schonste Madden, CD, NSD, NRD, BROM

Photo: R. George.

293

Show Champion *Ragstone Ryuhlan* (D) 873 BP.
Born: 8.2.79.
Breeders/Owners: Mr and Mrs A. Burgoin.
Winner of 15 CCs; Junior Warrant.

	US Ch. Kam's Tempest	*US/Can. Ch. Gwinner's Arco Wheel*
Ch. Kamsou Moonraker von Bismarck		*Kam's Redhill Reverie*
	US Ch. Kam's Dusty Moonshine	*US/Mex. Ch. Gretchenhof Silver Thor*
		US Ch. Kris Miss-Shadow, CD
	Ch. Ragstone Remus	*Derrybeg Argus*
Sh. Ch. Ludmilla of Ragstone		*Strawbridge Vanessa*
	Dinna vom Morebach	*Axel vom Wehrturm*
		Cilli von Tattendorf

Photo: A. Burgoin.

Show Champion *Jehnvar of Greyfilk* (D) 1686 BN.
Born: 15.11.74.
Breeder: Mr J. Harper. Owners: Mr and Mrs K. Absalom.
Winner of 4 CCs.

	Ch. Ragstone Remus	*Derrybeg Argus*
Sh. Ch. Gunther of Ragstone		*Strawbridge Vanessa*
	Dinna vom Morebach	*Axel vom Wehrturm*
		Cilli von Tattendorf
	Sh. Ch. Greyfilk Equerry	*Greyfilk Critic*
Greyfilk Ginza		*Sh. Ch. Greyfilk Sapphire*
	Greyfilk Emmaclan Angelique	*Sh. Ch. Monroes Nexus*
		Wildmoss Hestia

Photo: Garwood.

Champion *Shalina Sky Diver* (D) 2523 BN.
Born: 31.5.78.
Breeder: Mrs C. M. Cutting. Owner: Mr P. J. Bradley.
Winner of 3 CCs; Field Qualified.

	Monroes Upholder	*Sh. Ch. Cannylad Olympus Daedalus*
Sh. Ch. Midwil Zak		*Monroes Waidman Jane*
	Monroes Rosalka	*Sh. Ch. Monroes Nexus*
		Sh. Ch. Wolfox Nyria
	Sh. Ch. Cannylad Olympus Daedalus	*Ch. Ragstone Ritter*
Monroes Unity		*Cannylad's Bimbo of Merse-Side*
	Monroes Waidman Jane	*Monroes Invader*
		Ch. Andelyb's Balch

295

Show Champion *Verrami Aphrodite* (B) 3402 BN.
Born: 15.12.78.
Breeder: Mrs V. Clarke. Owner: Mrs D. Bushby.
Winner of 3 CCs; Junior Warrant.

	Fossana Algenon	*Willingstone Brandy* *Erika of Trafalgar*
Clackhill Christian		
	Clackhill Jade	*Sh. Ch. Kympenna's Tristan* *Waidman Gretel*
	Ghost of Gunsmoke	*Gunmetal Guy*, CDx, UDx *Teige of Whitsands*
Gerda of High Garrett		
	Silver Gretchen	*Greyfilk Silverstormee* *Gardenvale Bettina*

Photo: A. Burgoin.

Show Champion *Bredebeck Ilka* (B) 574 BP.
Born: 29.5.79.
Breeder: Mrs E. Hardman. Owners: Mr and Mrs A. Fairlie.
Winner of 7 CCs; Junior Warrant.

	Sh. Ch. Jehnvar of Greyfilk	*Sh. Ch. Gunther of Ragstone* *Greyfilk Ginza*
Sh. Ch. Greyfilk Knightsman		
	Greyfilk Haldana	*Greyfilk Gallant* *Greyfilk Elphine*
	Sh. Ch. Gunther of Ragstone	*Ch. Ragstone Remus* *Dinna vom Morebach*
Bredebeck Minna		
	Bredebeck Sophie	*Ch. Ragstone Ritter* *Manana Dorafila*

Photo: Pearce.

297

Champion *Fossana Quartz* (D) 616 BQ.
Born: 11.11.78.
Breeder: Mrs S. Fossey. Owners: Mr and Mrs M. C. Turner.
Winner of 9 CCs; Field Qualified.

	Sidwell Prospero	*Cartford Capricorn*, CDx *Manana Mandy's Quip*
Willingstone Brandy		
	Gunmetal Gameflusher	*Gunmetal Guy*, CDx, UDx *Teige of Whitsands*
	Ortega Opal Mint	*Fritz of Dunbriar* *Silverburn Shuna*
Erika of Trafalgar		
	Baynard Silver Cutie	*Ch. Ragstone Ritter* *Baynard Silver Belle*

Show Champion *Denmo Debutante* (B) 2576 BP.
Born: 1.3.78.
Breeder: Mrs D. Mosey. Owner: Mrs E. Smith.
Winner of 3 CCs.

	Sh. Ch. Jehnvar of Greyfilk	*Sh. Ch. Gunther of Ragstone* *Greyfilk Ginza*
Sh. Ch. Flimmoric Fieldday		
	Ch. Gifford's Lady	*Amfrid of Jacarini* *Greyfilk Caprice*
	Ortega Opal Mint	*Fritz of Dunbriar* *Silverburn Shuna*
Sh. Ch. Aisling Tuathach		
	Heronshaw Silver Chimes	*Ch. Ragstone Remus* *Sh. Ch. Monroes Nadine*

Photo: McFarlane.

Show Champion *Denmo Side-Car* (D) 1927 BP.
Born: 1.10.79.
Breeder: Mrs D. Mosey. Owner: Mrs J. Barry.
Winner of 10 CCs; Junior Warrant.

	US Ch. Kam's Tempest	*US/Can. Ch. Gwinner's Arco Wheel*
		Kam's Redhill Reverie
Ch. Kamsou Moonraker v Bismarck★		
	US Ch. Kam's Dusty Moonshine	*US/Mex. Ch. Gretchenhof Silver Thor*
		US Ch. Kris-Miss Shadow, CD
	Sh. Ch. Ragstone Rhion	*Ragstone Radames*
		Ragstone Rakete
Sh. Ch. Hansome Hirondelle		
	Sh. Ch. Hansom Hobby Hawk	*Sh. Ch. Cannylad Olympus Daedalus*
		Sh. Ch. Hansom Sylhill Odette

★ US Import.

Photo: Dalton.

Champion *Monroes Ambition of Westglade* (D), CDx, UDx, WDx, 416 BQ.
Born: 18.2.79.
Breeder: Mrs. J. Matuszewska. Owner: Mrs G. Sowersby.
Winner of 4 CCs; Field Qualified.

	Sh. Ch. Monroes Nexus	*Wolfox Monroes Hengist*
		Monroes Classic
Sh. Ch. Kympenna's Tristan		
	Flottheim's Kim (US)	*US Ch. Flottheim's Goldey*
		Pat von der Heide
	Sh. Ch. Monroes Nexus	*Wolfox Monroes Hengist*
		Monroes Classic
Sh. Ch. Monroes Aequo		
	Sh. Ch. Monroes Ubiquitous	*Sh. Ch. Cannylad Olympus Daedalus*
		Monroes Waidman Jane

Show Champion *Cleimar Country Cobbler of Flimmoric* (D) 0272 BR.
Born: 21.5.80.
Breeder: Mrs M. Tipney. Owner: Mrs S. Smith.
Winner of 6 CCs.

	Sh. Ch. Jehnvar of Greyfilk	*Sh. Ch. Gunther of Ragstone*
		Greyfilk Ginza
Sh. Ch. Greyfilk Knightsman		
	Greyfilk Haldana	*Greyfilk Gallant*
		Greyfilk Elphine
	Sh. Ch. Flimmoric Fieldday	*Sh. Ch. Jehnvar of Greyfilk*
		Ch. Gifford's Lady
Flimmoric Fairdinkum		
	Flimmoric Solitaire	*Ch. Ragstone Ritter*
		Ch. Gifford's Lady

Photo: B. D. L. R. Smith.

301

Show Champion *Denmo Raspberry Highball* (B) 1577 BQ.
Born: 1.10.79.
Breeder: Mrs. D. Mosey. Owner: Miss G. Averis, MRCVS.
Winner of 6 CCs.

	US Ch. Kam's Tempest	*US/Can. Ch. Gwinner's Arco Wheel*
		Kam's Redhill Reverie
Ch. Kamsou Moonraker v Bismarck (US)		
	US Ch. Kam's Dusty Moonshine	*US/Mex. Ch. Gretchenhof Silver Thor*
		US Ch. Kris-Miss Shadow, CD
	Sh. Ch. Ragstone Rhion	*Ragstone Radames*
		Ragstone Rakete
Sh. Ch. Hansom Hirondelle		
	Sh. Ch. Hansom Hobby Hawk	*Sh. Ch. Cannylad Olympus Daedalus*
		Sh. Ch. Hansom Sylhill Odette

Photo: A. Burgoin.

Show Champion *Hansom Brandyman of Gunalt* (D) 1616 BP.
Born: 26.7.79.
Breeder: R. M. W. Finch. Owners: Mr and Mrs S. J. Hollings.
Winner of 11 CCs; Junior Warrant.

	US Ch. Kam's Tempest	*US/Can. Ch. Gwinner's Arco Wheel*
		Kam's Redhill Reverie
Ch. Kamsou Moonraker von Bismarck		
	US Ch. Kam's Dusty Moonshine	*US/Mex. Ch. Gretchenhof Silver Thor*
		US Ch. Kris-Miss Shadow, CD
	Sh. Ch. Cannylad Olympus Daedalus	*Ch. Ragstone Ritter*
		Cannylad's Bimbo of Merse-Side
Sh. Ch. Hansom Hobby Hawk		
	Sh. Ch. Hansom Sylhill Odette	*Ch. Ragstone Remus*
		Ch. Theocsbury Abbie

Photo: A. Burgoin.

Show Champion *Hansom Hospitality* (B) 1580 BQ.
Born: 26.7.79.
Breeder: R. M. W. Finch. Owner: Mrs E. Kneebone.
Winner of 3 CCs.

	US Ch. Kam's Tempest	*US/Can. Ch. Gwinner's Arco Wheel*
		Kam's Redhill Reverie
Ch. Kamsou Moonraker von Bismarck		
	US Ch. Kam's Dusty Moonshine	*US/Mex. Ch. Gretchenhof Silver Thor*
		US Ch. Kris-Miss Shadow, CD
	Sh. Ch. Cannylad Olympus Daedalus	*Ch. Ragstone Ritter*
		Cannylad's Bimbo of Merse-Side
Sh. Ch. Hansom Hobby Hawk		
	Sh. Ch. Hansom Sylhill Odette	*Ch. Ragstone Remus*
		Ch. Theocsbury Abbie

Photo: Pearce.

Show Champion *Flashman of Flimmoric* (D) 0143 BR.
Born: 7.12.80.
Breeder: Mrs M. C. Tipney. Owner: Mrs C. Alston.
Winner of 8 CCs; Junior Warrant.

	Sh. Ch. Jehnvar of Greyfilk	*Sh. Ch. Gunther of Ragstone*
Sh. Ch. Flimmoric Fieldday		*Greyfilk Ginza*
	Ch. Gifford's Lady	*Amfrid of Jacarini*
		Greyfilk Caprice
	Bewohner of Hawsvale	*Monroes Supremo*
Sh. Ch. Wivelees Wicked Charmer		*Cannylad Olympus Hadria*
	Hawsvale Furstin	*Sh. Ch. Gunther of Ragstone*
		Uhlan Champelle of Hawsvale

Photo: A. Burgoin.

Show Champion *Denmo Prairie Oyster* (B) 0568 BQ.
Born: 1.10.79.
Breeder: Mrs D. Mosey. Owner: Mrs M. Brennan.
Winner of 3 CCs.

	US Ch. Kam's Tempest	*US/Can. Ch. Gwinner's Arco Wheel*
Ch. Kamsou Moonraker von Bismarck		*Kam's Redhill Reverie*
	US Ch. Kam's Dusty Moonshine	*US/Mex. Ch. Gretchenhof Silver Thor*
		US Ch. Kris-Miss Shadow, CD
	Sh. Ch. Ragstone Rhion	*Ragstone Radames*
Sh. Ch. Hansom Hirondelle		*Ragstone Rakete*
	Sh. Ch. Hansom Hobby Hawk	*Sh. Ch. Cannylad Olympus Daedalus*
		Sh. Ch. Hansom Sylhill Odette

Photo: Hartley.

305

Show Champion *Silvron Sonnet* (B) 2424 BQ.
Born: 26.11.80.
Breeder/Owner: Mrs J. B. Bates.
Winner of 3 CCs.

	Sh. Ch. Jehnvar of Greyfilk	*Sh. Ch. Gunther of Ragstone*
		Greyfilk Ginza
Sh. Ch. Greyfilk Knightsman		
	Greyfilk Haldana	*Greyfilk Gallant*
		Greyfilk Elphine
	Sh. Ch. Flimmoric Fieldday	*Sh. Ch. Jehnvar of Greyfilk*
		Ch. Gifford's Lady
Sh. Ch. Silvilee Lyra		
	Greymorn Cloud	*Sh. Ch. Gunther of Ragstone*
		Tallyham Silver Dream

Photo: McFarlane.

Show Champion *Denmo Broadway Melody* (B) 567 BQ.
Born: 5.8.78.
Breeder: Mrs D. Mosey. Owner: Mrs D. Hartley.
Winner of 3 CCs.

	US Ch. Kam's Tempest	*US/Can. Ch. Gwinner's Arco Wheel*
		Kam's Redhill Reverie
Ch. Kamsou Moonraker von Bismarck		
	US Ch. Kam's Dusty Moonshine	*US/Mex. Ch. Gretchenhof Silver Thor*
		US Ch. Kris-Miss Shadow, CD
	Sh. Ch. Ragstone Rhion	*Ragstone Radames*
		Ragstone Rakete
Sh. Ch. Hansom Hirondelle		
	Sh. Ch. Hansom Hobby Hawk	*Sh. Ch. Cannylad Olympus Daedalus*
		Sh. Ch. Hansom Sylhill Odette

Photo: McFarlane.

Champion *Czolkins Platinum Cirrus* (D) 3506 BP.
Born: 26.5.79.
Breeder: Mrs H. Jupp. Owners: Mr and Mrs P. A. Turner.
Winner of 3 CCs; Field Trial winner; Junior Warrant.
Weimaraner of the Year Award 1980.

	Sh. Ch. Jehnvar of Greyfilk	*Sh. Ch. Gunther of Ragstone*
		Greyfilk Ginza
Sh. Ch. Greyfilk Knightsman		
	Greyfilk Haldana	*Greyfilk Gallant*
		Greyfilk Elphine
	Willingstone Brandy	*Sidwell Prospero*
		Gunmetal Gameflusher
Fossana Etta		
	Erika of Trafalgar	*Ortega Opal Mint*
		Baynard Silver Cutie

Photo: McFarlane.

APPENDIX IX

Weimaraners Exported from Great Britain Gaining Overseas Championship Status*

COUNTRY	NAME	DATE OF BIRTH, BREEDER, SIRE AND DAM
Australia	*Halsall Brown Pheasant* (B)	15.7.63, Mrs K. E. Sharman, Strawbridge Oliver/Sandrock Coral.
	Penny Silver Dawn (B)	11.4.65, Mr and Mrs K. Stange, Ace of Acomb/Andelyb's Byth.
	Hansom Forward (D)	3.10.71, Mr R. M. W. Finch, Cannylad Olympus Daedalus/Hansom Sylhill Odette
	Monroes Zebedee (D)	7.5.73, Mrs J. Matuszewska, Kympenna's Tristan/Monroes Innisron Brunhilde.
	Monroes Accolade (B)	14.4.73, Mrs J. Matuszewska, Monroes Nexus/Monroes Vanadis.
	Strawbridge Fidget (B)	18.8.54, Mrs E. M. Petty, Thunderjet/Cobra von Boberstrand.
	Strawbridge Graf (D)	29.9.54, Mrs E. M. Petty, Bando von Fohr/Hella aus der Helmeute.
Austria	*Aruni Adria* (B)	19.5.73, Mrs A. Janson, Kympenna's Tristan/Monroes Waidman Jane.
	Merryhell Grampus (D)	25.4.75, Mrs V. Hawes, Bewohner of Hawsvale/Monroes Quicksilver.
Canada	*Abbisline Gabrielle* (B)	9.10.76, Mrs D. V. Brickl, Gunther of Ragstone/Webbdant's Arabesque.
Holland	*Acombdole Ami* (D)	14.10.68, Dr A. M. Mucklow, Arlebroc Brigand/Coninvale Greta of Acombdole.
	Monroes Supremo (D)	10.6.68, Mrs J. Matuszewska and Mrs B. Douglas-Redding, Monroes Orest/Wolfox Nyria.
	Hawsvale Cherry Brandy (B)	1.7.73, Mr V. B. Hawes, Kympenna's Tristan/Monroes Repartee of Hawsvale.
Hong Kong	*Merryhell Hermes* (D)	18.4.77, Mrs V. Hawes, Kympenna's Tristan/Monroes Quicksilver.
	Hawsvale Kay (B)	4.4.77, Mr V. B. Hawes, Hawsvale Impressario/Uhlan Champelle of Hawsvale.
Italy	*Hawsvale Fee* (B)	27.8.74, Mr V. B. Hawes, Gunther of Ragstone/Uhlan Champelle of Hawsvale.
Malaya	*Waidman Jezebel* (B)	4.1.67, Mrs L. Petrie-Hay, Monroes Invader/Andelyb's Balch.
Morocco	*Hawsvale Peso* (D)	27.6.79, Mr V. B. Hawes, Merryhell Havoc/Hawsvale Hero.

* Those notified to the author.

New Zealand	*Ragstone Rebhuhn* (B)	22.10.75, Mr and Mrs A. Burgoin, Richtkanonier of Ragstone/Ludmilla of Ragstone.
	Ragstone Ryulla (B)	8.2.79, Mr and Mrs A. Burgoin, Kamsou Moonraker v Bismarck/Ludmilla of Ragstone.
Singapore	*Hansom Bunny Girl of Westglade* (B)	3.10.71, Mr R. M. W. Finch, Cannylad Olympus Daedalus/Hansom Sylhill Odette.
South Africa & Zimbabwe	*Strawbridge Uhlan* (D)	19.9.58, Mrs E. M. Petty, Smokey/Vita von der Haraska.
	Tottens Telstar (D)	29.4.64, Mrs E. R. Kent, Derrybeg Argus/ Wolfox Andelyb's Awen.
	Ragstone Rhumbo (D)	4.7.74, Mr and Mrs A. Burgoin, Ragstone Ritter/Ragstone Rhossignol.
	Monroes A-Knightsman (D)	27.12.77, Mrs J. Matuszewska, Monroes Yarrow/Monroes Aequo.
	Monroes A-Katya (B)	27.12.77, Mrs J. Matuszewska, Monroes Yarrow/Monroes Aequo.
	Fatilla Romeo (D)	24.3.78, Mr N. Jones, Gunther of Ragstone/ Ambersbury Dorabella.
Spain	*Monroes Waidman Gustave* (D)	2.6.66, Mrs L. Petrie-Hay, Monroes Invader/ Andelyb's Balch.
Trinidad	*Wolfox Sabrewing* (B)	23.9.60, Mrs B. Douglas-Redding, Wolfox Kentrish Kanonier/Wolfox Silverglance.
USA	*Acombdole Archduke* (D)	14.10.68, Dr A. M. Mucklow, Arlebroc Brigand/Coninvale Greta of Acombdole.
West Indies	*Hawsvale Angostura* (B)	16.7.72, Mr V. B. Hawes, Kympenna's Tristan/ Monroes Repartee of Hawsvale.
	Merryhell Decoy, CDx (D)	26.5.72, Mrs V. Hawes, Monroes Supremo/Monroes Quicksilver.
Zambia	*Ragstone Ritzun* (D)	28.4.72, Mrs M. Wardall, Ragstone Ritter/Marta of Iken.
	Shiana Adamite (D)	26.9.73, Mrs P. J. Whitchurch, Ragstone Rupprecht/Sidwell Wife of Bath.

309

Export Pedigrees issued by the Kennel Club

NOTE: Many 'pet' dogs are exported without an official Kennel Club pedigree, therefore these figures should not be taken as representing numbers of Weimaraners exported, only those exported for which the Kennel Club issued a pedigree. Also, not all countries insist that imports from the UK should have an Export Pedigree so quite a number of potential show dogs leave without one. West Germany is just one such country and although a few dogs have been exported there, these are not shown in the figures.

COUNTRY	NO.	FIRST YEAR OF EXPORT	COUNTRY	NO.	FIRST YEAR OF EXPORT
Argentina	1	1979	Japan	5	1968
Austria	10	1974	Kenya	2	1970
Australia	29	1955	Lebanon	7	1972
Barbados	1	1983	Libya	2	1958
Belgium	11	1964	Malaysia	3	1967
Bermuda	1	1980	Morocco	1	1980
Brazil	3	1969	New Zealand	10	1976
Br. W. Indies	2	1961	North Africa	1	1956
Canada	7	1957	Norway	6	1961
Ceylon	1	1961	Pakistan	1	1963
Chile	1	1964	Portugal	3	1956
Denmark	9	1957	Saudi Arabia	2	1975
East Africa	1	1955	Singapore	2	1967
Finland	2	1969	South Africa	11	1957
France	27	1964	Southern Rhodesia	3	1955
Germany	5	1968	Spain	13	1967
Guernsey	2	1977	Sweden	6	1963
Holland	47	1969	Switzerland	4	1962
Hong Kong	6	1972	Trinidad	3	1966
India	6	1957	Turkey	1	1964
Indonesia	1	1977	USA	87	1953
Iran	3	1962	Venezuela	4	1973
Ireland	1	1977	West Indies	4	1966
Israel	2	1975	Yugoslavia	1	1981
Italy	14	1958	Zambia	6	1968
Jamaica	2	1982			

Schloss Grafenegg, home of the famous Austrian kennel of Prince Hans v Ratibor.

Linz 1956.

Förstrat. Ing. Otto Stockmayer with Frau Annie Hartl of the von der
Murwitz *affix, taken in 1956 at Internationale Hundausstellung, Linz.*
(Left: Rick v d Murwitz, right: Field Gray Cachet)

Oberforster Georg Stühlinger at the age of 79. He died aged 90 in 1979.

Totverbellen – *During the German Trials the dog must first track the deer over a considerable distance then bark on discovery, lie down and bay for a continuous period of fifteen minutes.*

This German Weimaraner is eight months old. Note the traditional oak leaves which are placed over the bullet hole and in the boar's mouth.

1957 City of Birmingham Show. B.O.B. Mrs Petty's Sandrock Ami handled by Miss T. Eland; judge Miss Rita Monkhouse; Mrs F. Bainbridge's Skyrose Typhoon handled by Miss Marcia Bainbridge.

Major Bob Petty taken shortly before his death in April 1980.

Mrs S. M. Milward with Gina, Ike and Mischa. Ike – Strawbridge Irene born 17.4.56 remains the only Obedience CC winner in the breed to date.

Manana Adonis (Ipley Apollo/Strawbridge Ermegard) owned by Mrs F. Maddocks.

Strawbridge Ermegard (Bando v Fohr/Vita v d Haraska) founder of the Manana affix.

Manana Athene (Ipley Apollo/Strawbridge Ermegard) founder of the Wolfox and Monroes affixes.

Ragstone Rasheba (Silver Eric/Hillandale Dina) founder of the Ragstone affix.

Manana Donna's Maxine (Manana Halsall Sea Count/Manana Beguine) founder of the Greyfilk affix. Here with Greyfilk Sapphire and Topaz.

Minka of Brundholme (Wolfox Monroes Hengist/Strawbridge Bracken)
founder of the Brundholme affix.

Marta of Iken (Ch. Ragstone Remus/Natasha of Abingdon) founder of the Ambersbury affix.

Cobra v Boberstrand (Casar v d Finne/Alma v Boberstrand) founder of the Strawbridge affix.

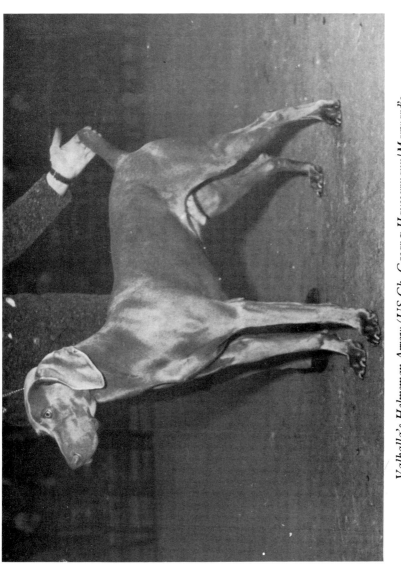

Valhalla's Helmsman Arrow (US Ch. Casar v Haussermann/Marward's Brenda) owned by Miss Rita Monkhouse of the Cabaret affix.

Laura Harding in 1966 with Bayonet Farm Sea Urchin (second from left) with her offspring by Ann's Pretty Boy Mike. (American)

Katie Go-Lightly (Ragstone Radamès/Lotti Go-Lightly) bred and owned by Lt Col H. D. Tucker pictured at the 1975 Crufts 'Personality Parade'. (Photo: Nicholas Meyjes)

Mars aus der Wulfsriede (Treff a d Grute/Cara v Schlossgehege) one of the first German exports to America. Born 25.4.38.

Ch. Burt v d Harrasburg (Sg Arco v d Filzen/Sgn Asta v Bruckberg) one of the three famous Harrasburg 'B' brothers exported from Germany to America.

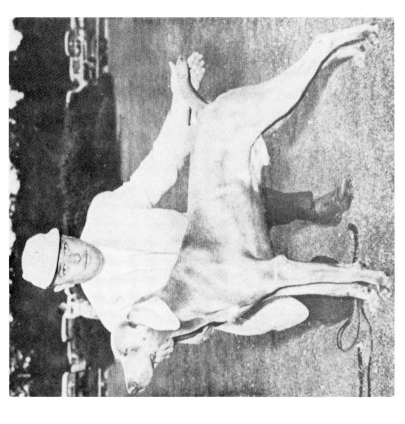

Ch. Bert v d Harrasburg (Sg Arco v d Filzen/Sgn Asta v Bruckberg) one of the finest dogs in America. Born 29.2.48 in Germany, bred by Max Baumler and owned by Mr & Mrs Elvin Deal.

Ch. Jamspirit Evolution NRD CD NSD RDX V (Ch. Arimar's Ivan/Ch. Jamspirit Complikate). Born 9.3.78, bred and owned by Mr & Mrs J. Simons. (America)

Can. Ch. & US Ch. Roschel's Fashion Impact (Ch. Colsidex Standing Ovation/Ch. Rajah's May Magic v Reiteralm). One of Canada's top dogs owned by Mr & Mrs Shoreman.

Aust. Ch. Fritz von Singen (Hans v Stedimar/The Lady Sachet von Gordon). Exported from America to Australia and an influential early sire.

NZ Ch. Puke Ataway (Thunder of Waldheim/Ch. Upton Fells Jenny Wren). Born 23.9.75, owned by Dianne Thomas, New Zealand.

NZ Ch. Silknsilver Royal Ace (Ch. Quailmaster Centurion/Ch. Weimas Sudlicher Stern). Owned by J. R. Martin. Exported from Australia to New Zealand.

Gunmettle Ritva with GSP and mixed bag of shelduck, quail and rabbit. Owned in New Zealand by John Tweedie.

Mrs Joan Matuszewska (Monroes) judging in South Africa. Dogs pictured left to right: Stahlberg's Mooncloud, Ch. Ansa van Migesta, Ch. Ragstone Rhumbo, Stahlberg's Moondust, Stahlberg's Moonraker.

Dog-sleigh racing in Sweden at the famous Åre-Draget. The bitch 'Decibell' would race over 10 km with cargo weight of 30 kg.

Ch. Bis do Canto de Pedra (Biruta d'Aldeia/Gr. Ch. Flicka do Jaraguá) bred by Mrs Marisa de Castro Lopes Corrêa in Brazil and owned by Samuel Waineraich.

Goodbye Bob, Cobra and Bando – and thanks for the legacy.